FM 3-34.5/MCRP 4-11B
February 2010

ENVIRONMENTAL CONSIDERATIONS

HEADQUARTERS, DEPARTMENT OF THE ARMY

Field Manual
No. 3-34.5/MCRP 4-11B (3-100.4)

Headquarters
Department of the Army
Washington, DC 16 February 2010

Environmental Considerations

Contents

Distribution Restriction: Approved for public release; distribution is unlimited.

*This publication supersedes FM 3-100.4/MCRP 4-11B, 15 June 2000.

Figures

Tables

Preface

Field Manual (FM) 3-34.5/Marine Corps Reference Publication (MCRP) 4-11B establishes and explains the principles of environmental support in full spectrum operations and the ways in which United States Army and United States Marine Corps (USMC) commanders develop and implement command environmental programs. This manual supports the doctrine found in Joint Publication (JP) 3-34, FM 3-0, FM 3-34, and FM 3-34.170/Marine Corps Warfighting Publication (MCWP) 3-17.4.

This manual provides guidance on integrating environmental considerations into the conduct of operations. It defines environmental considerations and provides guidance on their integration into the operations process. This manual also provides guidance on the development of command environmental programs and standing operating procedures (SOPs) to support operations and training.

Terms that have joint or Army definitions are identified in both the glossary and the text. Glossary terms: The glossary lists most terms used in FM 3-34.5/MCRP 4-11B that have joint or Army definitions. Terms with an asterisk in the glossary indicate that this FM is the proponent FM (the authority). Text references: Definitions printed in boldface in the text indicate that this FM is the proponent FM. These terms and their definitions will be incorporated into the next revision of FM 1-02/MCRP 5-12A. For other definitions in the text, the term is italicized, and the number of the proponent FM follows the definition.

Where the term "mission, enemy, terrain and weather, troops and support available, time available, civil considerations (METT-TC)" or "mission variables" is used, the USMC uses the term "mission, enemy, terrain and weather, troops and support available, time available (METT-T)." Civil considerations are inherently measured within the context of this acronym. The USMC title "environmental compliance officer" is generally the same as he Army term "environmental officer" as used throughout the manual. Unless this publication states otherwise, masculine pronouns do not refer exclusively to men.

This publication applies to the Active Army, the Army National Guard (ARNG)/Army National Guard of the United States, the United States Army Reserve (USAR), and USMC commanders and staffs, at all echelons of command, responsible for planning and executing operations. This doctrine applies to United States (U.S.) unilateral operations and U.S. Army and Marine Corps forces in multinational operations subject to applicable foreign nation laws and agreements.

The proponent for this publication is the United States Army Training and Doctrine Command (TRADOC). Send comments and recommendations on Department of the Army (DA) Form 2028 (*Recommended Changes to Publications and Blank Forms*) directly to Commander, Maneuver Support Center Directorate of Training, ATTN: ATZT-TDD-E, 320 MANSCEN Loop, Suite 270, Fort Leonard Wood, Missouri 65473-8929. Submit an electronic DA Form 2028 or comments and recommendations in the DA Form 2028 format by e-mail to <leon.mdottddengdoc@conus.army.mil>.

Introduction

The military's primary mission is to fight and win our nation's wars. Warfare, by its very nature, is destructive to humans and to the natural environment. Commanders are required to exercise judgment in applying combat power and limit damage inflicted to the extent that mission accomplishment allows. Commanders must plan to implement postconflict stability measures and always keep the health and safety of their Soldiers, Marines, DA civilians, and contractors foremost in their planning. Integrating environmental considerations into the planning process helps the military to identify, prevent, and mitigate potential threats to the environment (including those affecting historical and cultural resources) and potential environmental threats to Soldiers and Marines.

Environmental considerations are not solely focused on protection of the environment. For example, force health protection (FHP) issues may be directly linked to operational affects on the environment. FHP will significantly benefit from the integration of environmental considerations in the conduct of operations. Integrating environmental considerations also sustains resources, reduces the logistics footprint, promotes positive foreign nation relations, and supports postconflict stability efforts. All of these objectives contribute to the effectiveness of the mission and, when properly integrated, serve as force multipliers rather than mission distracters.

The most seamless integration will occur in organizations that foster an environmental ethic, practice active environmental sustainability, and perform an environmental risk assessment as early as possible when planning an operation. Environmental considerations in planning must encompass all aspects of the mission, from predeployment training through redeployment, and include such varied topics as targeting considerations, protecting hazardous material (HM) storage sites, and selecting base camp locations. Environmental considerations will apply to all operations, although a risk assessment may cause their relative importance to vary.

This manual is organized to aid commanders and staffs in their understanding of environmental considerations, and it describes how to integrate and apply them through existing staff procedures. Part One, Environmental Considerations, includes environmental planning in the conduct of operations. Part Two, Command Environmental Program, provides guidance on the development and execution of unit command environmental programs.

- Chapter 1 describes the way environmental considerations apply to operations—to include their implications at the operational and tactical levels.
- Chapter 2 supports FM 5-0 by covering the way that environmental considerations are integrated into planning activities of the operations process, to include their integration into environmental risk assessments and the military decisionmaking process (MDMP). This chapter also discusses integrating environmental considerations into plans, orders, and SOPs and includes a general discussion of environmentally specific planning.
- Chapter 3 discusses what and when to plan. This includes environmental considerations in predeployment, operations, and redeployment. This chapter also includes discussion of environmental considerations within the context of some specific focus areas, including topics such as predeployment environmental training; planning for HM storage, transportation, and disposal; targeting considerations; base camp operational issues; Soldier and Marine health considerations; and redeployment issues.
- Chapter 4 provides guidance on the establishment of unit-level environmental programs, including the development of SOPs and environmental training requirements.
- Chapter 5 provides information on integrating environmental considerations into unit operations in garrison, on deployments, and in training exercises.

- Chapter 6 describes the way that various staff sections plan for and integrate environmental considerations within various areas of expertise.
- Appendix A provides the primary environmental regulations and principal environmental laws applicable to military activities.
- Appendix B provides the formation for the environmental annex and the environmental appendix to the engineer annex.
- Appendix D discusses completing an environmental risk assessment.
- Appendix E provides guidance for conducting an environmental baseline survey (EBS).
- Appendix F discusses HM and hazardous waste (HW) management for field operations.
- Appendix G provides guidelines for integrating environmental considerations into base camp operations.
- Appendix H provides additional information for the environmental officer.
- Appendix I provides an example of an environmental policy letter.
- Appendix J provides an example of a unit environmental SOP.
- Appendix K discusses the information required to complete a material safety data sheet (MSDS).
- Appendix L provides a listing of resources for implementing and sustaining a unit environmental program.

This manual serves as a guide to aid planners in identifying environmentally related issues as they pertain to operations and enables them to integrate these issues into the operations process. While certain tactics, techniques, and procedures identify the way units will accomplish these tasks and vary depending on the situation, this manual provides a common frame of reference to guide commanders and their planners in integrating environmental considerations into the mission.

PART ONE

Environmental Considerations

Environmental considerations need to be integrated into the conduct of operations at all levels of command. While their relevance will vary depending on the particular situation, commanders and staffs must identify and integrate them as early as possible in planning an operation. This part of the manual describes how environmental considerations may influence operations and how they are integrated into planning and other activities in the operations process.

Chapter 1

Environmental Considerations Overview

The U.S. national security strategy now includes a focus on environmental and environmental security concerns. Lasting victories and successful end states will be measured in part by how well the military addresses environmental considerations, to include the protection and the conservation of natural and cultural resources; the improvement of citizens' living conditions in the affected nations; and FHP. Environmental considerations comprise a broad band of issues that must be integrated into all phases of military operations (from premobilization training, to the employment of forces, to the redeployment to home stations). Environmental considerations impact planning at all levels (from strategic to tactical) and at all echelons. Increasingly complex operations make the integration of environmental considerations even more challenging. Each operation presents a unique set of requirements that relates to and is influenced by the environment. Requirements vary according to the differences in the natural environment; the effects of military operations; the duration of the operation; and the various cultural, political, and religious sensitivities involved. While standards for environmental protection may not be as stringent in some overseas operations as they are in garrison, they are of great importance. Integrating these standards into full spectrum operations presents unique challenges. Senior commands must integrate environmental guidance into their operation plans (OPLANs) and operation orders (OPORDs). This guidance is essential to provide the balance between the operational framework and the environmental ethic within which subordinate commands conduct their operations. This chapter discusses environmental considerations and outlines their implications within the context of full spectrum operations.

DEFINITIONS

1-1. As doctrine continues to evolve, many doctrinally related definitions have been changed and updated. Defining environmental considerations and their associated terms gives a better understanding of their means of implementation.

CONTINGENCY OPERATIONS AND EXPEDITIONS

1-2. Since the Cold War, U.S. forces have conducted an increasing number of contingency operations and expeditions. U.S. forces are living and working outside of the established garrison environment, conducting operations in nations that previously saw limited U.S. military involvement.

1-3. A contingency operation, such as a response to a natural disaster conducted in the continental United States (CONUS), will require that the military follow U.S. environmental laws and regulations with limited exceptions. An expedition, which by definition is conducted in a foreign country, requires guidance and analysis from the senior command to determine the applicable policy and legal requirements.

ENVIRONMENTAL CONSIDERATIONS

1-4. *Environmental considerations* is the spectrum of environmental media, resources, or programs that may impact on, or are affected by, the planning and execution of military operations. Factors may include, but are not limited to, environmental compliance, pollution prevention (P2), conservation, protection of historical and cultural sites, and protection of flora and fauna. (JP 3-34) They include a myriad of specifics dealing with protection of the natural and cultural environment and environmental considerations in FHP. The **natural environment is the human ecosystem, including both the physical and biological systems that provide resources (clean air, clean water, healthy surroundings, and sufficient food), necessary to sustain productive human life. Included in the natural environment are man-made structures, such as water and wastewater treatment facilities and natural/cultural resources.** It represents more than habitat and living species; it includes a broad range of considerations, some of which are man-made. *Force health protection* is defined as measures to promote, improve, or conserve the mental and physical well-being of Servicemembers. These measures enable a healthy and fit force, prevent injury and illness, and protect the force from health hazards. (JP 4-02)

1-5. An **environmental area of interest is an environmentally sensitive area that may be deemed worthy of special consideration because of its unique and important qualities relative to adjacent areas (for example, the only forest within a large region) or the importance of its natural environment function (for example, a wetland, flood plains, permafrost area, or an endangered species critical habitat). The environmental area of interest includes man-made structures, such as wastewater treatment plants and dams**.

1-6. *Environmental stewardship* is the integration and application of environmental values into the military mission in order to sustain readiness, improve quality of life, strengthen civil relations, and preserve valuable natural resources. (JP 1-02) Environmental stewardship represents the reflection of leader and individual awareness of and commitment to protecting the environment. It is a proactive, values-based concept that helps to ensure the sustainability and conservation of resources.

1-7. Sustainability is a process by which resources are used in a manner that allows their continued availability. As applied to an environmental strategy, a sustainable Army simultaneously meets current as well as future mission requirements worldwide, safeguarding human health, improving quality of life, and enhancing the natural environment (see *The Army Strategy for the Environment* for additional information).

1-8. The principles of environmental stewardship and sustainability support environmental protection. **Environmental protection is the application of human ingenuity and resources, through the disciplines of science and engineering, as required by environmental protection laws, regulations, and policies, to protect the natural environment**. They accomplish this by adding the dimensions of human attitudes and values to the technical environmental protection process.

1-9. FHP is a vital concern for every commander. Many of the factors that affect the health of Soldiers and Marines may be directly related to environmental considerations within the theater and to the effects on the environment created by military actions. While FHP is not subordinate to environmental considerations, it does encompass many aspects of it.

1-10. The areas relating to preventive and curative health contain embedded environmental considerations as required by both national and international environmental protection laws. In addition, other aspects of FHP contain environmental components, such as managing *medical waste* **(defined as any waste that is generated in the diagnosis, treatment, or immunization of human beings or animals)**, blood supply, and HM related to medical operations. See JP 4-02, JP 4-02.1, and other Service-specific health service support manuals.

ENVIRONMENTAL HAZARDS AND RISK MANAGEMENT

1-11. A *hazard* is a condition with the potential to cause injury, illness, or death of personnel; damage to or loss of equipment or property; or mission degradation. (JP 3-33) Hazards are subcomponents of risks and, at times, the terms are used interchangeably.

1-12. *An environmental hazard* **is defined as all activities that may pollute, create negative noise-related effects, degrade archaeological/cultural resources, or negatively affect threatened or endangered species habitats. They also include environmental health-related hazards.** An environmental hazard is a subset of all hazards.

1-13. Hazards create risks that the military must anticipate, plan for, and mitigate. The composite risk management (CRM) process is one of detecting, assessing, and controlling risk arising from operational factors and balancing that risk with mission accomplishment. Environmental risks are those risks both to and from the environment that must be included in the CRM process. This would also include counter-proliferation and consequence management actions associated with chemical, biological, radiological, nuclear, and high-yield explosives (CBRNE), including toxic industrial materials (TIMs) and improvised explosive devices (IEDs). *Toxic* **is defined as capable of producing illness, injury, or damage to humans, domestic livestock, wildlife, or other organisms through ingestion, inhalation, or absorption through any body surface.**

ENVIRONMENTAL RECONNAISSANCE

1-14. The military conducts environmental reconnaissance to gather technical information pertaining to environmental conditions, including conditions relating to safety and FHP. *Environmental reconnaissance* **is defined as the systematic observation and recording of site or area data collected by visual or physical means, dealing specifically with environmental conditions as they exist, and identifying areas that are environmentally sensitive or of relative environmental concern, for information and decisionmaking purposes.** Commanders use this information to assess the impact of military operations in the environment and the effect that the environment may have on military and civilian personnel. Chapter 3 and Appendix E provide further guidance and information. Refer also to FM 3-34.170/MCWP 3-17.4 for further information.

ENVIRONMENTAL IMPLICATIONS

1-15. The military has a new appreciation for the interdependence between military missions, the global community, and the environment. Factors influencing international security and stability have dramatically changed. Global population and industrial activity have grown, and technological advances have accelerated. These phenomena have begun to shift the foundations of strategic analysis, altering the relationships between human populations and the supporting natural environment. As nations industrialize, they use more natural resources, which can lead to potential conflicts over the exploitation of scarce resources. In addition, rapidly industrializing nations frequently fail to implement adequate environmental controls. These inadequate environmental controls can lead to conflicts with neighbors and can present health concerns to their population and to U.S. military personnel conducting operations.

1-16. Protecting natural resources and the facilities exploiting them are now major components of planning. U.S. forces must plan to protect natural and cultural resources and mitigate conflicts driven by these issues. Failure to do so may have impacts far beyond the initial damage that results. Environmental considerations will impact operations at all levels of command and should be integrated, as appropriate, into the conduct of those operations. Integration of environmental considerations into activities at home stations provides a means for promoting the principles of stewardship and sustainability that will support environmental protection at home and abroad.

OPERATIONS PROCESS

1-17. When conducting full spectrum operations, commanders must balance environmental protection and mission requirements. Military environmental protection principles do not necessarily override other operational or mission variables; rather they are standard considerations for inclusion in the conduct of the operation. The mission variables for the operation determine and quantify the time and resources devoted to environmental protection. Commanders must analyze environmental considerations and impacts in concert with the operational and mission variables.

1-18. Environmental considerations and their relative importance will vary based on the type of operation, but the U.S. military must address them to ensure that it meets its objectives. Environmental considerations, regardless of the type of mission, are significant in each of the activities of the operations process and must be addressed throughout each phase of the operation. Issues such as site selection, target selection, HM transportation, FHP, risk management, base camp site selection, base camp operation, community relations, redeployment and camp closure actions, sensitive site exploitation, and environmental remediation in support of reconstruction efforts now play an important part in how the military plans and conducts operations.

1-19. Commanders and staffs must plan for and integrate environmental considerations into each phase of the operation as early as possible. While predeployment, deployment, employment, sustainment, and redeployment of forces each present different environmental challenges, the early integration of environmental considerations into the planning activities for each phase will enable building on the success of previous phases. Chapter 3 details the various aspects of integrating environmental considerations in each phase of an operation.

LEGAL FRAMEWORK

1-20. An extensive legal framework addresses environmental protection. Various international treaties, status-of-forces agreements (SOFAs), the overseas environmental baseline guidance document (OEBGD), final governing standards (FGS), and U.S. military Services regulations provide direction on conducting operations while protecting the environment. These laws/regulations impact military operations by preventing certain operations (such as environmental modification as prohibited by the 1977 Environmental Modification Convention) and by regulating others (such as the cross border movement of HM regulated by the Basel Convention). While the United States is not a party to the 1977 addition (Protocol I) to the 1949 Geneva Conventions, it states that combatants are required to "...protect the natural environment against widespread, long-term, and severe damage" during war. The United States and international communities each expect greater environmental protection during military operations than in the past.

1-21. The OEBGD prescribes implementation guidance and procedures for ***environmental compliance*** **(defined as the unconditional obeying of international, foreign nation, federal, state, and local environmental rules, regulations, and guidelines that affect current operations)** on Department of Defense (DOD) facilities outside the continental United States (OCONUS), but does not apply specifically to ships, aircraft, or the ground component in a selected contingency. It is meant for guiding the use of temporary and fixed facilities; however, the information may serve as a useful guideline for other situations. FGS developed for each foreign nation are country-specific and designed to provide guidance on particular aspects of environmental protection, such as effluent ***discharges*** **(defined as the accidental or intentional spilling, leaking, pumping, pouring, emitting, emptying, or dumping of a substance into or on any land or water)** or base camp-specific management practices.

1-22. Environmental considerations are not restricted to land operations. Maritime operations are also regulated by international law, such as the United Nations Convention on the Law of Sea (article 236), and by U.S. statutes, such as the Marine Mammal Protection Act.

1-23. U.S. forces must be aware of the environmental laws that may impact operations and plan accordingly. While the United States may not be signatory to some of these legal requirements, the political environment may still require the United States to adhere to them. Military members who violate environmental laws or regulations may be punished under the Uniform Code of Military Justice. Commanders and the personnel under their command must be aware of the requirements to avoid potential violations of international laws and to maintain the national environmental ethic. ***Environmental ethic* is defined as taking care of the environment because it is the right thing to do; this ethic is the operating principle and value that governs individual Soldiers, units, and the Army.**

COMPETITION FOR RESOURCES

1-24. Strategic resources such as oil, minerals, and water supplies have often been catalysts for conflict. The current struggle to obtain and secure adequate energy resources is the latest in a series of natural resource-driven conflicts. Historically, the United States was largely explored and founded by nations seeking to take advantage of its natural resources; wars were fought over such mundane but lucrative resources as the fur trade and access to timber. Adequate sources for ships' masts were as important then as oil supplies are today. As more nations industrialize, the list of potential resource-driven trouble spots around the globe increases.

1-25. As nations compete for resources, the potential for armed conflict increases. Water rights in the Middle East, access to diamond mines in Africa, and ownership of islands with access to oil deposits off the Philippines all present potential areas for future conflict. These conflicts may impact the United States, either through the requirement for armed intervention or the requirement for humanitarian assistance.

1-26. Theater-level planners consider the possibility of environmentally driven conflicts within their areas of responsibility (AORs). Planners must prepare for these sources of conflicts between states alongside conflicts based on political, economic, religious, ethnic, and other issues. These plans must address potential trouble spots and the effect environmental considerations may have on military action at the source of the conflict.

ENVIRONMENTAL DAMAGE

1-27. In addition to competition for resources, environmental and natural disasters may result in conflict. A nuclear plant accident or a major industrial ***spill* (defined as a generic term that encompasses the accidental and the deliberate but unpermitted discharge or release of a pollutant)** on a river that affects more than one nation may create economic damage to all parties and increase tensions between neighbors. The resulting claims for financial and legal settlements, along with the hostile feelings engendered, have the potential to lead to armed conflict. Man-made conflicts and disasters as well as natural disasters create tremendous impacts on the local populations and the environment.

1-28. In addition to overt armed conflict issues, the struggle for resources and the environmental damage resulting from human and natural events may lead to humanitarian crises. The loss of habitat, clean water sources, cropland, and mineral rights upsets economic, social, and cultural systems. The resulting poverty, disease, and malnutrition create the need for humanitarian-assistance operations. In addition, the flow of refugees within and across national borders can upset the balance of the population and increase ethnic and religious tensions between rival groups.

1-29. Contingency planning must address stability efforts in areas affected by environmental issues. These issues include the effect that local and regional conflicts and natural disasters have on the environment. Planners must develop contingency plans, which integrate environmental considerations into the response to environmental disasters.

vectors, and other contamination sources are prevalent. Soldiers and Marines exposed to these hazards may become sick or injured through these chemical and biological exposures.

1-36. Commanders and staffs must plan health protection and preventive medicine measures for their personnel. Immunizations, personal protective equipment (PPE), and training requirements must be addressed for individual Soldiers and Marines, while planners integrate health protection into operations such as base camp site selection. See FM 4-02 for additional information. The following vignette provides an example of how environmental hazards might affect FHP considerations.

Issue

The improper disposal of HW affects Soldier and Marine health and welfare (Operation Iraqi Freedom).

Discussion

U.S. forces occupying a base camp in Iraq failed to properly dispose of their HW. Insecticides; used vehicle batteries; petroleum, oils, and lubricants (POL); and other HW were dumped in the same area as solid waste. Additionally, fuel and gray water trucks were parked nearby and leaked their contents into the dump. The unit did not implement spill containment or cleanup procedures to prevent the hazardous fluids from potentially entering the water table. These wastes also posed an environmental health hazard to the Soldiers and Marines occupying the camp and to any civilians that might occupy the site later. Mixing wastes increased the likelihood of spontaneous combustion. Additionally, enemy fire hitting this area increased the risk of toxic and noxious vapors against which the Soldiers' and Marines' protective gear would be ineffective.

Techniques and Procedures

Commanders must—

- Practice environmental management during operational deployments.
- Appoint and train an environmental officer for both garrison and operational environments.
- Conduct environmental assessments and environmental risk assessments.
- Apply the laws, regulations, and other guidance documents pertaining to the disposal of solid and HW (to include foreign nation laws).
- Establish local environmental and waste-management policies and procedures.
- Use the deployed base camp mayor, Directorate of Public Works (DPW), or unit environmental officer to report environmental and waste-management issues.
- Train personnel within the unit on HM/HW handling and procedures.
- Consult with preventive medicine units for monitoring support.
- Ensure that tenant units have access to sufficient quantities of proper HW storage containers.

FORCE SUSTAINMENT

1-37. U.S. forces consume large quantities of materials. HM and POL products in particular are used in large quantities. All of these materials require proper transportation, handling, storage, and disposal techniques. Military operations also generate large quantities of waste products. *Waste* **is defined as any discarded material.** Human waste, medical waste, *hazardous waste* **(defined as a solid waste that is either listed as such in federal law or exhibits any of the four hazardous characteristics—ignitability,** corrosiveness, reactivity, or toxicity), damaged or destroyed military material, construction materials, and even household/consumer products all require proper disposal. Base camp facilities supporting operations need to be constructed, maintained, and closed at the end of operations. These sites should address FHP issues, waste disposal, and HM/HW storage.

1-38. Commanders and staffs should develop plans to address the environmental component of force sustainment. Much of the effort is resource-intensive, requiring spill cleanup, storage containers, and construction materials. Adequate subject matter experts (SMEs) provide advice and help plan and manage operations; legal and contracting experts arrange for transportation and disposal by foreign nation or civilian contractors. These requirements may present significant challenges to conducting operations. Commanders and staffs must also integrate P2 concepts and technology to help reduce waste disposal requirements. See the following vignette pertaining to the effect of environmental considerations on force sustainment.

Issue

The disposal of used motor oil involves excessive cost and effort.

Discussion

Before May 2002, all of the Army's used oil products were transported from the Balkans to Germany for disposal, requiring a large logistical support structure. Recently, a problem with used oil has been identified in Afghanistan and Iraq. Weekly oil generation there is estimated at 10,000 to 20,000 gallons. The U.S. military currently spends a significant amount of money collecting, storing, and disposing of used motor oil. These costs are even more dramatic overseas and in forward-deployed locations.

Techniques and Procedures

The Army has identified a technology called oil reutilization that will transform used motor oil into usable fuel without spending resources on collection, storage, or disposal of the oil. This technology removes the oil from the crankcase, filters the mixture, blends it with fuel from the vehicle fuel tank, and deposits it into the vehicle for use as fuel.

The oil reutilization process has proven to eliminate used oil from the waste stream and results in fuel cost savings. Aside from cost savings relating to waste-oil disposal and fuel purchases, the reduced manpower resulting from the oil reutilization process was an added benefit. Before the use of an oil reutilization unit, the Balkans' disposal process required handling the waste eight separate times by multiple individuals. The waste reutilization unit cycle is a one-person, three-step process conducted in a local maintenance shop.

STABILITY OPERATIONS

1-39. Stability operations, whether conducted after major combat operations or in support of natural-disaster recovery, present many environmental challenges. These challenges include areas such as remediation of environmental damage, sensitive-site exploitation, environmental *restoration* (defined as the systematic removal of pollution or contaminants from the environment, especially from the soil or groundwater, by physical, chemical, or biological means; also known as remediation or environmental cleanup), and environmental considerations as they apply to construction operations.

1-40. During these types of operations, environmental protection requirements will most likely be more stringent than during combat operations. The military may require additional equipment, materials, and expertise to support these requirements. Planners will need to integrate requirements as early as possible to ensure that adequate resources are available.

LINKAGE TO THE ARMY UNIVERSAL TASK LIST

1-41. The Army Universal Task List includes two tasks that specify support to environmental considerations, although environmental considerations are inherent in a number of other Army tactical tasks. These two tasks, Develop a Command Environmental Program and Conduct Actions to Control Pollution and Hazardous Materials (see FM 7-15 for current task numbers), include specific aspects of environmental considerations that must be integrated into and the conduct of operations, providing measures of effectiveness for each task.

Chapter 2

Integrating Environmental Considerations

Military operations integrate environmental considerations into planning throughout the operations process, regardless of the echelon or type of operation. What will differ are the specifics of the planning guidance received to support a given operation, the risks associated with the environmental considerations relative to the other mission requirements, and the echelon at which the risks are addressed. Failure to consider the environmental impact of military activities may adversely affect the operation. Potential impacts include endangering Soldier, Marine, and civilian health; causing operational delay; creating adverse public opinion; and incurring excessive financial costs. This chapter discusses the integration of environmental considerations early during planning and the use of the CRM process to aid with the assessment and management of environmentally related risk. Integrating environmental considerations does not require a new process or system. The military can include environmental considerations within the same activities used in the conduct of the operation. For specifics on the joint/multi-Service planning process, see Chairman of the Joint Chiefs of Staff (CJCS) Manual 3122.03C, Volume II; FM 5-0; and JP 5-0.

ENVIRONMENTAL COMPOSITE RISK MANAGEMENT

2-1.   CRM is the process of identifying, assessing, and controlling risks arising from operational factors and making decisions that balance that risk with mission benefits (see FM 5-19). The five steps (see Appendix D) are performed throughout the planning and the rest of the operations process.

2-2.   It is crucial to identify environmental risks associated with an operation early. The earlier the risk is identified, the easier it is to avoid or mitigate. Since many environmental risks have significant impacts on the health of Soldiers, Marines, and civilians, it is especially important to identify these early enough in the process to avoid negative health effects and to take the necessary precautions.

2-3.   Risk is characterized by both the probability and the severity of a potential loss that may result from the presence of an adversary or a hazardous condition. During mission analysis, the commander and staff assess the two following kinds of risk:

- *Tactical risk* (defined as the risk concerned with the hazards that exist because of the presence of either the enemy or an adversary).
- *Accident risk* (defined as all operational risk considerations other than tactical risk. Includes risks to friendly forces and risk posed to civilians by an operation, as well as the impact of operations on the environment).

2-4.   The CRM process addresses safety and other operational issues, and the environmental CRM process is performed in the same manner. Risks to the environment and to the health of Soldiers, Marines, and civilians are identified and analyzed, and mitigation measures are developed to minimize the risks. These risks are included in the course of action (COA) development and selection process, to assist in determining the best COA for a given operation or mission. Appendix D provides additional guidance. The following vignette shows how using CRM can prevent financial expenditure and environmental hazards.

Issue

Fuel leaks from an aboveground storage tank threaten the source of drinking water.

Discussion

Fuel supplies for the heating systems in the barracks of an overseas installation were located in an aboveground storage tank. The storage tank was located 200 meters from a creek, and a buried fuel line supplying the storage tank was leaking, threatening the installation's drinking water supply. Although the storage tank was located in the unit's company area, the unit did not routinely inspect its infrastructure, believing it to be the installation's responsibility.

The unit could have detected the leak by noticing the stains on the ground and the strong smell of fuel oil. Based on these indicators, the unit should have reported the situation to the facility engineers. Because the unit failed to report the situation in a timely manner, the facility engineers were forced to install an expensive extraction fuel/water separator to recover more than 700 gallons of fuel oil.

Techniques and Procedures

- Commanders must conduct risk assessments for items containing HMs located within their unit areas even though the equipment is maintained by other agencies.

- Units should include an inspection procedure in their environmental SOP for aboveground storage tanks.

- Unit environmental officers should be appointed and trained to conduct weekly environmental inspections of the unit areas.

- Individuals may contact the installation environmental management office or during deployment the next higher command environmental officer for more information and assistance.

PLANNING PRINCIPLES AND CONCEPTS

2-5. Integration of environmental considerations begins with planning and must be included in the planning focus at each echelon. Higher echelon environmental planning guidance provides a foundation for corresponding planning at lower echelons. *Environmental planning* **is defined as efforts that consider the impact of operation, training, exercises, or weapon system introduction on the environment and, where necessary, allow decisionmakers to take early action to eliminate or mitigate those impacts.** Planning guidance provides the foundation of information for subordinate commanders and staffs to effectively integrate and implement environmental considerations into their planning and operations.

2-6. Planning at the strategic level involves developing strategic military objectives and tasks in support of the national security strategy and developing force and materiel requirements necessary to accomplish those tasks. This is the level that policy is translated into strategic military objectives. Combatant commanders plan at this level by participating in the development of the national military strategy, the theater estimate, and theater strategies. At this level, planners determine broad policy on environmental considerations. These considerations may include making decisions on the rules of engagement for targeting cultural sites, developing guidance for targeting industrial infrastructure as pertains to environmental considerations, deciding which environmental laws and treaties pertain to the situation, and determining the level at which the military may conduct environmental remediation and restoration.

2-7. Planning at the operational level links the tactical employment of the forces to their strategic objectives through design, organization, integration, and implementation of campaigns, major operations, and battles. At this level, planners review and decide how to specifically apply environmental policy and general procedures. Operational-level decisions may include items such as selecting (or not selecting) potential targets, developing guidance for base camp site selection, developing guidance on recycling programs, and planning for the transportation of HM.

2-8. Planning at the tactical level is how units employ tactics to fight and win engagements and battles. These engagements and battles are the means by which units carry out operations. In a similar vein, environmental considerations at the tactical level are the tactics, techniques, and procedures units use to implement guidance from higher headquarters. These tactical-level environmental decisions include items such as unit environmental SOPs, field sanitation, landfill construction, and steps to protect HM and POL stockpiles.

JOINT PLANNING PROCESS

2-9. Operational planning (see JP 5-0, JP 5-00.1, and JP 5-00.2) encompasses all phases required for conducting operations to include mobilization, deployment, employment, sustainment, and redeployment of forces. JP 3-34 provides the framework for the integration of environmental considerations into joint operational engineer planning. Joint operations planning includes deliberate, campaign, and crisis action planning. Although the specific steps are different, these three processes are similar and interrelated.

Deliberate Planning

2-10. Deliberate planning takes place primarily during peacetime to develop OPLANs for contingencies identified in strategic planning documents. It relies heavily on assumptions regarding the political and military circumstances existing when the plan is implemented. Integrating probable environmental considerations during this time is important. Planning for environmental considerations should take into account numerous possibilities, from the likelihood of environmentally driven conflicts, to possible enemy COAs that may impact the environment, to decisions regarding the *environmental protection level* **(defined as the varying level of environmental protection that can reasonably be afforded at any particular time during military operations, given the absolute requirement that such a diversion of resources away from the mission at hand does not adversely affect that mission, any friendly personnel, or indigenous or refugee populations)** enforced by U.S. forces. Deliberate planning is a highly structured process that engages commanders and staffs in methodically developing fully coordinated plans for contingencies and transitioning to and from war or other operations. Plans developed because of deliberate planning provide a foundation for campaign and crises action planning.

Campaign Planning

2-11. Campaign planning is employed by the military when the scope of operations requires more than a single operation. Integrating environmental considerations into campaign planning is largely the same as integrating them into deliberate planning. During campaign planning, the standards and guidance for environmental considerations in one or more of the OPLANs may involve significantly different planning guidance given different operational areas or different situations within an assigned area of operation (AO). Causes for these differences include variations within full spectrum operations, international agreements or similar documents, specific operational objectives, and other aspects of the operating environment.

Crisis Action Planning

2-12. Crisis action planning involves developing OPLANs and OPORDs in response to an imminent crisis in a time-sensitive manner. It follows prescribed crises action procedures for formulating and implementing an effective response within the time permitted by the crisis. Planners base this plan on the circumstances existing at the time of the event.

2-13. The military adapts and employs a basic process for planning and executing operations in crises. An adequate and feasible military response to a crisis demands a flexible adaptation of this process. For a crisis, planners follow established crisis action plan procedures to adapt previously prepared OPLANs to meet the specific situation or develop new OPLANs based on the crisis. Maintaining environmental considerations and related information in existing plans becomes critical when dealing with crisis plans.

2-14. Planners integrate environmental considerations into crisis action plans, using environmental considerations already identified in the deliberate planning process or information already obtained regarding a potential AO. As with any operation, the scope of the relevant environmental considerations will vary with the type of mission being executed. In a situation such as a hostage rescue operation, the environmental considerations would be limited to certain targeting or cultural issues. In other situations, such as the response to an environmental disaster, the environment is the key component of the mission. The more information staff sections have about environmental considerations affecting their respective AO, the faster they can integrate them into the OPLAN.

MULTINATIONAL OPERATIONS PLANNING

2-15. Multinational operations planning requires that the staff be aware of the environmental constraints placed on multinational operations by international agreements applicable to U.S. forces. Military material restrictions, such as limitation on depleted uranium ammunition, may also limit the method by which U.S. forces conduct multinational operations. Additionally, the military must consider foreign nation cultural and historical sensitivities as a factor in planning multinational operations. Many international forces with which U.S. forces operate may have different standards for integrating environmental considerations. U.S. forces will have to coordinate and sometimes assist multinational forces in integrating environmental considerations to ensure consistent standards and levels of protection for the environment, the civilian population, and deployed Soldiers and Marines.

MILITARY DECISIONMAKING PROCESS

2-16. Each supporting OPLAN, regardless of the military Service, requires the military to complete a formal planning process. This process, which varies among Services, includes at a minimum a mission analysis, running estimates, COAs, and a command approval process. These supporting plans reflect each Service's specific requirements, including their specific measures for dealing with and integrating environmental considerations. Just as the joint planning process requires staffs to work together to analyze environmental considerations, Service staffs work together to analyze and integrate environmental considerations into their planning documents.

2-17. Staff sections use the guidance provided in their higher headquarters plans and orders to develop their own supporting plans. The military integrates environmental CRM and environmental considerations in varying levels of detail, based on the higher headquarters plan, the situation, and the planning echelon.

2-18. MDMP is a planning tool that establishes procedures for analyzing a mission and producing a plan or order. This process applies across the spectrum of conflict. Table 2-1 depicts the seven steps in the MDMP (see FM 5-0 for more information). Each step begins with input that builds on the previous steps. The output of each step drives subsequent steps; therefore, any initial errors or omissions impact later steps in the process. It is important to integrate environmental considerations into each step of the process.

2-19. Table 2-1 uses the MDMP framework to discuss how to integrate environmental considerations into the MDMP. Environmental considerations are generally addressed as a function of risk, much like safety considerations.

Table 2-1. MDMP environmental considerations

Input	Steps	Output
• The environmental appendix or annex from higher-level order • Foreign nation agreements and OEBGD • Lessons learned	Step 1. Receipt of mission	• Commander's initial guidance • Warning order
• Higher headquarters order/plan/intelligence preparation of the battlefield (IPB) • Running estimates • Geospatial information and products resulting from terrain analysis • Facts and assumptions	Step 2. Mission analysis	• Environmental areas of interest • Specified, implied, and essential environmental tasks • Specialized assistance for an EBS, such as an environmental or contingency real estate support team • Tactical and accidental environmental risks (see the discussion of CRM in this chapter and in Appendix D) • Initial environmental reconnaissance • Environmental considerations in restated mission • Commander's intent • Commander's guidance • Warning order
• Restated mission • Initial commander's intent • Planning guidance • Commander's critical information requirements (CCIR) • Updated running estimates	Step 3. COA development	• Updated environmental risk controls • Refined commander's intent and planning guidance • Enemy environmental COA
• Updated environmental risk controls • Refined commander's intent and planning guidance • Enemy COA	Step 4. COA analysis (war game)	Environmental protection level matrix
Environmental protection level matrix	Step 5. COA comparison	• Residual risk • Environmental considerations significant enough to appear in commander's intent or guidance

Table 2-1. MDMP environmental considerations (continued)

Input	Steps	Output
Decision matrix	Step 6. COA approval	• Approved residual risk with implementing controls • Refine commander's intent and guidance
• Approved COA • Refined commander's intent and guidance • Refined CCIR	Step 7. Orders production	OPORD

INTEGRATING ENVIRONMENTAL CONSIDERATIONS INTO PLANS, ORDERS, AND STANDING OPERATING PROCEDURES

2-20. Plans and orders are the means by which commanders express their vision, intent, and decisions. Plans and orders form the basis by which commanders synchronize military operations. They encourage initiative by providing the "what" and "why" of a mission, while leaving the "how" of the mission up to subordinates. They provide subordinates with the operational and tactical freedom to accomplish the mission by providing the minimum restrictions and details necessary for synchronization and coordination. SOPs provide units with standardized procedures for the execution of routine actions.

OPERATION PLANS AND OPERATION ORDERS

2-21. Plans and orders normally include environmental considerations in coordinating instructions. This can be as special or coordinating instructions and may be included in either an annex or appendix based on the level of the operation. When specific command procedures dictate, staff officers include some environmental considerations in other annexes. Unit planning at brigade level and below will normally include only those elements required by the higher headquarters order or plan and are not included in a unit SOP. Table 2-2 lists some of the annexes and appendixes including environmental considerations within the Joint Operation Planning and Execution System (JOPES) format. These areas of concern will be similar for all branch-specific orders, regardless of the particular order format. Chapter 6 further describes staff section input for environmental considerations.

2-22. The engineer is the primary staff integrator for environmental considerations. However, environmental concerns are addressed by every staff officer, as applicable, in respective annexes and appendixes. Joint plans or orders following the JOPES format contain a separate annex (annex L, Environmental Considerations). In the context of an Army order following the format in FM 5-0, the specified appendix is appendix 5, Environmental Considerations, to annex G, Engineering. The format for annex L is included in appendix B, and a sample of appendix 5 to annex G is included in appendix C of this manual. Table 2-2 provides information concerning JOPES annexes and appendixes containing significant environmental considerations.

Table 2-2. JOPES annexes and appendixes with significant environmental considerations

JOPES Location	Proponent Staff	Principal Staff and Special Capabilities	Comments
Annex B Appendix 1	Intelligence staff officer (J-2)	All, primarily civil affairs (CA), engineer, and surgeon	Contains the environmental priority intelligence requirements (PIR), which may include information on planned base camps and other sites.
Annex C	Operations staff officer (J-3)	All, primarily CA, engineer, and surgeon	Ensures that elements to perform critical environmental missions are included in the task organization, especially engineer, medical, and CA deployment sequence may be critical to perform missions in a timely fashion.
Annex B, Appendix 4	J-2	CA, engineer, fire support element (FSE), staff judge advocate (SJA)	Addresses cultural considerations and the environmental effects of specific targeting.
Annex C, Appendix 2	Chemical, biological, radiological, and nuclear (CBRN) officer	SJA, surgeon	Addresses riot control agents and herbicides requiring the integration of environmental considerations.
Annex C, Appendix 7	J-3	CBRN, engineer, J-2	Addresses reconnaissance in general, to include specific engineer and CBRN reconnaissance assets and the necessary expertise to verify base camp or other similar locations.
Annex C, Appendix 8	Engineer	CBRN, explosive ordnance disposal (EOD)	Addresses clearing of hazards for air base operability with environmental considerations.
Annex C, Appendix 13	Engineer	CBRN, EOD	Addresses clearing of unexploded explosive ordnance (UXO) for base camps and other similar sites, which may be necessary.
Annex D, Appendix 1	Logistics staff officer (J-4)	Engineer, J-4, surgeon	Addresses POL, which always contains significant embedded environmental considerations. Plan for HM/HW transportation, storage, and disposal.
Annex D, Appendix 2	J-4	Engineer, surgeon	Addresses water sampling, well-site selection, and preparation for containing environmental considerations.
Annex D, Appendix 6	Engineer	CA, J-4, SJA, surgeon	Addresses the engineer support plan, which must integrate environmental considerations.
Annex E, Appendix 4	SJA	Engineer, FSE, J-3, J-4	Includes those considerations associated with the environmental law of war (LOW).
Annex F	Public affairs officer (PAO)	CA, engineer, SJA, surgeon	Addresses environmental considerations of concern to the PAO.
Annex G	CA	Engineer, SJA, surgeon	Covers the spectrum of environmental considerations, with a primary focus on cultural considerations.
Annex L	Engineer	J-4, SJA, surgeon	Addresses CA, engineer, legal, and medical considerations that may involve all members of the Joint Environmental Management Board (JEMB).
Annex M	Engineer	J-2, J-3, J-4, any staff requiring geospatial information to support planning	Addresses geospatial information for base camps and other similar sites.
Annex P	J-4	CA, engineer, SJA, surgeon	Addresses environmental considerations and guidance to be included where applicable.

Table 2-2. JOPES annexes and appendixes with significant environmental considerations (continued)

JOPES Location	Proponent Staff	Principal Staff and Special Capabilities	Comments
Annex Q	Surgeon	Surgeon	Addresses numerous areas with environmental considerations embedded, other than in appendix 6 and appendix 10.
Annex Q, Appendix 6	Surgeon	CA, engineer	Addresses FHP, a principal component of environmental considerations. Remediation is often linked to engineer actions.
Annex Q, Appendix 10	Surgeon	Engineer	Addresses medical intelligence critical to the planning phase and especially critical to support EBSs and environmental health site assessments (EHSAs) for base camps and other similar sites.

STANDING OPERATING PROCEDURES

2-23. To enhance effectiveness and flexibility, commanders standardize routine or recurring actions not requiring their personal involvement in SOPs, which detail the way forces execute these unit-specific techniques and procedures. Commanders develop SOPs from doctrinal sources, applicable portions of higher headquarters procedures, a higher commander's guidance, and experience. These SOPs are as complete as possible, allowing new arrivals or newly attached units to quickly become familiar with the unit's routine. SOPs apply until commanders change them. The benefits of SOPs include—

- Simplified, brief combat orders.
- Enhanced understanding and teamwork among commanders, staffs, and troops.
- Standard synchronized staff drills.
- Standard abbreviated or accelerated decisionmaking techniques.

2-24. Unit commanders are responsible for complying with the applicable environmental requirements established by the commander in the environmental considerations annex or appendix of the OPLAN or OPORD. Subordinate commanders should keep the higher command staff informed of conditions that may result in noncompliance or the potential for noncompliance. Unit SOPs (see Appendix J) at battalion and company levels must incorporate specific responsibilities. The operations officer is responsible for tactical and administrative SOPs that include preparing, coordinating, authenticating, publishing, and distributing them. Other staff sections provide input.

ENVIRONMENTALLY SPECIFIC PLANNING

2-25. Environmentally specific planning focuses on providing units with the additional environmentally related resources and information+ necessary to accomplish their missions. This planning includes identifying environmental hazards/risks posed by an operation and considering ways to reduce these hazards/risks through planning. Environmentally specific planning is included, as appropriate, in the running estimates produced at all echelons during the planning process. Chapter 3 includes further guidance for integrating specific environmental considerations into operations.

ELEMENTS OF ENVIRONMENTAL PLANNING

2-26. Staffs should plan the operation to achieve mission objectives while minimizing adverse affects on the environment. Although not all of the following elements are applicable to all operations, they should prove helpful in planning. These elements include—

- Identifying operational objectives and the activities that are proposed to obtain those objectives, to include logistics and HM.
- Identifying potential alternative means of obtaining operational objectives. Alternatives may include using new technologies to minimize impacts on the environment.

- Identifying the environmental requirements applicable to the AO.
- Identifying adverse environmental health and environmental impacts resulting from an operation.
- Establishing formal relationships and coordinating with other disciplines with roles in environmental planning and operations.
- Linking environmental considerations to CA planning.
- Identifying the environmental characteristics of the affected area.
- Identifying possible environmental emergencies that may occur.
- Determining how an environmental emergency would affect the environment in the AO and the way in which the military could prevent or mitigate it.
- Determining the environmental and operational risk associated with the operation.
- Negotiating applicable agreements to allow for the unimpeded transit of HM/HW by military and contracted assets.
- Determining contractor status, to include privileges and immunities, in support of the operation.
- Identifying environmental resources and reach capabilities.

KEY ENVIRONMENTAL PLANNING FACTORS

2-27. Commanders should consider the environment and FHP during each phase of the operation. In planning and conducting military operations, regardless of geographic location, commanders should give appropriate consideration to—

- Legal requirements and constraints.
- Cultural, historical, and religious factors.
- The presence of environmentally sensitive ecosystems.
- Potential environmentally related health risks to Soldiers and Marines.
- Potential for environmental terrorism on the part of enemy forces.
- Targeting considerations to avoid damage to cultural, historical, or religious sites or damage to facilities resulting in environmental damage or health risks to Soldiers and Marines.
- Site selection for base camps and other facilities.
- Camp closure and site cleanup.
- Transportation, storage, and disposal of HM, HW, and POL.
- Spill prevention, containment reporting, and cleanup requirements.
- Transportation, storage, and disposal of medical and infectious waste.
- Solid and human waste management.
- Water and wastewater management.
- P2 and recycling efforts to reduce waste generation and logistics efforts.
- Possible environmental remediation/restoration of damaged areas.
- Environmental requirements pertaining to sensitive site exploitation.
- Environmental controls pertaining to construction operations.

This page intentionally left blank.

Chapter 3

Environmental Considerations and Force Projection

Environmental considerations play a part in all phases of an operation. Planners must consider the effect environmental considerations have and how they may constrain or influence various actions and decisions. In the predeployment, deployment, and redeployment phases of operations, these considerations will be rather clear, and units will have to adhere to the laws and regulations with little margin for noncompliance. In the employment and sustainment phases of the operation, units will have greater latitude (based on the situation and the commander's guidance) in integrating environmental considerations into the operation. Integrating environmental considerations early into the planning activities and effectively identifying and managing environmental risk are key elements of the process.

PREDEPLOYMENT

3-1. Predeployment environmental considerations include training with a focus on environmental principles, analysis of operational and mission variables (including initial environmental risk assessment and integrating environmental considerations into IPB and other planning activities), and logistics planning. Integrating environmental considerations early establishes the foundation for future success and allows subordinate units to begin planning for environmental considerations earlier in their planning process.

TRAINING

3-2. Predeployment environmental training is essential for personnel to gain the proper skill sets to conduct operations in a manner supporting environmental principles. This training includes not only individual skills but also collective training in the integration of environmental considerations into planning and operations.

Individual Skill Sets

3-3. Protecting the environment, Soldiers, Marines, and civilians from environmental health hazards begins with training the individual. This includes the training conducted as a part of the Soldier's and Marine's individual job and the training related to specific additional duties and deployment considerations. Commanders must ensure that their assigned personnel maintain the necessary skills to protect themselves and the environment. Staffs must plan and integrate this training into routine training schedules to ensure that Soldiers and Marines possess the required expertise before deployment. Predeployment environmental training assists in the deployment of military units by reducing the requirement to conduct additional environmentally specific training during deployment, thereby allowing units to focus on mission-specific requirements. While each Service includes specific requirements for both routine job-related and additional duty-specific training, the following areas should generally be addressed to ensure adequate numbers of trained personnel:

- The environmental protection portion of the unit SOP.
- Environmentally related additional duty-specific training.
- Spill prevention and response.

- *Hazard communication* (HAZCOM) **(defined as the responsibility of leaders and supervisors concerning possible hazards in the workplace and notification of hazards and necessary precaution to their Soldiers).**
- HW operations and emergency response.
- HM/HW transportation, storage, and handling certifications.
- Environmental officer training.
- HM/HW certifier courses.
- Field sanitation.
- Satellite accumulation point operation.
- MSDS recognition and use.
- First aid procedures for HM/HW exposure.
- Installation environmental awareness training.
- Geneva Convention and LOW training.
- Personal health and hygiene.

Collective and Staff-Level Training

3-4.   In addition to individual Soldier and Marine skills, units integrate environmental considerations into unit and staff training. While units are already required to integrate environmental considerations into FTXs, they can also integrate these considerations into simulation training exercises. Simulation exercises allow staffs to include planning for environmental considerations, to include those not normally encountered in CONUS field training. The more experienced staffs are at identifying and planning for environmental factors, the more proficient they will become at integrating these factors into the conduct of operations.

3-5.   In addition to collective staff training, certain staff positions require that individuals be aware of various environmental considerations impacting their running estimates. SJA, CA, and contracting officers in particular must be aware of pertinent environmental laws, regulations, and treaties that may impact military operations. Predeployment training is essential to ensure the rapid integration of environmental considerations into the running estimates.

3-6.   Once units are alerted for deployment to a specific AO, they must ensure that personnel are trained in specific aspects of environmental considerations pertaining to that area. The location of the operation, intermediate staging locations en route, and other foreign nations that supply lines may run through will have differing requirements for environmental protection and present different health hazards to the Soldiers and Marines. Training at all echelons may be necessary to prepare personnel for deployment. This training may include—

- Environment health hazards in the area.
- Cultural, religious, and political sensitivities.
- Recognition and protection of *endangered species* **(defined as those species designated by the Secretary of the Interior that are in danger of extinction throughout all or a significant portion of their range)** or habitats.
- Recognition of cultural or archaeological artifacts and buildings.
- Specific environmental laws, regulations, and treaties.
- Transportation requirements for HM/HW.
- Theater-specific training for handling, storing, transporting, and disposing of HM/HW, *solid waste* **(defined as any material or substance [solid or liquid] that is inherently waste-like by being no longer suitable for its originally intended purpose)**, medical waste, gray water (water that has been used for dish washing, cooking, showers, or laundry, but does not include water used for wash racks or latrine facilities), and recycling programs.
- Rules of engagement.
- Infrastructure assessment.

3-7. The following vignette displays the importance of integrating environmental considerations into training.

Issue

The Joint Readiness Training Center (JRTC) integrates environmental considerations into its tactical scenarios.

Discussion

JRTC takes a proactive approach to environmental considerations by writing scenarios with socioeconomic implications rather than treating "no-dig" areas as administrative restrictions. For example, units are advised that the local population has reservations about U.S. forces being in the area. Units are also informed that a power line providing electrical power to the local town is buried somewhere in the area and if severed would adversely affect their units' ability to accomplish the mission. To create defensive positions and avoid digging in this area, units constructed berms by hauling soil from less sensitive areas.

This JRTC scenario forces units to consider the long-term effects of their actions. The mission end state may be impaired when units do not consider socioeconomic and environmental impacts.

Techniques and Procedures

Commanders must—

- Integrate environmental considerations into the mission analysis phase of the MDMP. During mission analysis, the commander and his staff conduct a risk assessment, which includes identifying all environmentally related hazards.
- Develop innovative solutions to limit training distracters, which may be the result of environmental considerations (for example, making environmental considerations part of the tactical scenario).
- Consult the unit environmental officer throughout the planning process.

ANALYSIS OF OPERATIONAL AND MISSION VARIABLES

3-8. Combatant commanders are responsible for a specific AOR. This responsibility entails planning for various contingency operations. As a part of the predeployment phase of the operations, staffs must integrate environmental considerations into contingency planning. This planning includes information gathering on specific countries within the AOR and the integration of environmental considerations into specific plans. Each staff section must take into consideration a myriad of concerns, listing them in their running estimates and intelligence collection plan/IPB for specific countries or operational situations. In addition, planners must include environmental considerations in their risk assessment for conducting operations. This information is essential to allow commanders and staffs to develop plans that protect the environment against undue harm and the health of Soldiers and Marines and support stability operations (as required) in a fashion that adheres to U.S. national values.

3-9. Topics or areas of concern include:

- What are the applicable laws, treaties, FGS, and regulations?
- Are there any *threatened species* (**defined as those species that are likely to become endangered within the foreseeable future throughout all or a significant portion of their range**) or endangered species and/or designated *critical habitats* (**defined as a designated area declared essential for the survival of a protected species under authority of the Endangered Species Act [ESA]**)?
- What are the cultural, ethnic, and religious sensitivities?
- What are the environmental health hazards?
- What is the status of the infrastructure that supports environmental considerations?
- What effect will terrain and weather have on operations (as they pertain to the environment)?
- What types of industry, agriculture, and natural resources are present?
- What types of industry or agriculture that generate HM/HW are present?
- Are there specific environmental issues (such as water rights) that may be catalysts for conflict?
- Are there potential targets for environmental terrorism? If so, what are the anticipated results of the damage?
- What is the attitude of the public toward environmental matters in the affected foreign nation?
- Are specific forces, such as facility engineer teams, required to support environmental activities?

LOGISTICS PLANNING

3-10. Early planning is essential to ensure adequate time to obtain and transport resources. Predeployment planning helps identify the logistic requirements in time to make the necessary arrangements for procurement, storage, and transportation. Adequate provision for environmental considerations may have a significant impact on the logistics system in the areas of transportation, material procurement, and contracting. Much of this information will be provided to subordinate commands in the higher headquarters OPLAN/OPORD. The development of environmentally sustainable logistics and the use of new products and technology will enhance logistics support.

3-11. During predeployment, unit personnel must prepare a basic load list of equipment and other supplies required to protect the health of personnel and the environment until the supply system is established. Equipment and supply considerations include—

- Adequate PPE for use when handling HM/HW.
- Spill response equipment. The basic planning guidance is to have enough material to contain the substance in the largest container. Ensure that team members are trained and aware of procedures to request additional assistance.
- Material and waste containers (including secondary containment), overpack containers, labels, markers, placards, signage, and bung wrenches.
- Fueling operations equipment. Ensure that spark-proof tools, PPE, and other equipment is available.
- Trained personnel to handle the HM/HW. Ensure that HMs (explosives and POL) are properly labeled and MSDS is on hand.
- Trained personnel to handle solid waste.

3-12. A sample of a basic packing list is provided in table 3-1. This list may not be all-inclusive, and unit personnel must adjust their lists as necessary.

Table 3-1. Sample basic packing list

Item	Number Packed
55-gallon drums	2
Bags for sand bags (secondary containment)	150
Block and brace material	60
Bung wrenches	6
Drip pans	12
Eye wash	22
Labels, markers, placards, and signage	15
Large funnels	5
Locks	17
MSDSs	18
Nonspark tools (shovel and pick)	5
Overpack drums	3
PPE	55
Rags	75
Rolls of plastic	25
Spill kits	5
Used bladder material/canvas	12
Wooden pallets	10

Transportation

3-13. Transporting HM/HW is subject to various laws, regulations, and treaties. Relevant requirements and procedures must be addressed to ensure the safe and legal movement of these materials. Since the movement of HM across international boundaries requires coordination, initial planning must include provisions to enact or establish procedures with foreign governments to transport them. Planners must determine these requirements early in the planning process to avoid unexpected delays when the materials become essential. In addition to coordination requirements, planners must include planning for adequate resources to transport HM/HW to and from HW accumulation sites. A *hazardous waste accumulation site* **is a specially designed site for the temporary collection of hazardous wastes where no container may remain onsite for more than 90 days** (the definition was shortened, and the complete definition is printed in the glossary).

Material Procurement and Contracting

3-14. Planning for environmental considerations includes procuring and contracting materials. These materials may be nonpolluting or may be to support other aspects of environmental protection, such as spill response. Purchasing reusable or nonpolluting alternatives reduces the logistics burden by reducing the quantity of HW that must be stored, handled, or transported. Logistics planners must plan to purchase and transport these materials as early as possible to ensure that units maintain adequate, accessible stockpiles. In addition to purchasing materials, military forces must be prepared to implement recycling programs. These programs help to reduce the waste stream by reusing serviceable materials, such as construction materials, tents, and shipping containers.

DEPLOYMENT

3-15. As military forces deploy, specific environmental considerations become more obvious. The additional specific training and resources required are supported by the various installations that support the deployment. In addition, further transportation requirements will become necessary for HM/HW. Adequate predeployment planning mitigates the impact for deploying units and supporting installations for additional environmental requirements. If this planning is not done during predeployment, it will create a greater burden on the deploying force because of time constraints. Guidelines for deployment are listed in table 3-2.

Table 3-2. Deployment guidelines

Adhere to general guidelines (applies to training and OCONUS deployments)	<ul><li>Forward the EBS to higher headquarters after it has been performed</li><li>Ensure that all unit personnel comply with off-limits area restrictions</li><li>Ensure that hazard signs are standardized and personnel are briefed on their meaning</li><li>Verify that units dig (fighting positions and tank ditches) only in approved areas</li><li>Ensure that all personnel know and comply with special environmental requirements</li><li>Use downtime for conducting opportunity training on environmental concerns</li><li>Ensure that leaders monitor high-risk operations and activities</li><li>Report spills and maneuver damage to the proper headquarters immediately</li><li>Verify that leaders are making on-the-spot corrections</li><li>Conduct periodic environmental conditions reports (ECRs) as necessary, and pass them to the proper headquarters in a timely fashion</li></ul>
Reduce Noise	<ul><li>Ensure that leaders are explaining and marking the noise-restricted areas</li><li>Ensure that units are complying with community/installation noise abatement hours</li></ul>
Minimize Vehicle Movement Damage	<ul><li>Ensure that personnel drive vehicles on secondary roads and bypass when possible to minimize off-road damage</li><li>Ensure that personnel move vehicles into bivouac or assembly areas in columns</li><li>Designate personnel to remove mud and debris from roadways</li><li>Drive carefully in wooded areas to avoid vehicle damage to vegetation</li><li>Stay on approved and marked trails and routes when driving off-road, minimizing cross-country movement</li><li>Cross streams and ditches only at approved crossings</li></ul>

Table 3-2. Deployment guidelines (continued)

Protect Wetlands (Marshes, Swamps, and Bogs)	• Obtain a special permit, if required, to train in wetland areas • Ensure that sensitive and off-limits areas are designated, well marked, and avoided • Limit the use of vehicles and other destructive activities when possible • Ensure that drivers use designated bridges and crossing sites • Ensure that units observe prohibitions against discharging wastewater into wetlands or waterways • Prohibit refueling or field maintenance operations near or in wetlands or surface waters • Ensure that units observe prohibitions against filling any wetlands areas
Protect Threatened Endangered Species and Other Protected Wildlife, Vegetation, and Habitats	• Ensure that personnel exercise care to avoid disturbing threatened and endangered species, habitats, and sensitive areas • Verify that sensitive areas are marked
Protect Natural/Cultural Resources	• Ensure that units avoid digging in or near sites or structures designated as cultural resources • Verify that personnel follow instructions not to modify or destroy these sites in any way • Confirm that personnel understand that destroying or defacing archaeological sites, including collections of artifacts, is a violation of the law • Ensure that personnel immediately report the discovery of any artifacts and wait for clearance to resume training • Ensure that sensitive and off-limits areas are designated and avoided
Discern Use of Camouflage	• Ensure that units exercise care to prevent ground covering from being stripped of vegetation • Verify that units use camouflage nets instead of live vegetation, whenever possible • Brief personnel regarding local guidance on the use of vegetation for camouflage
Dispose of Waste Properly	• Ensure that each unit polices its area • Establish designated accumulation points for proper trash disposal • Dispose of field kitchen wastes only as authorized • Dispose of medical and human wastes in an approved manner • Verify that units correctly dispose of liquid waste from kitchens, showers, and baths • Ensure that units properly dispose of reverse osmosis water purification unit discharges

Table 3-2. Deployment guidelines (continued)

Dispose of HM and HW Properly	• Comply with OPORD/installation environmental management office procedures for HW turn-in and disposal • Obtain approval before using chlorobenzalmalononitrile (tear gas) and smoke • Properly mark and report unexploded munitions • Minimize the use of hazardous substances • Place HW and POL waste products in separate containers • Ensure that containers requiring long-term storage before disposal are protected from weather and inspected to prevent container failure • Ensure that waste description records are handed off to replacement units • Deliver HW and POL waste to a designated waste collection point • Ensure that POL and vehicle maintenance waste products are not dumped into sewers, ditches, or streams • Ensure that spill teams are available on-site • Confirm that adequate spill response equipment and material are available • Ensure that spill teams respond immediately to reported spill locations • Report spills as required by local regulations and the unit SOP
Refuel and Maintain Vehicles	• Refuel vehicles only at designated sites • Protect ground surfaces by using POL drip pans • Use POL-absorbing compounds during refueling operations
Perform Recovery Operations	• Use only designated vehicle wash facilities and equipment • Confirm that fighting positions, gun emplacements, and other excavated areas are properly refilled • Collect communications and obstacle wires for proper disposal or reuse • Properly police and remove all wastes and recyclables • Mark and report unexploded munitions • Report, contain, and clean up hazardous spills according to directives • Coordinate for and perform an environmental site closure survey to document the condition of the AO • Inspect all sites before departing the AO

MOBILIZATION

3-16. As forces increase their training tempo in preparation for deployment and as additional forces (including ARNG and USAR forces) are mobilized, demands on training facilities, areas, and ranges will increase. This training will place additional strain on installations and may stress installation sanitation, maintenance, and recycling facilities. These strains will be most apparent on overseas installations that do not regularly host large numbers of military personnel. Planners need to analyze the effects that this increase in personnel will have on installations supporting these operations. In some circumstances, it may prove necessary to request excusal from or modification to certain environmental requirements for the mission. These issues must be addressed early to allow time for the legal and regulatory issues to be resolved, for engineer and facility planners to develop solutions, and for logistic specialists to acquire the needed materials. The installation environmental, engineering, and logistic offices are essential points of contact for coordinating mobilization planning.

3-17. Questions that affect mission planning pertaining to mobilization activities include—

- What are the applicable laws, treaties, regulations, FGS, and installation operational procedures?
- Will it be possible to obtain adjustments or exemptions to laws and regulations? What are the procedures for this?
- Will the installation infrastructure support added personnel—in particular water, wastewater, sewage treatment, solid waste disposal, medical waste, and recycling centers? What steps need to be taken to increase capacity?
- How will training areas and ranges be impacted by increased use? What mitigation steps are necessary to reduce damage?
- Are there adequate billeting areas? If not, are additional structures (for example, warehouses, hangars, and bunkers) safe for extended occupation by military personnel?
- Are dining facilities adequate? Are new food service personnel properly trained to avoid food contamination and the spread of food-borne illnesses?
- Are adequate facilities available for personnel hygiene? If not, have arrangements been made to increase them?
- Are medical facilities adequate for the increased population?

TRANSPORTATION

3-18. The deployment of military forces requires a tremendous allocation of transportation assets. It involves transporting vehicles, equipment, materials, and personnel to distant locations. Units must transport various forms of HM/HW, including POL products and ammunition, in a manner safe for the environment and for military personnel and civilians. This process involves training in the proper procedures and handling, storing, inspecting, and certifying loads. Planners must negotiate transit agreements with other nations as well to ensure the legal movement of materials. Considerations in the movement of material include—

- Negotiating international transit agreements.
- Identifying HM/HW.
- Ensuring that adequate numbers of personnel are trained to certify HM.
- Preparing vehicles and equipment for shipment.
- Implementing safety procedures for HM/HW specific hazards (flammable, combustible, corrosive, reactive, and health).
- Coordinating with local authorities to transport HM/HW and ammunition.
- Arranging the security for HM/HW and ammunition shipments.
- Conducting customs inspections of personnel and equipment.
- Ensuring that the correct documentation for HM/HW is acquired.

3-19. The following vignette demonstrates the importance of complying with environmental requirements with regard to vehicles, equipment, materials, and rear detachment personnel.

Issue

Rear detachment personnel were unprepared to comply with environmental requirements.

Discussion

Many deploying units fail to realize the importance of maintaining environmentally trained personnel as part of their rear detachment.

The rear detachment is responsible for the continued maintenance of existing facilities and HM storage areas and compliance with installation and state environmental requirements. Failure to maintain trained personnel increases environmental/safety risk and decreases the ability to meet regulatory requirements.

Techniques and Procedures

Deploying unit commanders must ensure that stay-back personnel maintain the necessary training, facility access, and equipment to carry on the unit's rear detachment mission.

Develop an environmental SOP that encompasses rear detachment responsibilities and procedures, to include—

- Training rear detachment personnel to assume environmentally related duties.
- Ensuring that the rear detachment has a trained environmental officer.
- Conducting an inventory and walk-through inspection of facilities/supplies between the deploying unit commander and the rear detachment officer in charge. Note all environmentally related issues.
- Ensuring that adequate spill kits are available for rear detachment use.
- Ensuring that rear detachment personnel have access to HM lockers, container express (CONEX), or POL storage bins.

EMPLOYMENT

3-20. The employment of military forces often creates a significant impact on the environment. While much of this impact is unavoidable, commanders must seek to minimize its impact to the greatest practical extent. Reducing or mitigating environmental damage serves to support U.S. goals. Protecting the environment and the health of military and civilian personnel reduces long-term reconstruction and medical costs, supports IO, and aligns with U.S. national values.

INTELLIGENCE PREPARATION OF THE BATTLEFIELD

3-21. Identifying environmental risks early and developing mitigation plans is essential to avoid unwarranted environmental damage. The IPB process identifies aspects of the operating environment crucial to the commanders' decisionmaking. The engineer and CA staffs must work with the intelligence staff to integrate environmental considerations into the IPB. Geospatial engineers can generate geospatial data, provide geospatial information, and create terrain visualization products to further the staff's analysis of the physical environment and help them visualize those aspects of the terrain that may require additional environmental consideration. By identifying environmental considerations, the other staff elements can develop plans, which take into account various environmental factors (such as terrain, weather, infrastructure, and civil considerations). These considerations may include:

- Potential weapons of mass destruction (WMD) sites.
- Potential targets that the enemy may attack to inflict environmental damage.
- Industries and factories that emit, produce, or store TICs/TIMs.
- Location of oil and gas pipelines.
- Potential second- and third-order effects of damage to industrial facilities and WMD sites.
- Endangered species or critical habitats.
- Historic, cultural, or religious sites or structures.
- Ability of the local infrastructure to support environmental considerations (such as sewer and water treatment plants).
- Effect of the weather and the terrain on the potential spread of contaminants.
- Potential force beddown and operating base locations.
- Material and technology used in the AOR that may be hazardous.

ENVIRONMENTAL RECONNAISSANCE

3-22. Environmental reconnaissance focuses on the collection of technical information on existing environmental conditions and the identification of environmentally sensitive areas or areas of relative environmental concern. Planners use the information they collect to assess the impact of military operations on the environment and identify potential environmental impacts on safety and other aspects of protection. With adequate information on both risks, planners can mitigate the impact of environmental concerns on the operation. (See the vignette on page 3-12 for an example.)

3-23. Environmental reconnaissance is a multidisciplinary task best conducted by a base team augmented as necessary with additional expertise. The engineer will likely be responsible for coordinating environmental reconnaissance but should rely on other branches for help, depending on expected areas of concern and required expertise. In many circumstances, however, a team may consist of one to two personnel with limited experience. To obtain effective results, commanders and staffs must work to coordinate for and obtain additional expertise or, at a minimum, additional training support before conducting an environmental reconnaissance.

3-24. Many operations require fixed facilities, structures, or other real property as logistics, command and control, administration, communications, billeting, and maintenance areas. Planners must ensure that any hazards from HM/HW, POL, CBRN contamination, disease vectors, and other contamination sources (such as open sewers or medical waste) are identified and mitigated, if possible, before the unit occupies the site. Planners must also understand the site layout and the layout of the surrounding civilian infrastructure to help determine overall site suitability and to plan for locating various base camp/installation functions. In addition to protecting military personnel and civilians, an *environmental baseline survey* (**defined as an assessment or study done on an area of interest [a property] in order to define the environmental state or condition of that property prior to use by military forces. Used to determine the environmental impact of property use by military forces and the level of environmental restoration needed prior to returning the property upon their departure**) will also help determine site condition before occupation, thereby limiting liability to U.S. forces for any damage incurred. If the tactical situation permits, commanders conduct or direct an EBS before occupying any of these sites. An EBS is typically performed by or with support from engineer elements. However, units may conduct an initial site assessment without assistance from engineer elements. Ideally, units will conduct a full EBS in conjunction with an EHSA. Appendix E provides additional information.

Issue

EBS prevents Soldiers' and Marines' exposure to toxic substances during Operation Enduring Freedom.

Discussion

U.S. and coalition forces occupied former Soviet bases during Operation Enduring Freedom. They discovered a stockpile of leaking electrical transformers. The commanders' risk assessment determined that due to their age, these transformers potentially contained carcinogens. Subsequently, the commanders determined that the risk to Soldiers and Marines, the cost of cleanup, and the value of the real estate parcel to mission needs did not warrant immediate removal of the transformers. However, as a risk mitigation procedure, the site was effectively marked and posted as a hazardous area and recorded on the EBS document.

During its real-world mission, the unit employed proper risk assessment procedures acquired through training scenarios. By taking the necessary precautions, the commanders protected Soldiers and Marines from an environmental hazard and helped safeguard the mission and Soldier and Marine health and well-being. Doing the right thing came as second nature.

Techniques and Procedures

To help safeguard the health and well-being of Soldiers and Marines, leaders must—

- Ensure the completion of an EBS before occupying base camps or existing facilities. (Appendix E contains information on conducting an EBS and initial site survey.)
- Conduct a risk assessment to include environmentally related risk before and during operations.

TARGETING CONSIDERATIONS

3-25. Destroying various targets may result in environmental or civil consequences. Throughout the planning process, staffs and commanders must determine if the damage inflicted is worth the relative cost. In most cases, environmental considerations will be of second- or third-order importance in target selection. However, certain targets must be analyzed based on their effect on the environment.

3-26. Destroying industrial and WMD facilities may result in significant environmental impacts. These impacts may be long-lasting and impact the conduct of U.S. military operations. Releasing TICs/TIMs could spread contamination over U.S. forces, impeding operations, and possibly posing severe health issues to exposed military and civilian personnel. This contamination may affect air, water, and soil. In addition, these negative impacts could create significant political repercussions, especially if the contamination plume affects neighboring nations. The destruction of these targets and the possible resulting long-term effects must be evaluated against the relative gain. Whenever possible, the military should avoid targeting these types of facilities or consider alternate means to disable them. Other means may include precision targeting by specific weapons (which disable the facility without creating some of the detrimental effects) or disabling ancillary and supporting structures and systems (which render actual target destruction unnecessary). In some instances, it may be necessary to conduct detailed target analysis and to consult civilian experts in the field to determine the best means of disabling the facility while still preventing the excessive release of contaminants.

3-27. Destroying other targets that make up the national infrastructure may be desirable based on military necessity. For instance, it may be beneficial to destroy power generation stations, denying enemy forces reliable electrical power. As with other industrial sites, planners must weigh the costs and benefits. If the operation is going to later include stability operations, the military may have to rebuild what was destroyed. This process may cost considerable sums of money and impede the progress of the stability operation. This may in turn fuel continued hostility toward U.S. forces and interests.

3-28. The enemy may use various historic, cultural, and religious sites as sanctuaries. These targets may have particular significance for certain populations. While the enemy may be using them for protection from U.S. forces, destroying them may result in negative reactions among the local and world populations. While U.S. forces have the right under the LOW to attack otherwise-protected targets if used by the enemy, commanders should still be aware of the potential implications of unnecessarily damaging or destroying these targets. In some circumstances, it may be better to avoid targeting certain sites to avoid adverse reactions. Other measures, such as isolating the target or using local security forces to secure the site, may be more beneficial to long-term U.S. interests.

COMBAT OPERATIONS

3-29. As forces engage in combat operations, a certain amount of environmental damage will occur. The steps the military takes to reduce and mitigate that damage will vary with the situation and the operation. In major combat operations, the importance of environmental considerations may be less compared to other concerns. In other operations, such as peacekeeping or peace enforcement, the situation may allow for more comprehensive safeguards. Nevertheless, certain steps may be necessary to avoid damage impacting the ability of U.S. forces to conduct the operation and to safeguard the health of Soldiers and Marines. By integrating environmental considerations into the IPB and conducting environmental risk assessment, commanders and staffs may identify and avoid unnecessary impacts. These vary from the targeting considerations addressed above, to practicing good field sanitation measures, protecting HM/HW and POL stockpiles, and securing vital infrastructure against damage. In addition, international law as prescribed in the Geneva Convention and the 1977 Engineer Modification Convention specifically forbids modifying the environment or deliberately destroying the environment as a means of waging war. Some of the considerations in conducting combat operations include—

- Identifying and securing vital infrastructure against damage and looting, to include power plants, water treatment plants, hospitals, dams, and pumping stations.
- Securing locations that may be targets for environmental terrorism.
- Identifying and protecting historic, cultural, and religious sites, to include museums, schools, and universities.
- Avoiding damage (where possible) to agricultural land.
- Avoiding damage (where possible) to threatened and endangered species and their habitats and important habitats such as wetlands and estuaries.
- Securing HM/HW and POL stockpiles against damage.
- Ensuring that personnel wear and use the proper PPE.
- Practicing good field sanitation and personal hygiene.

SUSTAINMENT

3-30. The military's concern for environmental considerations must extend throughout the operation. Environmental considerations must be integrated into plans and daily operations, as U.S. forces establish base camps, continue to pursue combat operations, and conduct stability operations. These include areas such as logistics operation; base camp and installation operations; sensitive site exploitation; historical, cultural, and religious site protection; and reconstruction operations.

3-31. Units perform inspections, ensure that environmental protection measures are in place, and ensure that HM/HW areas are clean and orderly during the sustainment phase. Units also note, document, and report changes in conditions if necessary. These changes may be significant enough to include with the EBS, such as finding new conditions at the site or increasing the area of the site. Use an *environmental conditions report* (defined as a concise summary of environmental conditions at a base camp site, based on the environmental baseline survey, supported by maps and backup documents, prepared by base camp commanders for each base camp; the environmental conditions report documents conditions at the site if claims or other legal challenges arise against the government) to document these findings. Use table 3-3 as a guideline during the sustainment phase.

Table 3-3. Sustainment guidelines

Maintenance Area	
Containment	• Place drip pans or absorbent pads under vehicles and refueling nozzle in the drip pan • Ensure that POL storage and waste areas maintain secondary containment and are in good condition • Empty water from secondary containment and dispose as HW
HM/HW Locations	• Ensure that POL and fuel storage areas are located away from populated areas and are kept clean and orderly • Ensure that warning signs can be read from 50 feet away • Ensure that lids are on (no funnels), areas are secure, and proper labels are on containers
Environmental Documentation	• Maintain MSDSs for all material, and keep spill response and unit SOPs readily available • Label and date all waste containers as soon as the first drop hits • Maintain turn-in documents and waste manifests
Containers	• Keep lids shut tightly when not adding or removing material. Ensure that there are no leaks or corrosion • Empty containers in the vehicle maintenance HW accumulation site when they are full or nearly full • Keep incompatible materials separated to prevent reactions
Kits	• Order new PPE, dry sweep, prevention tools, and spill kits when necessary • Use gloves and goggles during fueling operations
HW Collection	
Containment	• Ensure that secondary containment is in good condition • Empty water accumulating in secondary containment as HW
HW Accumulation Site	• Locate HW accumulation sites away from populated spaces • Keep sites clean and orderly • Ensure that warning signs can be read from 50 feet away
Environmental Documentation	• Keep spill response plans and unit SOPs available • Label and date all waste containers when the first drop hits • Keep inventory of incoming and outgoing wastes
Containers	• Check for leaks • Empty containers when full or nearly full • Keep lids tightly closed when not in use • Keep wastes segregated
Kits	• Order new PPE, dry sweep, prevention tools, and spill kits when necessary • Keep spill response equipment in good condition, and make sure it is accessible

Table 3-3. Sustainment guidelines (continued)

HM Supply and Storage Area	
Containment	• Ensure that secondary containment is in good condition • Empty water that accumulates in secondary containment as HW • Make sure tent heaters, pot belly stoves, generators, and light sets have secondary containment
HM Locations	• Locate HMs away from populated areas • Ensure that warning signs may be read from 50 feet away • Keep locations clean and orderly, and eliminate trip hazards
Environmental Documentation	• Keep spill response plans and unit SOPs readily available • Label and date all waste accumulation containers • Keep inventory of incoming/outgoing materials
Containers	• Keep items orderly • Store incompatible materials separately • Make sure lids are on tightly when not in use
Kits	• Order new PPE, dry sweep, spill kits, and prevention tools when necessary • Keep spill response equipment in good condition, and make sure it is accessible
Other Wastes	• Locate wastes away from populated areas • Keep locations clean and orderly • Ensure that wastes are segregated • Recycle as appropriate • Ensure that burning is conducted downwind of the population

LOGISTICS OPERATIONS

3-32. Providing logistics support to military operations requires extensive planning. The more material required for military forces, the greater the transportation effort. This effort translates into greater cost and more personnel. The more personnel required to support logistics operations, the higher the demand on base camps and protection requirements. The more planners reduce the logistics burden, the more they can reduce the overall mission support requirements.

3-33. Reducing the quantity of HM/HW can significantly reduce logistics requirements. Using available nonpolluting materials reduces the time and expense of adhering to extensive requirements that protect against spills and the process of transporting the HW out of the theater. Fuel conservation measures can also reduce the amount of POL required. In addition, recycling programs for materials (in particular Class II and Class IV) can reduce the amount of material shipped into and out of the theater.

3-34. Logistics planners must also ensure that they make adequate provisions for environmental and health-related products. These products range from spill containment materials to PPE and to contracting for portable latrine and shower units. Integrating these considerations as early planning factors is important to ensuring that adequate resources are available when needed. See the following vignette to better understand the importance of sound sustainment operations.

Issue

Lack of contract oversight results in improper disposal of HW.

Discussion

During operations in support of the War on Terrorism, the United States hired a local national contractor to haul waste oil from U.S. force positions. The contractor dumped the oil in a local landfill and sold the barrels. Lack of direct oversight of the contractor resulted in a $1.25 million claim by the foreign nation for compensation (later negotiated down to a reasonable fine). The U.S. government should have hired a reputable contractor to dispose of the waste oil according to applicable disposal standards (typically foreign nation or U.S. standards). Contracting officer representatives and contracting officers in theater must ensure that contractors are supervised for compliance of the contract terms.

Units must remain aware of contract personnel working in their area. They should inform their command and the local contracting agency if they see contractors performing illegal, improper, or unethical actions.

Techniques and Procedures

To prevent illegal, improper, or unethical contractor actions, the following must occur:

- The contracting officer will include the proper procedures for waste removal into the contract statement of work.
- The contracting officer's representatives and occasionally the unit receiving the services will ensure the proper execution of the contract statement of work.
- Unit leaders will remain cognizant of contractors working in their area and report all incidents that create potential safety, health, or environmental risk.

BASE CAMP AND INSTALLATION OPERATIONS

3-35. Establishing base camps and occupying existing facilities (such as ports and airfields) require extensive integration of environmental considerations. These sites, sometimes approaching the size of small cities, require tremendous allocations of resources. In addition, they generate waste in quantities similar to small cities, only without the existing infrastructure to support them. Planning for base camp and installation operations must begin as early as possible in the operation—to include establishing environmental guidelines, oversight authority, site selection, and camp operating procedures. Appendix E and Appendix G provide detailed guidance on base camp site selection, construction, and operation.

SENSITIVE SITE EXPLOITATION

3-36. Exploiting sensitive sites may be a significant part of operations. In some circumstances, the existence of these sites may be the primary reason for the use of military force. These sites include WMD storage sites, research facilities, and sites that include possible evidence of criminal actions, such as mass graves.

3-37. Investigating these sites presents inherent environmental considerations, particularly with regard to FHP. The presence of CBRNE contamination presents significant hazards regarding conventional WMD hazards and TIM and IED hazards. The military must take measures to identify and contain the possible spread of contaminants and to protect Soldiers and Marines involved in the mission. Investigating other sites (such as mass graves) may also present health hazards, and personnel must be properly trained in site recognition, exploitation, and evidence preservation.

3-38. Planners involved in exploiting these sites must plan to include personnel who are properly trained in the safety and health measures required. In addition, special detection equipment and PPE may be required to determine the possible contaminants present, to prevent or monitor the potential spread of the contaminants, and to assist in site cleanup.

HISTORICAL, CULTURAL, AND RELIGIOUS SITE PROTECTION

3-39. Historical, cultural, and religious sites are often vital to a nation's sense of identity. As such, protecting these sites may be crucial to furthering stability. Hostile forces, including organized military forces, insurgents, and criminals, may damage or loot these locations (such as archaeological sites and museums). This creates a need to provide adequate security forces to safeguard these sites.

3-40. Planners must anticipate which sites may be present and which may be the greatest targets for damage or looting. The planning process must include identifying and allocating security assets to these locations to support stability operations. Military personnel assigned to these missions should be briefed on the importance of the site and recognizing and protecting the critical aspects of each site. Forces should also avoid establishing long-term operating bases at these locations to avoid damage and to return them to the foreign nation as soon as possible.

3-41. Despite the best efforts of U.S. forces, damage to these sites may occur. Units must report the damage immediately and take steps to protect them from further degradation. In addition, military forces should not undertake the restoration of these sites without coordination with foreign nation representatives and SMEs.

RECONSTRUCTION OPERATIONS

3-42. Reconstruction operations will play a significant part in stability operations. These efforts may include repairs to damage caused during the conflict and damage resulting from previous practices. In some circumstances, these operations may be focused on environmental issues, such as restoring and protecting specific habitats and cleaning up contaminated areas.

3-43. Damage to, or a general lack of, infrastructure supporting environmental considerations is typical for much of the developing world. Stability operations may include the reestablishment or creation of sewer, water, electrical, academics, and trash cleanup services. Planners must assess the need for experts in infrastructure rehabilitation and identify those assets to ensure that they are in place early in the reconstruction process. In addition, adequate funding and financial contracting safeguards are established to ensure efficient construction efforts.

3-44. Reconstruction efforts must also integrate environmental protection measures into practice. Environmental risk assessments are conducted in support of reconstruction projects, and proper environmental protection measures are instituted.

REDEPLOYMENT

3-45. As military forces redeploy, they must dispose of large quantities of waste and materials or return them to their home stations. In some cases, forces may hand over material to replacement units or to the local government. In other cases, it may be necessary to return large quantities to home stations. In addition, forces may need to clean up any contamination resulting from the activities of U.S. forces. Planners must include the time, forces, and material resources in their redeployment planning and the guidelines to ensure that appropriate measures are taken. Early decisionmaking on the disposal of materials and good environmental stewardship during the operation will speed up the redeployment process. In addition to the environmental issues, departing military personnel will require postdeployment health surveys to document their overall health and ensure that possible exposures to environmental hazards are recorded. Redeployment guidelines are provided in table 3-4.

Table 3-4. Redeployment guidelines

Category	Guidelines
General	• Return the area to its predeployment state when contingency operations end • Return the area to the foreign nation, and ensure that it is not contaminated • Turn in all HW to the designated accumulation site for proper shipment
Waste Transportation	• Label and package HW properly for safe transport • Label all containers and transporting vehicles with the Department of Transportation (DOT) label/placard • Make sure contents are compatible with all other contents • Check MSDS for proper packaging requirements • Block and brace for shipping

Environmental Documentation	Provide the following:
	  • Installation and background (a brief description of the installation)
	  • Base camp map (a map to indicate spill sites, septic tanks, and other environmental hazards)
	  • Summary of environmental conditions (a list of significant environmental events)
	Findings and determinations:
	  • Provide an assessment on whether the camp area will impact the environment
	  • Document all environmental damage before departing to enable a comparison to the original EBS. The report should include the following:
	    ▪ Installation and background
	    ▪ Base camp map
	    ▪ Summary of environmental considerations
	    ▪ Findings and determinations
	  • Return the area to its predeployment state when contingency operations end
	  • Return the area to the foreign nation, and ensure that it is not contaminated
	  • Turn in all HW to the designated accumulation site for proper shipment

ECR to Replacement Unit	Provide the following:
	  • Base camp map (a map to indicate spill sites, septic tanks, and other environmental hazards)
	  • Summary of environmental conditions (a list of significant environmental events)

BASE CAMP AND INSTALLATION CLOSURE

3-46. Closing or transferring operating base camps may present significant environmental issues. In many circumstances, forces will need to deal with HM/HW, landfills, sewage systems, and POL spills. Planners should develop redeployment camp closure guidance as early as possible to allow tenant units adequate time to make preparations. In certain circumstances, planners may develop this guidance in cooperation with the foreign nation. In addition, as units redeploy from camps that are to remain in operation, it is necessary to plan for them to recover, clean up, or transfer materials to incoming units. Units must perform an environmental site closure survey to track and document all critical environmental issues and related remedial activities before closing or transferring camps and installations. This survey will document conditions at the time of closure compared to conditions at the opening of the camp or installation, to protect U.S. forces against undue liability. The vignette on page 3-20 highlights an example of environmental issues that may affect base camp closure. Some issues to consider in planning to close base camps and installations include—

- Developing closure guidance.
- Executing the closeout survey.
- Returning HM/HW to the nearest appropriate accumulation point.
- Removing survivability measures, to include filling in fighting positions and removing wire.
- Cleaning up HM/HW and POL spills.
- Disposing of medical supplies and infectious wastes.
- Closing latrine and gray water facilities.
- Establishing, and later closing of, vehicle and aircraft wash racks.
- Removing structures, to include making decisions on material recycling or transferring/selling to foreign nation representatives.

Issue

Unreported fuel spill affects base camp expansion during Operation Iraqi Freedom.

Discussion

A 300-gallon fuel tanker overturned on a U.S. forces base camp. A supervisor coordinated for a unit to clean up the spill site and haul the contaminated soil to a temporary storage location. Due to mission priorities, a senior supervisor countermanded the cleanup. The spill was never officially reported, and the site was not properly marked.

Base camp planners were not aware of the spill and planned to construct troop-sleeping areas over the spill site. As the first tents went up, the original supervisor notified base camp officials, leaving the camp planners with two options: 1) remediate the site or 2) resite the troop sleeping areas. Either option would cost the unit additional time and resources.

During the time of inaction, the size of the plume increased and required a more costly remediation effort. Furthermore, Soldiers and Marines unaware of the spill might have used dirt from the spill site to fill sandbags and HESCO Bastion Concertainers® placed around their living facilities. In addition to safety and remediation cost concerns, a spill of this magnitude could seep into the ground and contaminate the local water supply. This can have long-term effects on friendly forces and civilian populations.

Techniques and Procedures

Use the following measures to assist in the prevention of a reoccurrence:

- Ensure that command emphasis is placed on proper environmental procedures and CRM.
- Ensure that all Soldiers and Marines are trained to comply with spill response procedures as outlined in Graphic Training Aid (GTA) 05-08-017.
- Incorporate all spill procedures into unit SOPs. An example of a unit environmental SOP can be found in Appendix J.
- Ensure that the unit has the proper equipment on-site to respond to spills.
- Report all spills using the electronic spill report message format found in FM 6-99.2.

TRANSPORTATION

3-47. Transportation of vehicles, equipment, and material to the home station is subject to the same requirements as initial deployment. Equipment must be inspected, and personnel must address proper safety, legal, and administrative issues. In addition, planners must integrate customs inspections of personnel and equipment into the deployment plan to prevent the transport of prohibited materials. These include war trophies and possible biological contaminants, such as foreign plants and insects. Planners should also integrate recycling centers into redeployment camps to reduce the amount of material returned to the home station and to put usable items back into the supply system. Equipment must also be washed before returning to home station, and the wash racks used must meet environmental restrictions.

PART TWO

Command Environmental Program

Unit commanders develop command environmental programs to ensure that their units are prepared to meet environmental requirements in garrison, in field training, and during deployments. These programs ensure that personnel have the required training to protect themselves and the environment. This part of the manual describes the establishment of the command environmental program, its integration with installation and deployment considerations, and the environmental responsibilities of commanders and staff at various echelons.

Chapter 4

Establishing the Command Environmental Program

Whether conducting operations on a training installation, supporting a disaster recovery mission, or conducting contingency operations, the military's actions impact the environment and the environment impacts the mission. The Army and the Marine Corps manage millions of acres of land that may be scrutinized by public regulators, Congress, or the courts. The military needs that land to conduct training and other mission activities. In addition, there is the very practical need to sustain environmental resources in a manner that supports the mission and provides a high quality of life for our Soldiers and Marines; their families; and others that live on, work on, or visit those facilities. As well as sustaining resources on installations, the military must protect and sustain resources in foreign nations during deployments and contingency operations. The military also has legal requirements to conserve, protect, and restore natural and cultural resources while accomplishing its mission. By integrating proper environmental management into the mission, the military not only complies with federal, state, local, and foreign nation regulations but also enhances its mission through sustaining operations and realistic training conditions.

FOSTERING ENVIRONMENTAL STEWARDSHIP

4-1. Fostering environmental stewardship and sustainability in units provides a framework for Soldiers and Marines to integrate environmental considerations into daily operations. When Soldiers and Marines automatically analyze environmental impacts and keep environmental issues in mind, they avoid adverse actions and conditions. The command climate of a unit is the basis for fostering a sound environmental ethic.

COMMAND CLIMATE

4-2. From every philosophical or moral perspective, environmental stewardship and sustainment is the right thing to do. As humans make more demands on the shrinking resource base, ethical issues become clearer. Senior leaders must create ethical climates in which subordinate leaders recognize that the natural resources of the earth are exhaustible, that the environment has an impact on human health, and that they must take responsibility to protect the environment. This ethical climate also guides decisions in areas such as the law of land warfare. Ethical behavior is not restricted to the letter of the law when it comes to specific written laws, regulations, and treaties. Instead, it captures the ethos that generated those laws in the first place. By educating subordinates and setting the example, leaders enable their subordinates to make ethical decisions that in turn contribute to excellence.

4-3. Acknowledging considerations for environmental protection during training, operations, and logistics activities reduces environmental damage and costs. Consistently protecting the environment ensures that land will continue to be available to conduct realistic training and environmental problems will not disrupt operations. In short, environmental considerations must be instilled as an institutional and personal ethic. To be successful, the military must incorporate environmental considerations as a proactive measure rather than a reaction to laws and regulations. Commanders must train their subordinate leaders on stewardship and sustainability, counsel them on doing what is right, lead by example, and enforce compliance with laws and regulations.

4-4. Commanders must promote an ethical climate to ensure that subordinates make good decisions concerning environmental issues. Routine decisions may be as simple as emptying a bucket of solvent onto the ground or carrying it to an appropriate accumulation point. A commander must encourage his subordinates to make ethical decisions by ensuring that each of them ask the following questions when confronted with an environmental dilemma:

- What are my orders? Look to leaders for guidance and ensure that you understand what they expect. If instructions are unclear or confusing, ask for help. Review unit SOPs for environmental guidance.
- What have I been trained to do? Ask this question in the absence of specific orders or guidance.
- What does my concept of right and wrong tell me to do? Ask this question in the absence of training and orders. Most personnel know when an action will harm the environment. Do not perform environmentally related tasks without the proper guidance, especially if you have not been trained on the task or you doubt it is correct.

POLICY

4-5. Commanders establish a command environmental policy (see appendix I) to set forth procedures and responsibilities for integrating environmental considerations into planning and operations. Command policies help ensure that all military personnel and civilians in the unit make informed decisions regarding compliance with laws and regulations.

STANDING OPERATING PROCEDURES

4-6. SOPs provide units with standardized procedures for the execution of routine actions. Units develop SOPs that contain a detailed list of actions that are necessary to fulfill the daily environmental responsibilities of the unit to maintain environmental compliance with federal, state, local, and foreign nation laws and regulations (see appendix J).

ESTABLISHING THE PROGRAM

4-7. A unit's command environmental program is the basis by which unit commanders ensure that their personnel adhere to laws, regulations, and procedures and promote the sustainable use of natural resources. In addition, command environmental programs help to ensure that proper techniques and procedures are implemented and that unit members receive proper environmentally related training.

ESTABLISHING A UNIT-LEVEL PROGRAM

4-8. To establish effective unit environmental program requirements, the unit leader should—

- Assess the unit to understand the activities that affect the environment and the state of the command environmental program.
- Ensure that all unit personnel have had environmental awareness training.
- Designate an environmental officer who is properly trained and qualified. The Marine Corps has a specific military occupational specialty (MOS) 9631 (Environmental Engineering Management Officer) who deals with environmental matters. These individuals interface with appropriate environmental personnel and ensure that their units comply with environmental laws and regulations. Appendix H provides an example.
- Meet with key higher-unit staff counterparts (operations staff officer [S-3]/logistics staff officer [S-4] for a battalion-size organization), installation, and base camp personnel who deal with environmental issues. Find out their requirements concerning environmental training, qualifications, and certification of unit personnel; the *Environmental Performance Assessment System (EPAS)* (defined as the examination of an installation's environmental program review to identify possible compliance deficiencies [the definition was shortened, and the complete definition is printed in the glossary]) inspections affecting the unit and common environmental problem areas; and problem avoidance.
- Ensure that the unit SOP addresses environmental issues and procedures applying to the unit (coordinate environmental requirements with appropriate installation/chain-of-command personnel). Appendix J provides an example.
- Conduct environmental risk assessments before training and deployment operations.

4-9. The following are common unit, installation, and base camp environmental programs that commanders establish:

- HAZCOM.
- HM management.
- HW management.
- POL management.
- P2 and HW minimization.
- Recycling program.
- Spill prevention and response training.
- Sustainable range program.

TRAINING

4-10. The best use of available resources toward adequately training selected groups or individuals will positively impact quality of life, sustainment efforts, and unit compliance status. Personnel should know how to accomplish their tasks in a manner that has no or minimal impact on the environment, while complying with environmental regulations. Army Regulation (AR) 200-1 and Marine Corps Order (MCO) P5090.2A require that the military provide training to appropriate personnel and maintain training and certification records according to governing laws and regulations.

4-11. Many environmental laws require specific training requirements for personnel performing certain tasks or activities. These details are normally within federal or state regulations, which usually include refresher training requirements and specific recordkeeping. Sometimes the qualifications of the trainer are specified in the regulations. Required training types include the following:

- HW generators and accumulation points, shipping, and permitted storage or waste treatment. Annual training is required.
- Packing, receiving, transporting, and certifying HM shipments. Refresher training is required every two years.

- Working with hazardous or toxic chemicals (except for personnel performing military-unique tasks). Some specific chemicals require training even if workers are infrequently exposed to the hazards. Initial training must be supplemented if hazards change.
- Uncontrolled HW site investigations and cleanup. Annual training is required for individuals working, visiting, or supervising workers at these sites.
- Asbestos demolition and removal, maintenance, and repair work involving asbestos disturbance and asbestos sampling. Refresher requirements vary.
- Exposure to lead-based paint during building maintenance, repair, demolition, or removal. Refresher requirements vary.
- Discovery and response to spills of oil or hazardous substances. Annual training is required.

ENVIRONMENTAL PROGRAMS

4-12. Units are required to implement or establish training for a variety of environmental programs to ensure that their units meet the necessary requirements and promote sustainability. The extent of these programs will vary with the nature of the unit and the unit's specific requirements, along with the requirements of the installation or base camp where the unit is located.

HAZARD COMMUNICATION

4-13. An effective HAZCOM program will assist leaders in determining what hazardous chemicals are present in their units, how to protect their personnel from hazards those chemicals present, and how to properly store and use those chemicals. The installation or base camp safety officer is the point of contact for most HAZCOM matters, the MSDS program, and the HAZCOM training program.

Key References

4-14. The following laws and regulations are source documents that support the HAZCOM program:
- AR 40-5.
- AR 385-10.
- AR 700-141.
- Part 1910, Title 29, Code of Federal Regulations (CFR) (29 CFR 1910).
- United States Army Center for Health Promotion and Preventive Medicine (USACHPPM) Technical Guide (TG) 217.
- Technical Bulletin (TB) Medical (MED) 593.

Unit Actions

4-15. In support of HAZCOM, unit leaders should—
- Ensure that their subordinates receive adequate training on the HM to which they are exposed, according to the Occupational Safety and Health Standards, Occupational Safety and Health Administration (OSHA) requirement.
- Maintain an up-to-date list of all HM/HW known to be present in the area.
- Ensure that containers of hazardous chemicals are labeled, tagged, or otherwise marked to identify the material and warn personnel of hazards.
- Maintain an MSDS for every HM in the unit (see Appendix K).
- Ensure that personnel are trained to recognize, understand, and use the MSDS and labels for the HM to which they are exposed.
- Ensure that personnel use proper procedures when working with hazardous chemicals and wear PPE.
- Refer to applicable HAZCOM references.

HAZARDOUS MATERIALS MANAGEMENT

4-16. The military's objective is to minimize health hazards and environmental damage caused by the use and misuse of HM. *Hazardous material* **is defined as any substance that has a human health hazard associated with it; special storage, use, handling, and shipment safety procedures and protocols must be followed to help protect against accidental exposure; hazardous materials are specifically identified under federal law.** It is a material that, due to its 1) quantity; 2) concentration; or 3) physical, chemical, or infectious characteristics, may—

- Cause or significantly contribute to an increase in mortality in serious, irreversible, or incapacitating reversible illness.
- Pose a substantial present or potential hazard to human health or the environment when improperly treated, stored, transported, disposed of, or otherwise managed.

Key References

4-17. The following source documents provide guidelines for the proper handling of HM:

- AR 200-1.
- AR 700-141.
- AR 700-68.
- MCO P5090.2A.
- 29 CFR 1910.
- Part 761, Title 40, CFR (40 CFR 761).
- Technical Manual (TM) 38-410.
- USACHPPM TG-217.
- DOD 4715.05-G.

Unit Actions

4-18. To effectively manage HMs, leaders should—

- Ensure that the best management practices are followed for all HM.
- Comply with all applicable regulations, policies, inspections/evaluations, and procedures.
- Order and use only what is required; do not stockpile HM.
- Use nonhazardous substitutes to the maximum extent practicable.
- Conserve resources through recovering, recycling, and reusing.
- Maintain records of all material on hand, received, or issued, to include MSDSs.
- Report HM use, storage, and acquisition by established policy.
- Establish procedures to identify and correct management deficiencies.
- Establish a training program and ensure that required personnel are properly trained.
- Ensure that drivers transporting HM are qualified. According to DOT HM 181 and 126F (see 49 CFR), transporters of HM must (by law) be trained.
- Ensure that adequate spill prevention and control equipment is on hand.
- Coordinate training requirements with the chain of command and the environmental management or safety office.
- Ensure compliance with special disposal and turn-in procedures for batteries.
- Establish HM spill procedures.
- Establish HM fire/explosion procedures.
- Establish emergency first aid procedures.
- Ensure that adequate protective equipment is available.
- Refer to applicable HM references.

HAZARDOUS WASTE MANAGEMENT

4-19. The presence of HW is a cause for concern among installation/base camp personnel and nearby residential populations. However, hazardous chemicals are an unavoidable part of military activities and ultimately result in some waste generation. The proper handling and disposal of these wastes will minimize hazards and ensure the safety of people and the environment.

Key References

4-20. The following laws and regulations are source documents that provide guidelines for properly handling and disposing of HW:

- AR 200-1.
- MCO P5090.2A.
- Department of Defense Instruction (DODI) 4160-21-M.
- 29 CFR 1910.
- Parts 259, 260-281, 300-302, 761; Title 40; CFR (40 CFR 259, 260-281, 300-302, 761).
- Parts 106-178, Title 49, CFR (49 CFR 106-178).
- USACHPPM TG-217.
- TB MED 593.

Unit Actions

4-21. When a unit generates HW, it must take the following actions:

- Establish an HW management program to comply with HW regulations.
- Identify HW properly. Label accumulated waste and the containers that hold HW with the correct hazard warning labels. Inspect containers for leaks, corrosion, or damage.
- Ensure that wastes do not accumulate beyond allowable quantity and time limits. Ensure that accumulation areas contain secondary containment.
- Maintain records of all material on hand, received, or issued.
- Employ HW minimization techniques as a part of P2 efforts.
- Comply with off-post HW transportation requirements. Public road use increases transportation requirements. Contact and coordinate with the installation Directorate of Logistics (DOL) or Facilities Management Office and the Defense Reutilization and Marketing Office (DRMO).
- Ensure that drivers transporting HW are qualified. According to DOT HM 181 and 126F, transporters of HM must (by law) be trained.
- Establish an HW training program and ensure that personnel attend proper training. Most installations conduct HW train-the-trainer programs.
- Maintain a liaison with key chain of command and installation/base camp personnel.
- Ensure that unit personnel use their PPE when handling HW.
- Ensure that adequate spill prevention and control equipment is on hand.
- Establish HW fire/explosion procedures.
- Establish HW spill/leak procedures, and ensure that the unit conducts drill procedures annually, at a minimum.
- Establish emergency first aid procedures.
- Ensure that unauthorized storage or disposal of HW does not occur. HW must be stored only in authorized containers and disposed of as directed by the environmental management office, DRMO, or as directed in the OPORD (for contingency operations).

PETROLEUM, OIL, AND LUBRICANTS MANAGEMENT

4-22. Requirements for POL are an unavoidable consequence of modern military operations. Products sustaining the military each day (such as motor oils, paints, cleaning compounds, and aircraft fluids) are significant health, safety, and environmental issues and management challenges. At a minimum, personnel must know how to handle, transport, and dispose of POL products.

Key References

4-23. References for managing POL products are similar to those applicable to HM/HW, HAZCOM, P2, HW minimization, recycling, and spill prevention and response. They also include CFR (40 CFR 110, 112, and 302); FM 10-67; FM 10-67-1; Parts 110, 112, and 302 (Hazardous Substances); and Title 40.

Unit Actions

4-24. The following actions are required when receiving, storing, and using POL products:
- Requisition only the amount of POL products required.
- Practice inventory control, to include *monitoring* **(defined as the assessment of emissions and ambient air quality conditions** [the definition was shortened, and the complete definition is printed in the glossary]) HM shelf life and HW accumulation dates.
- Store POL products in approved containers and locations.
- Maintain an MSDS for each POL product.
- Provide proper PPE for products handled by personnel.
- Supply labeled 55-gallon liquid-waste containers for the following waste streams:
  - Used oil.
  - Waste fuel.
  - Waste antifreeze.
  - POL-contaminated solids.
- Ensure that adequate spill prevention and control equipment is on hand.
- Ensure that adequate secondary containment exists for HM/HW storage facilities.
- Ensure that containers are properly marked and in good condition.
- Provide drip pans for vehicles and refueling operations.

POLLUTION PREVENTION AND HAZARDOUS WASTE MINIMIZATION

4-25. This program complements the HM, HW, and HAZCOM programs. HW minimization reduces the amount and toxicity of the HW generated or produced. P2 reduces the amount of material, hazardous or not. For example, recycling reduces the amount of trash that goes into landfills. The reduction in waste supports deployment operations by reducing transportation, storage, and landfill requirements and helping to reduce financial liability resulting from claims against U.S. forces.

Key References

4-26. P2 and HW minimization references include the following:
- AR 200-1.
- MCO P5090.2A.
- Executive Order (EO) 12856.
- Section 41, Part 262, Title 40, CFR (40 CFR 262.41).
- Pollution Prevention Act.

Unit Actions

4-27. Unit leaders should ensure that their units conduct proper inventory control. A unit should not stockpile HM. If an HM has an expired shelf life, it can cost much more to dispose of the item than it did to obtain it since the HM will have to be handled as an HW.

4-28. Product substitution is an easy way to reduce the HW a unit generates. Unit personnel should review the HM inventory in their areas and check to see if nonhazardous or less hazardous substitutes are available. Examples are using biodegradable degreasers instead of solvents or replacing the sand used in sandblasting operations with plastic beads, which last longer and can be recycled.

4-29. A process change can reduce the amount of HW generated. For example, a vapor degreaser could be replaced by a soap and hot water parts cleaner.

RECYCLING PROGRAM

4-30. *Source reduction* **is the decrease of hazardous waste generation at its sources. This reduction is to be achieved through product substitution, recycling, and inventory control and by developing new industrial processes that use less hazardous materials, such as bead blasting rather than solvents to remove paint.** The military promotes 1) separating products, substituting materials, and changing procedures to avoid using hazardous substances and 2) recycling to reduce the volume of solid waste. Most permanent installations have a recycling program that units should incorporate into their SOPs. While recycling programs during contingency operations may be minimal, most established base camps will develop programs to recycle Class II and Class IV materials.

Key References

4-31. The following references provide the basis for recycling programs:
- AR 200-1.
- MCO P5090.2A.
- EO 13101.

Unit Actions

4-32. To support the recycling program, unit personnel should—
- Recycle all recyclable materials. Recyclable materials include computer printouts (after ensuring all sensitive material is shredded), corrugated cardboard, card stock, newspaper, high-grade white paper, aluminum cans, plastics, oil, solvents, glass, steel, and brass. Check with the installation environmental office to verify the material recycled locally.
- Separate materials to be recycled by type.
- Refer to applicable recycling references.

SPILL PREVENTION AND RESPONSE PLANNING

4-33. It is military policy and a Clean Water Act requirement to prevent oil and hazardous-substance spills and to provide prompt response to contain and clean up spills. A spill response plan must be available at each operation storing or accumulating HM/HW, such as maintenance facilities, supply activities, and tactical-refueling areas. The plan should address, at a minimum, site-specific response procedures and spill response equipment requirements for each operation. Exceptions will be made in cases of extreme emergency, where the discharge is—
- Considered essential to protect human life.
- Authorized by a discharge permit or installation on-scene coordinator during a spill incident response.

Key References

4-34. The following references are applicable to spill prevention and response plans:
- AR 200-1.
- MCO P5090.2A.
- 40 CFR 110.
- 40 CFR 302.
- Part 355 (Extremely Hazardous Substances), Title 40, CFR (40 CFR 355).
- TB MED 593.

Unit Actions

4-35. Units should take every reasonable precaution to prevent oil and hazardous-substance spills. The unit leader should—

- Provide facilities that store, handle, or use oils and HMs, and implement proper safety and security measures.
- Appoint (in writing) a spill coordinator and members of the unit spill response team.
- Maintain an up-to-date spill response plan. This requirement is generated by the installation.
- Conduct appropriate training and periodic spill response drills.
- Ensure that sufficient equipment and supplies (PPE and absorbent materials) for spill responses are on hand and pre-positioned in the unit.
- Locate all drains, drainage ditches, streams, ponds, and other water sources/outlets in the area, and plan how to prevent a spill from reaching them.
- Coordinate with the installation safety office, preventive medicine office, and environmental management office to determine proper PPE. Know when to attempt to clean up a spill and when to leave the area and contact the installation spill response team for cleanup. The installation environmental management office or installation on-scene coordinator will determine when to dispatch a spill response team.
- Maintain a copy of the installation spill contingency plan. This plan, available from the environmental management office, contains critical/necessary information.
- Maintain a current point of contact list of who to contact in case of an emergency (for example, the fire department, safety office, provost marshal, preventive medicine, and environmental management office).
- Maintain an up-to-date inventory of all HM/HW, and provide a copy to the installation fire department for use in case of a chemical fire.
- Ensure that pollutants are not discharged into storm or wash rack drains or poured on the ground.
- Ensure that small spills are properly attended to, cleaned up, and collected and disposed of.
- Strictly control the discharge of ballast water from watercraft.
- Ensure the management of waste or used oil complies with all applicable federal, state, and local requirements.
- Ensure that wastes produced during the cleaning of fuel storage tanks and combustion engine components are collected and managed as required before disposal.
- Monitor wastewater discharges containing oil or hazardous substances to comply with permit limits.
- Ensure that oil, fuel, or other hazardous pollutant spills are reported to the environmental management office and higher headquarters. The S-4/Assistant Chief of Staff, Logistics (G-4) and the post environmental management office can provide information on reportable spill quantities.
- Establish HM/HW fire/explosion procedures.
- Establish emergency first aid procedures.
- Refer to applicable spill prevention references.

SUSTAINABLE RANGE PROGRAM

4-36. Unit mission training presents a difficult environmental challenge. Unit leaders must exercise caution with noise pollution, waste disposal, spill prevention, water pollution, and cultural and natural resource protection.

Key References

4-37. When conducting an FTX, references relating to HM/HW, HAZCOM, HW minimization, recycling, and spill prevention apply. The following also apply:

- AR 350-19.
- AR 385-10.
- USACHPPM TG-217.
- Local regulations for range operation.
- Unit SOP.

Unit Actions

4-38. As the unit prepares for FTXs, leaders and the environmental officer must coordinate with installation training staff to obtain environmental guidance due to differing local, state, or foreign nation regulations. They—

- Review the OPLAN/OPORD for environmental requirements/considerations.
- Ensure that a recent environmental risk assessment has been performed.
- Confirm coordination with installation and operational staffs concerning applicable environmental laws, regulations, and considerations.
- Determine whether a recent site reconnaissance has been performed.
- Conduct rehearsals to ensure that all safety and environmental considerations are satisfied.
- Review the environmental protection portion of the unit SOP, especially those areas concerning spill response and reporting.
- Make provisions for handling medical wastes.
- Make provisions for handling human and solid wastes.
- Ensure that HMs (explosives/POL) are properly labeled and that an MSDS is on hand for each chemical/product before transporting.
- Have tools, equipment, PPE, and materials available to respond to environmental emergencies.
- Ensure that personnel designated for the spill response team(s) are properly trained and aware of their assignment.
- Ensure that team members are aware of the procedure for requesting additional spill assistance when required.
- Verify areas of environmental concern during site reconnaissance.
- Ensure that personnel understand their responsibilities with regard to reducing HW generation and minimizing damage to the environment.
- Brief all personnel on range or maneuver restrictions; endangered species; vegetation use; and archaeological, cultural, and historic resource considerations.
- Discuss the identified environmentally related risks during planning.

PROGRAM ASSESSMENT

4-39. With the implementation of the Federal Facility Compliance Act, federal or state regulators may inspect an installation without prior notice. Often, the first indication that federal, state, or other inspectors are on post is when they visit the installation environmental management office or the provost marshal's office, asking for directions to a specific site on the installation. Preparing for regulatory inspections should be a necessary part of the day-to-day routine.

Note. If an environmental regulator arrives for an inspection without an escort from the installation environmental management office, contact the environmental management office or commander immediately.

4-40. Regular meetings between the commander and the environmental management team (which may consist of the environmental coordinator, the PAO, the legal advisor, the safety and occupational health manager, the preventive medicine officer, the resource manager, and the land manager) can demonstrate command emphasis and serve to nourish a healthy environmental program. The environmental management team should brief the commander regularly on specific installation environmental issues.

4-41. Installation environmental compliance status may be determined in two ways. The first is through a formal inspection by a regulatory agency, such as the Environmental Protection Agency (EPA) and state agencies. The second way and the Army's preference is through the EPAS.

4-42. OCONUS commanders determine the scope for the EPAS within their commands. They often implement procedures to ensure compliance with applicable foreign nation, SOFA, FGS, AR 200-1, and MCO P5090.2A requirements.

4-43. The commander ensures that the unit's environmental program is effective through self-assessment. The unit may use a self-assessment general checklist to assess its environmental compliance status. Units also use EPAS checklists as a supplement to the self-assessment checklist. Unit leaders, with the assistance of the installation's environmental staff, determine the frequency of self-assessment checks.

4-44. The environmental officer uses self-assessment checklists to check the following unit areas:

- Program management.
- Accumulation sites.
- HM/HW management.
- Solid waste management.
- Spill prevention and response.
- Recycling program.
- Wash racks.
- Storm water management.
- P2/HW minimization.
- Environmental training.

This page intentionally left blank.

Chapter 5

Garrison and Training Considerations

This chapter discusses environmental considerations in routine unit actions while in garrison and during training activities. Integrating environmental considerations is a constant in planning, as is CRM, but specific risks or considerations may be of reduced importance. During garrison and training activities, environmental considerations typically receive higher priority and are more focused on sustainability. Federal, state, and local environmental laws and regulations tend to dictate unit actions. Violating these statues may result in punitive actions. Commanders must be aware of the various installation and other requirements and integrate these requirements into their command environmental programs.

GARRISON CONSIDERATIONS

5-1. Military units occupy installations, which contain varying environmental requirements. In addition, USAR units must comply with their own federal, state, and local requirements. Commanders develop command environmental programs to ensure unit compliance with outside requirements and in support of unit operations during deployment.

5-2. Installations must adhere to a multitude of federal, state, and local laws and regulations in which most are integrated into various Service manuals. As commanders develop their command environmental programs, they must be aware of these requirements—which are generally much more stringent than during force projection operations and can impact the way in which units conduct their daily administrative, logistic, maintenance, and training operations. Units must be familiar with installation, range, and training area requirements and maintain a liaison with installation environmental and public works managers to ensure that the development of command environmental programs meets the necessary requirements.

5-3. Industrial operations, acquisition services, and training area management support the installation's routine missions. They also provide significant support to operations during mobilization/demobilization and deployments/redeployments. Units may avoid unanticipated costs and delays with proper environmental considerations and integrated planning functions. They must therefore coordinate with installation personnel when support requirements are expected to increase, as in the following circumstances:

- Number of troops. Large numbers of troop units may cause an installation to exceed its air, wastewater, and storm water discharge permit levels.
- Operational pace. Additional natural resource or special use permits are required as the operational pace in the training area increases.
- Transportation. Temporary marshalling areas are required at points of departure or railheads to relieve overcrowded transportation facilities.
- Temporary storage. Offloading fuel and POLs at points of departure and railheads increases the likelihood of spills and places additional requirements for temporary storage on installation industrial operations.

Environmental Management System

5-4. To comply with EO 13423 and other environmental laws and regulations, the Army uses an Environmental Management System based on the International Organization for Standardization (ISO) 14001 model. The ISO 14001 provides a set of internationally recognized criteria for an Environmental Management System. It employs a continual cycle of environmental policy, planning, implementation, and operation; checking and corrective actions; and management review. An Environmental Management System helps to avoid environmental problems by increasing awareness and developing sustainable activities and processes. Units must be aware of the installation's Environmental Management System program and develop their command environmental programs accordingly.

Installation Sustainability

5-5. Many installations have recently embraced the concept of sustainability and taken initial steps toward creating a sustainable military. A sustainable military simultaneously meets mission requirements worldwide, safeguards human health, improves quality of life, and sustains the natural environment. This comprehensive revision of doctrine, force structure, training, and equipment provides a unique opportunity and the obligation to integrate and institutionalize environmental protection and stewardship with installation sustainability throughout the military. Commanders develop plans to support installation sustainability goals, including the following areas:

- Energy conservation.
- Fuel conservation.
- P2.
- Recycling programs.
- HM/HW minimization.
- Soil and water conservation.
- Installation natural resource management plans.

5-6. Figure 5-1 describes the continual improvement process. The continual improvement process forms an integral part of installation sustainability.

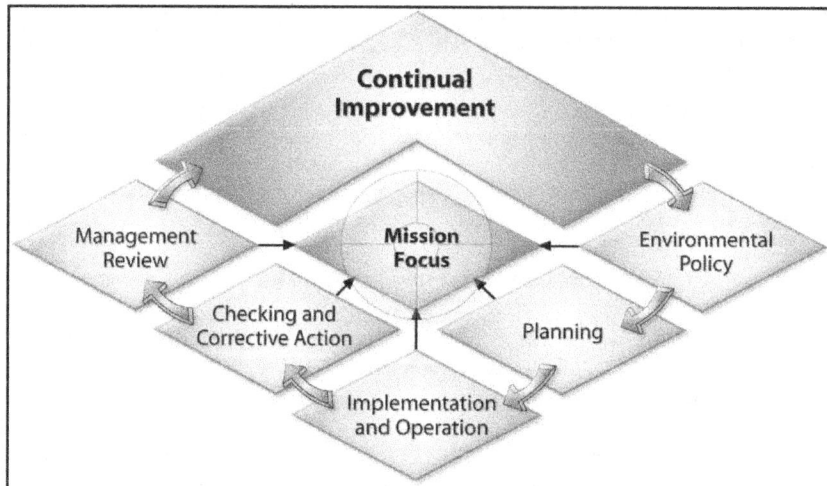

Figure 5-1. Continual improvement

TRAINING CONSIDERATIONS

5-7. Operational readiness depends on sufficient land for training individuals and units. Without adequate training areas, training opportunities would rapidly diminish. This decline would cause a reduction in military ability to effectively train to conduct its mission across full spectrum operations. Therefore, to ensure that the military maintains a highly trained force, it must identify ways to sustain the natural environment while executing its mission across full spectrum operations.

5-8. Integrated training area management (ITAM) is a key part of the Army's commitment to realistic training according to doctrinal-based standards and under realistic combat conditions. The purpose of ITAM is to achieve optimum sustainable use of training lands by implementing a uniform program that includes—

- Inventorying and monitoring land conditions.
- Integrating training requirements with carrying capacity.
- Educating land users to conduct their activities in a way that minimizes adverse impacts.
- Providing for land rehabilitation and maintenance.

5-9. Along with the ITAM, units must consider all aspects of the natural environment. Laws impacting training are integrated into installation regulations and impact the way that units train. These laws include the following:

- National Environmental Policy Act (NEPA).
- Clean Air Act.
- Clean Water Act.
- ESA.
- Sikes Act.
- National Historic Preservation Act.
- Noise Control Act of 1972.
- Resource Conservation and Recovery Act (RCRA).

5-10. To help ensure sustainable practices and to comply with these and other environmental policies, laws, and regulations, leaders and personnel should—

- Avoid operations in or near cultural, archaeological, or historical sites, artifacts, and structures.
- Identify and reduce sources of air pollution (such as dust control in training areas, excessive emissions from poorly maintained vehicles, or parts washer emissions).
- Ensure that riot control and smoke agents are used only in authorized training/tactical scenarios.
- Plan and conduct training and operations to avoid **surface water (defined as all water naturally open to the atmosphere [rivers, lakes, reservoirs, ponds, streams, impoundments, seas, or estuaries] and all springs, wells, or other collectors directly influenced by surface water)** and **groundwater (defined as a body of water, generally within the boundaries of a watershed, that exists in the internal passageways of porous geological formations [aquifers] and flows in response to gravitational forces)** areas where possible.
- Supervise to ensure that released or spilled vehicle fluids do not contaminate surface water or groundwater by taking immediate corrective action should a spill occur.
- Plan missions to reduce the possibility of erosion, and prohibit using live vegetation for camouflage (unless permitted), driving or parking vehicles close to trees, and cutting trees without permission from range control or from the installation forester.
- Avoid tactical maneuvers in erosion-susceptible areas and refill fighting positions.
- Make maximum use of existing roads and trails.
- Recognize threatened and endangered species habitat, and avoid it during training and operations. Also, avoid actions that could harm protected plants and animals and their habitats.
- Mark environmentally sensitive areas as restricted movement areas during field training.

- Write HM/HW and solid waste collections, disposals, and turn-ins into the training scenarios as they would be experienced in the operation (local landfills, recyclers, transport to centralized facility) to enforce realistic training. Compliance with U.S./installation policy should be transparent to the unit.
- Incorporate restricted areas into training/tactical scenarios (for example, identify them as minefields or other restricted terrain).

Chapter 6

Environmental Responsibilities and Duties

Commanders, staffs, subordinate leaders, and individual Soldiers and Marines must understand their individual duties and responsibilities for environmental sustainment and become environmental stewards. To practice stewardship, all personnel must understand the basic environmental management responsibilities that apply to their work area or assigned duties. They must also understand what their roles and responsibilities are with respect to incorporating environmental considerations into the conduct of operations. This includes not only the specific planning process for those missions but also the integration of environmental considerations into all the training their unit undertakes.

COMMAND RESPONSIBILITIES

6-1. Command and staff environmental responsibilities vary by echelon and position. While certain elements include more extensive or better-defined environmental responsibilities, almost all positions contain an environmental component.

BRIGADE/BATTALION LEVEL

6-2. An effective brigade/battalion environmental program begins with the establishment of command policies and SOPs. These documents integrate installation and operational requirements into daily routines. Command environmental programs always include guidance for subordinate commanders, staffs, subordinate leaders, and personnel.

COMMANDER

6-3. AR 200-1; AR 700-141; DA Pamphlet (Pam) 700-142, Part 651, Title 32, CFR (32 CFR 651); and MCO P5090.2A specify the commander's environmental responsibilities. These include—

- Complying with the installation environmental policy and appropriate federal, state, and local laws and regulations (see appendix A).
- Developing an environmental SOP (see Appendix J) and ensuring that it contains all environmental considerations and regulatory requirements right for the level of command.
- Promoting environmental stewardship.
- Understanding the links between environmental considerations and the associated impact on safety and other aspects of protection and FHP.
- Appointing an environmental officer (see Appendix H) and an HW coordinator (these duties may be combined into a single position) at the proper level and ensuring that they are properly trained.
- Ensuring that all environmental training mandated by law occurs.
- Addressing environmental concerns throughout the training cycle.
- Conducting an environmental self-assessment or an internal environmental performance assessment.

6-4. When deployed, commanders will often work with base camps. Base camps—though not installations—are comparable to small towns and require many of the considerations applied to installations. A mayor assists the base camp commander with the control of base operations. A base camp coordination agency may provide expertise and support to the commander, largely through its subordinate base camp assistance/assessment team. This team maintains environmental expertise, supports the base camp commander and the designated mayor of the base camp, provides technical recommendations, and maintains appropriate standards.

EXECUTIVE OFFICER

6-5. As the commander's principal staff officer, the executive officer directs staff tasks and coordination and ensures efficient and prompt staff response. The executive officer is responsible for integrating CRM into operations planning and execution. As a supervisor, the executive officer also ensures that all staff members analyze operational effects on the environment and assess the environmental status, while the S-3 integrates environmental planning and execution into the operations.

COMMAND SERGEANT MAJOR

6-6. The command sergeant major is the senior enlisted trainer and spokesperson, who enforces established environmental policies and standards for enlisted personnel and ensures that subordinate noncommissioned officers (NCOs) do the same. Command sergeant major duties include—

- Providing advice and making recommendations to the commander and staff on matters pertaining to environmental sustainability.
- Assisting with inspecting command activities and facilities as prescribed by the commander.
- Ensuring adherence to command environmental policies.
- Ensuring that newly assigned enlisted personnel are instructed in command regulations or policies relating to environmental stewardship.
- Assessing environmental training at all levels and providing feedback to appropriate commanders and leaders.
- Noting environmental deficiencies and initiating appropriate corrective action.

PRIMARY STAFF

6-7. Whether developing the running estimate, the protection levels, or the EBS, environmental protection requires that each staff member actively participate. Environmental factors may influence a wide range of activities or require a significant expenditure of resources. A single point of contact for all environmental considerations is neither effective nor efficient.

6-8. Unit staffs are responsible for certain environmental actions within their areas of expertise. While some of these responsibilities may depend on the command or commander, all staffs undertake many of them. Unit SOPs at battalion and company levels incorporate specific responsibilities.

6-9. Unit staffs also integrate environmental considerations into the planning and execution processes. Common staff duties provide the basis for some environmental responsibilities while FM 5-0 provides a basis for others.

PERSONNEL STAFF OFFICER

6-10. As the principal staff officer for all matters concerning human resources and personnel, the personnel staff officer (S-1) ensures that the command maintains the requisite expertise to fulfill environmental requirements. Depending on the level of the command, experts may include both military and civilian personnel. The S-1 is the coordinating staff officer for the medical officer, the SJA, and the PAO and coordinates environmental issues between these personnel and across the staff.

INTELLIGENCE STAFF OFFICER

6-11. As the staff officer responsible for conducting IPB and defining and characterizing the AO, the intelligence staff officer (S-2) is responsible for incorporating significant environmental factors.

Additionally, the S-2 must collaborate with other staff officers to effectively coordinate environmental intelligence requirements.

OPERATIONS STAFF OFFICER

6-12. The S-3 is responsible for ensuring that any significant collateral environmental damage caused by command-directed operations is understood and approved by the commander in the MDMP. The S-3 establishes and supervises the command training programs. These programs include providing environmental skill and awareness training to support the unit's mission. The S-3 also ensures that the unit protects and maintains training areas. As the overall ground manager and planner for troop movements, bivouacking, and quartering, the S-3 understands and considers environmental vulnerabilities during operations. The S-3 also requires and coordinates for the initial and the final EBSs before occupying or leaving a site.

6-13. The S-3 may assign special missions to tactical units to secure and safeguard critical environmental resources, such as wastewater treatment plants in urban areas. When appropriate, the S-3 prepares counterterrorism and security plans to combat possible environmental sabotage. The S-3 must coordinate with the engineer coordinator (ENCOORD), the S-2, the CA staff officer, and the unit surgeon to establish environmental vulnerability protection levels.

LOGISTICS STAFF OFFICER

6-14. As the principal staff officer integrating supply, maintenance, and services for the command, the S-4 oversees many functions with a potential for generating HW. Significant environmental issues for logisticians include procurement, transportation, storage, distribution, and disposal of HM/HW. The S-4 establishes procedures for requisitioning, storing, reducing, and controlling HM and recommends command policies for solid waste and HM/HW disposal. The S-4 also recommends command policies for P2 and, in coordination with the S-3, oversees and coordinates the preparation of spill prevention and response plans.

6-15. In staff planning and in supervising food, bath, and laundry services, the S-4 ensures that the staff exercises and implements appropriate controls over wastes and effluents. The S-4 is responsible for constructing facilities and installations and for controlling real property, including EBSs, upon occupation and redeployment.

6-16. The S-4 coordinates property disposal actions (such as the disposal of HM/HW and medical waste) and establishes the authority to conduct nonstandard supply operations for HM requisitioning. The S-4 office tracks disposal actions on the unit's document register, prepares the proper turn-in documentation, and maintains turn-in receipts. To perform these actions, the S-4 coordinates with the appropriate DOD activities, to include DRMO, the Defense Logistics Agency, and the Logistics Civilian Augmentation Program.

CIVIL AFFAIRS STAFF OFFICER

6-17. As the principal staff officer for all matters concerning CA, the CA officer is familiar with the relationships between the local populace and their environment. These relationships include an understanding of the underlying causes of the conflict, the threats to public health, and knowledge of critical vulnerabilities to the disruption of environmental services, such as clean water or useable croplands. *Environmental services are defined as the various combinations of scientific, technical, and advisory activities (including modification processes such as the influence of man-made and natural factors) required to acquire, produce, and supply information on the past, present, and future states of space, atmospheric, oceanographic, and terrestrial surroundings for use in military planning and decisionmaking processes or to modify those surroundings to enhance military operations.*

6-18. In conjunction with the SJA, the CA officer advises the commander of the legal and moral obligations regarding the long- and short-term effects (economical, environmental, and health) of military operations on civilian populations. The CA officer also must coordinate with the fire support coordinator to protect culturally significant sites and targets. In many areas of the world, these obligations include protecting critical environmental resources. Along with the SJA, the CA officer should also be familiar with local environmental laws, especially in overseas deployment areas. The CA officer may supervise CA units assisting local governments with environmental protection services. Finally, the CA officer also serves as the coordinator for foreign nation support and indigenous labor and coordinates with the SJA on civilian claims against the U.S. government for environmental damage.

SPECIAL STAFF

6-19. Special staff officers have functional environmental responsibilities. The following are the key special staff officers with environmental protection expertise and responsibilities.

MEDICAL OFFICER

6-20. The medical officer advises the commander and the staff on regional health matters within the commander's area of interest. The medical officer will—

- Advise on medical threats, including environmental, endemic, and epidemic diseases.
- Conduct pre- and post-health assessments.
- Conduct medical surveillance activities.
- Monitor environmental and occupational health hazards, pest management, food service sanitation, drinking water supplies, field hygiene, and sanitation activities.

6-21. The medical officer also maintains direct access to environmental, preventive medicine, and public health services. He provides health risk assessment guidance to support the commander's CRM decisionmaking process. The medical officer relates the effects of environmental hazards to the environmental health of personnel. In more demanding situations, the medical officer may rely on the capabilities of the Army Medical Laboratory and USACHPPM to assist in providing recommendations to the commander. The commander and the unit staff may call on the medical officer to assist in determining the public health implications of damage to critical environmental resources.

CHEMICAL, BIOLOGICAL, RADIOLOGICAL, AND NUCLEAR OFFICER

6-22. The CBRN officer is the special staff officer responsible for using and requiring chemical assets, CBRN defense, and obscuration operations. A CBRN officer exists at every echelon of command and integrates chemical reconnaissance assets to assist in performing site assessments. In conjunction with the medical officer, the CBRN officer advises the commander with information to understand the current and predicted situation while providing actual and potential impacts of CBRN hazards and their effects on personnel and equipment.

ENGINEER COORDINATOR

6-23. The ENCOORD is the special staff officer for coordinating engineer assets and operations for the command. As the senior engineer officer in the force, the ENCOORD will—

- Advise the commander on environmental issues.
- Work with other staff officers to determine the impact of operations on the environment.
- Assist the commander in integrating environmental considerations into the MDMP.
- Integrate geospatial engineering throughout the operations process.
- Plan and coordinate environmental protection, critical areas, and protection levels.

6-24. The ENCOORD works with the S-4 in performing site assessments for installations and facilities. He and the SJA advise the commander on the necessity for *environmental assessment* (defined as a study to determine if significant environmental impacts are expected from a proposed action). When a project has mitigating environmental impacts that do not call for a complete environmental impact statement, the agency can develop an environmental assessment for site-specific projects to meet foreign nation or EO 12114 requirements. The ENCOORD is also responsible for advising the S-2 on significant environmental factors and integrating these impacts into the IPB process.

TRANSPORTATION OFFICER

6-25. The transportation officer plans and supervises administrative movements. When these movements contain HM/HW, the transportation officer ensures that unit personnel follow applicable laws and regulations. These requirements include the following:

- Training personnel.
- Manifesting cargo.
- Inspecting loads.
- Segregating loads.
- Marking vehicles.
- Arranging for hazardous cargo routes (as necessary).

MAINTENANCE OFFICER

6-26. The maintenance officer plans and supervises maintenance and repair activities. In many instances, these activities require significant quantities of HM and generate HW. The maintenance officer ensures safe use, storage, and disposal of these materials—which often includes operating temporary storage areas for products, such as used oils, contaminated fuels, paint residues, spill cleanup residues, and solvents. Since maintenance personnel work with hazardous chemicals, the maintenance officer must ensure that all personnel comply with HAZCOM requirements.

PERSONAL STAFF

6-27. Some staffs involve personal staff officers who work under the immediate control of the commander, giving him direct access to them. The commander establishes guidelines or gives specific guidance to the personal staff officer who informs or coordinates with the chief of staff or other members of the staff.

STAFF JUDGE ADVOCATE

6-28. The SJA advises the commander on compliance with environmental laws, regulations, treaties, and conventions. He also writes or interprets SOFAs. The SJA provides legal advice and assistance concerning contracts, health care, environmental matters, and compensation matters. The SJA helps other staff officers to understand the legal aspects involved in their respective specialties.

PUBLIC AFFAIRS OFFICER

6-29. Public perceptions of environmental threats may be more significant to mission accomplishment than the threat itself. The PAO advises the commander on methods of conveying information and responding to information from the public. When deployed overseas, the PAO coordinates with appropriate staff and commanders to plan and execute public relations efforts in support of the mission objectives. In CONUS, various environmental laws require public involvement. The PAO identifies and prepares plans for meeting these requirements.

UNIT-LEVEL RESPONSIBILITIES

6-30. In addition to senior command and staff responsibilities, small units must meet similar requirements. In general, these requirements mirror those of senior commands but are directed to a different scale and echelon.

UNIT COMMANDER

6-31. The commander's role in environmental sustainment centers on building an environmental ethic within personnel by training and counseling subordinates on environmental stewardship, leading by example, and enforcing compliance with laws and regulations. Commanders will—

- Communicate environmental ethics to assigned personnel while training them to be good environmental stewards.
- Develop and sustain a positive and proactive commitment to environmental protection.
- Protect the environment during training and other activities.
- Train peers and subordinates to identify the environmental effects of plans, actions, and missions.
- Counsel personnel on the importance of protecting the environment and the possible consequences of noncompliance.
- Understand the links between environmental considerations and the associated impacts on safety and other aspects of protection and FHP.

EXECUTIVE OFFICER/OPERATIONS OFFICER

6-32. As the commander's principal company officer, the executive officer is responsible for the day-to-day operations of the company. The executive officer/operations officer will—

- Identify environmental risks associated with individual, collective, and mission-essential tasks.
- Plan and conduct environmentally sustainable actions and training.
- Analyze the influence of environmental factors on mission accomplishment.
- Integrate environmental considerations into unit activities.
- Ensure that personnel are familiar with unit SOPs and supervise their compliance with laws and regulations.
- Incorporate environmental considerations into after-action reviews (AARs).
- Oversee the environmental officer's performance.

FIRST SERGEANT

6-33. As an essential member of the command team, the first sergeant must be tactically and technically competent and totally committed to the Soldiers and Marines, their mission, and the military. The first sergeant will—

- Manage the field sanitation section of the unit SOP (see Appendix J).
- Train the field sanitation team.
- Incorporate personal hygiene and preventive medicine measures.
- Maintain water supply in the field.
- Maintain waste disposal in the field.
- Inspect unit activities and facilities to identify environmental issues and discrepancies and initiate corrective action.
- Assist the commander in planning, conducting, evaluating, and assessing unit environmental training.
- Ensure that personnel providing environmental training are training to standard.

MAINTENANCE OFFICER

6-34. The maintenance officer/NCO plans and supervises maintenance and repair activities. In many instances, these activities use significant quantities of HM and generate HW. The maintenance officer/NCO ensures that personnel are safely using, storing/accumulating, and disposing of these materials. This may include operating temporary storage areas for products such as used oils, contaminated fuels, paint residues, spill cleanup residues, and solvents. Since maintenance personnel work with hazardous chemicals, the maintenance officer must ensure that all personnel comply with HAZCOM requirements. Maintenance supervisors—

- Maintain MSDS for their AO (see Appendix K).
- Provide required PPE.
- Set up field expedient satellite accumulation points for HW collection.
- Ensure that personnel wear the proper PPE.
- Ensure that maintenance personnel properly manage HM/HW (see Appendix F).
- Ensure that sufficient HW containers are available.
- Prepare a spill response plan.
- Provide trained spill response teams.

SUPPLY PERSONNEL

6-35. HM and HW should be managed through the unit supply channel. Support platoons within the maneuver and forward support battalions supply HM to tactical units at designated logistics release points and should, at the same time, retrograde HW for proper storage and disposal. Supply personnel—

- Supply HM within the company.
- Retrograde HW from the company to the battalion storage area.
- Maintain a log of all HW accumulated within the company storage area (see Appendix F).
- Coordinate with the unit environmental officer, as appropriate.
- Complete the appropriate turn-in documents for HW generated by the company.
- Coordinate with the battalion S-4 for final transport or disposal of HW.

PLATOON LEADER/SERGEANT

6-36. The platoon leader/sergeant role in environmental sustainability centers on building an environmental ethic in their Soldiers and Marines by training and counseling subordinates in environmental stewardship, leading by example, and enforcing compliance with laws and regulations. Leaders—

- Communicate the environmental ethic to Soldiers and Marines while training them as good environmental stewards.
- Develop and sustain a positive and proactive commitment to environmental protection.
- Understand the links between environmental considerations and their associated impact on safety and other aspects of protection and FHP.
- Identify environmental risks associated with individual, collective, and mission essential tasks.
- Plan and conduct environmentally sustainable actions and training.
- Analyze the influence of environmental factors on mission accomplishment.
- Integrate environmental considerations into unit activities.
- Counsel Soldiers and Marines on the importance of protecting the environment and the possible consequences of noncompliance.
- Ensure that Soldiers and Marines are familiar with unit SOPs (see Appendix J) and supervise their compliance with laws and regulations.
- Incorporate environmental considerations into AARs.
- Coordinate with unit environmental officer(s), as appropriate.

ENVIRONMENTAL COMPLIANCE OFFICER

6-37. The environmental compliance officer accomplishes environmental compliance requirements on behalf of the commander. While this position is not a formal staff position, the environmental compliance officer is critical to the commander's environmental program (see Appendix H).

SOLDIERS AND MARINES

6-38. Soldiers and Marines maintain inherent professional and personal responsibility for understanding and supporting the unit environmental program. Soldiers and Marines—

- Comply with environmental requirements in unit and installation SOPs (see Appendix J).
- Attend the required environmental awareness training.
- Maintain environmental awareness throughout daily activities.
- Provide recommendations to the chain of command on techniques to ensure compliance with environmental regulatory requirements.
- Identify the environmental risks associated with individual and team tasks.
- Support recycling programs.
- Report HM/HW spills immediately.
- Make sound environmental decisions based on guidance from the chain of command, training received, and individual concepts of right and wrong.

Appendix A

Environmental Regulations, Laws, and Treaties

Environmental issues are a major concern for our military forces. With new laws and regulations emerging, environmental protection will continue to have a growing impact on operations. Violations of federal, state, or local environmental laws can result in both civil and criminal penalties. Military personnel and leaders must understand these laws and respond accordingly. They must apply the respective regulations, ensure that unit personnel are properly trained, and ensure that all legal and regulatory guidance and requirements (military and civilian) are met. This appendix provides a brief description of the primary environmental regulations and principal environmental laws applicable to military activities. It is not inclusive of all requirements; some regulations are applicable to overseas or force projection operations, while others apply primarily to CONUS requirements. Military facilities are subject to federal, state, local, and foreign nation environmental laws. When requirements differ, facilities should apply the most stringent regulations. The U.S. military does not expect commanders to be legal experts, but they must understand the requirements of environmental laws and regulations. The unit's supporting environmental management office staff is the best source of assistance to ensure unit compliance with environmental laws and regulations.

SOURCES OF ENVIRONMENTAL LAWS AND REGULATIONS

A-1. Federal, state, local, and foreign nation governments have established laws and regulations to protect human health and to protect natural and cultural resources from environmental degradation. Heightened public and federal environmental awareness has led agencies to develop policies to support regulatory compliance and stewardship. The President of the United States also directs the federal government through the use of EOs, and DOD complies with these directives, as it does with any other federal law. The regulations, orders, and pamphlets identified in this appendix provide additional guidance for commanders. The U.S. military will comply with these laws and regulations as they pertain to individual localities or installations, deployments, or operations.

A-2. At most locations, installation environmental support personnel are available to help unit leaders understand the various laws and regulations. These support personnel include the chain of command and key installation personnel (DPW/environmental officer, SJA attorneys, and range officers). Unit leaders should consult with these environmental personnel on the specific requirements for each location. Given state and local differences in environmental laws, military personnel must understand that what is environmentally permissible on one installation may not be permissible on another.

LAWS, REGULATIONS, AND EXECUTIVE ORDERS RELATING TO PREDEPLOYMENT AND DEPLOYMENT OPERATIONS AND TRAINING

A-3. Preparation is the key to any endeavor. As military forces prepare for deployment, various laws and regulations govern the conduct of the operations. Reviewing these requirements will assist military forces in the early integration of environmental considerations.

ARMY REGULATION 200-1

A-4. This regulation implements federal, state, and local environmental laws and DOD policies for preserving, protecting, conserving, and restoring the quality of the environment. This regulation provides guidance on the following areas:

- Environmental components of installation sustainability.
- Environmental support to the Army training and testing mission.
- Environmental support during deployments and contingency operations on and off the installation, and operations at Army facilities that are not officially designated as installations.
- Compliance-related cleanup program.
- Army Defense Environmental Restoration Program.
- Formerly used defense sites.
- Defense and State Memoranda of Agreement/Cooperative Agreement Program.
- P2.
- Compliance with environmental legal mandates.
- Natural resources.
- Cultural resources.
- Environmental protection aspects of pest management.
- Environmental training for military and civilian personnel.
- Base realignment and closure environmental program.
- NEPA requirements.
- Operational noise.
- Environmental quality technology.
- Environmental Legislative/Regulatory Analysis and Monitoring Program.
- Environmental reporting and information management.
- Environmental considerations in real estate and materiel acquisition programs.
- Army Environmental Management System.

ARCHAEOLOGICAL RESOURCES PROTECTION ACT OF 1979

A-5. This act stipulates that anyone excavating archaeological resources on federal lands must have a permit or be subject to civil or criminal penalties. Persons requesting an Archaeological Resources Protection Act permit should be directed to the installation archeologist or the United States Army Corps of Engineers (USACE) district engineer. Installation law enforcement personnel should be aware of archaeological resources in need of protection, and sites should be monitored regularly.

A-6. Unit leaders—

- Avoid digging or conducting operations in or near cultural sites or structures.
- Brief military personnel on the importance of avoiding, protecting, and safeguarding archaeological sites, to include refraining from collecting artifacts.
- Report the discovery of any artifacts and wait for clearance to resume training.

COMPREHENSIVE ENVIRONMENTAL RESPONSE, COMPENSATION, AND LIABILITY ACT OF 1980

A-7. This act, known as Superfund since its enactment in 1980, regulates the past releases of HM into the environment and establishes personal liability for the release of HM. In 1986, the Superfund Amendments and Reauthorization Act (SARA) amended the Comprehensive Environmental Response, Compensation, and Liability Act of 1980 (CERCLA). Together, these laws establish the Superfund program for the cleanup of HW sites. The corresponding DOD program for SARA and CERCLA laws is the installation restoration program. This program helps to identify, investigate, and clean up the contamination that occurs on DOD property.

4

A-8. Unit leaders—

- Report suspected contamination sites to the chain of command.
- Ensure that military personnel understand the environmental ethic and apply it to avoid future liabilities.
- Dispose of all HM/HW properly.

EMERGENCY PLANNING AND COMMUNITY RIGHT-TO-KNOW ACT OF 1986

A-9. The Emergency Planning and Community Right-to-Know Act (EPCRA) provides a mechanism for informing local populations about possible chemical hazards in the community. Also known as the SARA Title III, the law originally applied only to industry. EO 12856 extended the EPCRA to federal facilities, including DOD. The law requires military installations to plan for effective emergency procedures in the event of a spill or an uncontrolled release of HM.

A-10. The EPCRA also requires local governments to prepare for the emergency release of HM by appointing a local emergency planning committee. Facilities with HM operations submit nonclassified inventories and immediately notify the committee when any release of HM occurs in quantities greater than permissible levels. Installations prepare annual reports of HM released through accidents and normal operations.

A-11. With regard to EPCRA, unit leaders—

- Train military personnel on spill prevention planning, reporting, and cleanup according to the installation spill contingency plan.
- Maintain a current HM inventory and an MSDS for each HM in the unit. Unit leaders provide a copy of the HM inventory to the fire department or installation environmental management office.
- Comply with the installation spill contingency plan.

ENDANGERED SPECIES ACT OF 1973

A-12. As amended, the ESA protects threatened or endangered plants and animals, to include fish, insects, and invertebrates. All federal agencies are to ensure that any action (authorized, funded, or carried out by it) is not likely to jeopardize the continued existence of any listed species or result in destruction or adverse modification of the critical habitat. The National Defense Authorization Act for fiscal year 2004 amended the ESA by allowing installations to be excluded from critical habitat if such designation would impact national security.

A-13. The ESA prohibits anyone from "taking," which includes harassing or harming, a listed fish and wildlife species unless permitted by the law. Additionally, the ESA makes it unlawful to remove or maliciously damage or destroy listed plants in areas under federal jurisdiction. Laws imposed on federal agencies include requirements to—

- Conserve listed species.
- Not jeopardize listed species or cause destruction or adverse modification of critical habitat.
- Consult on actions that may affect listed species or critical habitat or to confer if the species is proposed for listing.
- Conduct biological assessments for major construction activities.
- Not take listed species.

A-14. The ESA prohibits the destruction, capture, trading, selling, or buying of the listed species. DOD consults with the appropriate agency (National Oceanic and Atmospheric Agency–Fisheries or the United States Fish and Wildlife Service) before taking any action that may affect, adversely or beneficially, a listed species or designated critical habitat.

A-15. It is Army policy to proactively manage species at risk to prevent ESA listings that could severely degrade military readiness. The Army identifies species at risk as those species that are official candidates for ESA listing, classified as critically imperiled on a global scale, or a concern for the ESA listing in the foreseeable future. Implementing proactive measures to prevent the listing of a species at risk would be beneficial to both the Army and the species.

A-16. Unit leaders—

- Enforce range control and installation environmental regulations.
- Avoid actions that could harm protected plants and animals and their habitats on the installation and on any off-post training areas.
- Recognize threatened and endangered species' habitats and avoid them during training, operations, and logistics activities.
- Avoid actions that could harm species at risk and their habitats on Army property, if feasible.
- Mark environmentally sensitive areas as restricted movement areas during field training.
- Consult and coordinate with the environmental office for other local requirements relating to wildlife and natural vegetation.
- Avoid brush and tree cutting for camouflage.
- Coordinate with preventive medicine personnel.
- Avoid damage to marked wildlife food plots and watering areas.
- Comply with the installation endangered species management plan.
- Provide the environmental office with information, when applicable, on the impacts that critical habitat designated on the installation would have on the mission.

EXECUTIVE ORDER 11987

A-17. EO 11987 directs all federal agencies to prevent the introduction of exotic species (all plants and animals not occurring, either presently or historically, in any ecosystem of the United States) into the natural ecosystems of the United States (United States means all 50 states, the District of Columbia, the Commonwealth of Puerto Rico, American Samoa, the Virgin Islands, Guam, and the Trust Territory of the Pacific Islands). This order is of special importance when addressing redeployments to the United States from areas OCONUS.

EXECUTIVE ORDER 11990

A-18. EO 11990 addresses the actions federal agencies must take to identify and protect wetlands. Additionally, it directs agencies to take into consideration the effects of actions within wetlands. The intent is to preserve and enhance the natural values of wetlands and to minimize the risk of wetland destruction.

EXECUTIVE ORDER 12088

A-19. EO 12088 links federal environmental regulations with federal facilities. It directs all federal facilities to control and monitor *environmental pollution* (**defined as the condition resulting from the presence of chemical, mineral, radioactive, or biological substances that alter the natural environment or that adversely affect human health or the quality of life, biosystems, the environment, structures and equipment, recreational opportunities, aesthetics, or natural beauty**) according to federal environmental regulations.

A-20. This order also established the A-106 (1383) reporting process, now referred to as environmental program requirements. In November 1988, the EPA issued The Yellow Book: Guide to Environmental Enforcement and Compliance at Federal Facilities, which establishes a comprehensive and proactive approach by which federal facilities may comply with federal regulations.

EXECUTIVE ORDER 12580

A-21. EO 12580 (amended EO 12088) delegates CERCLA duties and powers (as amended by the SARA). It provides for a national contingency plan to provide national and regional response teams to plan and coordinate HM/HW preparedness and response actions. The response teams may include representatives from state and local governments.

EXECUTIVE ORDER 13007

A-22. EO 13007 provides direction to federal agencies on managing Native American sacred sites. It requires that federal agencies allow Native Americans reasonable access to lands that contain sacred sites. Further, federal agencies must avoid adversely affecting the "physical integrity" of sacred sites and ensure that reasonable notice is provided to Indian tribes when land management policies may restrict future access or adversely affect sacred sites.

EXECUTIVE ORDER 13101

A-23. EO 13101 (replaced EO 12995 and EO 12873) requires federal agencies to incorporate waste prevention and recycling into their daily operations and implement cost-effective procurement preference programs for recycled and environmentally preferable products and services. P2 whenever feasible is national policy. Pollution that cannot be prevented should be recycled; pollution that cannot be prevented or recycled should be treated in an environmentally safe manner. Disposal should be employed only as a last resort. Federal agencies shall comply with executive branch policies for the acquisition and use of environmentally preferable products and services and implement cost-effective procurement preference programs favoring the purchase of these products and services.

EXECUTIVE ORDER 13423

A-24. EO 13423 requires federal agencies to lead by example in advancing the nation's energy security and environmental performance by achieving goals in the area of—

- Vehicles. Increase purchase of alternative fuel, hybrid, and plug-in hybrid electric vehicles when commercially available.
- Petroleum conservation. Reduce petroleum consumption in fleet vehicles by 2 percent annually through the year 2015.
- Alternative fuel use. Increase alternative fuel consumption at least 10 percent annually.
- Energy efficiency. Reduce energy intensity by 3 percent annually through the year 2015 (30 percent by the year 2015).
- Greenhouse gases. Reduce energy intensity by 3 percent annually (30 percent by the year 2015) in order to reduce greenhouse gas emissions.
- Renewable power. At least 50 percent of current renewable energy purchases must come from new renewable sources (in service after 1 January 1999).
- Building performance. Construct or renovate buildings according to sustainability strategies, including resource conservation, reduction, and use; siting; and indoor environmental quality.
- Water conservation. Reduce water consumption intensity by 2 percent annually through 2015.
- Procurement. Expand purchases of environmentally sound goods and services, including biobased products.
- P2. Reduce use of chemicals and toxic materials and purchase lower-risk chemicals and toxic materials from the top priority list.

- Electronics management. Annually, 95 percent of electronic products purchased must meet Electronic Product Environmental Assessment Tool standards where applicable; enable Energy Star® features on 100 percent of computers and monitors; and reuse, donate, sell, or recycle 100 percent of electronic products using environmentally sound management practices.
- Environmental management systems. Implement Environmental Management System at all appropriate organizational levels to ensure use of Environmental Management System as the primary management approach for addressing environmental aspects of internal agency operations and activities.

FEDERAL FACILITY COMPLIANCE ACT OF 1992

A-25. The Federal Facility Compliance Act applies only to RCRA requirements. However, this act represents a growing consensus that federal facilities should comply with environmental laws in the same manner as private, nongovernmental civilian agencies.

A-26. Originally passed in 1992, the Federal Facility Compliance Act subjects DOD employees at all levels to personal criminal liability for environmental violations of any federal or state solid waste or HW law. Criminal sanctions under federal HW law (the RCRA) include a maximum fine of up to $250,000, a jail sentence of up to 15 years, or both. The Federal Facility Compliance Act also allows regulatory agencies to issue *notices of violation* (NOVs) (defined as a formal written document provided to an installation by a regulatory agency as a result of environmental noncompliance) and impose civil fines and administrative action for solid waste and HW violations. Unit leaders—

- Cooperate with environmental inspectors.
- Perform assessments of the military personnel work areas to ensure compliance with environmental guidelines.
- Inform the chain of command when environmental problems are discovered.

FEDERAL INSECTICIDE, FUNGICIDE, AND RODENTICIDE ACT OF 1972

A-27. The Federal Insecticide, Fungicide, and Rodenticide Act requires pesticide products to be licensed or registered by the EPA. It also requires proper management of pesticide use, storage, and disposal. Only certified personnel or someone under the direct supervision of a certified person may use restricted-use pesticides.

A-28. Unit leaders—

- Ensure that field sanitation teams are properly trained in the use of HM in the field sanitation kit (for example, pesticides, rodenticides, insecticides [insect repellent], and fungicides [foot powder]).
- Employ procedures according to FM 21-10 and FM 4-25.12.
- Notify the installation DPW or G-4 concerning pest control in unit billets and dining facilities.

FEDERAL HAZARDOUS MATERIALS TRANSPORTATION LAW OF 1975

A-29. Formerly known as the Hazardous Material Transportation Act, this federal HM law authorizes the U.S. DOT to issue interstate and intrastate regulations related to transportation of HM. DOT oversight applies to packing and repacking, handling, labeling, marking, placarding, and routing.

A-30. In addition, the Federal Hazardous Materials Transportation Law establishes recordkeeping requirements and a registration program for shippers, carriers, and container manufacturers. Units most commonly haul HM in the form of POL products and ordnance. Units comply with these requirements during operations and deployments requiring vehicle movement or convoys on federal and state highways. Unit leaders—

- Train military personnel on proper transportation procedures, to include vehicle placarding, material packaging, vehicle loading, operator requirements, safety precautions, and spill procedures.

- Ensure accountability for all HM.
- Apply the CRM process to each unit movement requirement.

MARINE CORPS ORDER P5090.2A

A-31. MCO P5090.2A provides policy and responsibilities for cultural resources management and identifies applicable statutory and regulatory requirements for cultural resource and Native American programs. It provides guidance to Marine forces operating ashore after disembarking. For guidance while afloat, see Naval Warfare Publication (NWP) 4-11 to incorporate environmental considerations into naval doctrine and reference Chief of Naval Operations Instruction (OPNAVINST) 5090.1B for specific guidance.

A-32. This MCO also establishes specific Marine Corps policy and responsibilities for compliance with federal, state, and local environmental legislative and regulatory requirements. It addresses the following major areas:

- Protection of human health and the environment.
- Compliance with appropriate laws and regulations.
- Remediation of past contamination.
- P2.
- Preservation of natural, historical, and cultural resources.

MILITARY MUNITIONS RULE OF 1997

A-33. This rule amends RCRA and identifies when conventional and chemical munitions become HW under the law. It is a minimum federal standard for the management of waste military munitions and provides new procedures for the storage, transport, and disposal of such waste. DOD, other federal agencies, and government contractors who produce or use military munitions for DOD are affected by this rule. States may adopt military munitions requirements more stringent than the federal rules.

A-34. Unused munitions become waste when abandoned (for example, buried, placed in landfills, or dumped at sea); detonated (except as a consequence of intended use); burned, incinerated, or treated before disposal; removed from storage for treatment/disposal; deteriorated or damaged beyond repair; recycled or reused; or declared as waste by an authorized military official.

A-35. Military munitions are not waste when used for their intended purpose, such as training; as a part of research, development, testing, and evaluation activities; or during range clearance activities on active and inactive ranges. This rule excludes unused munitions that are repaired, reused, recycled, reclaimed, disassembled, reconfigured, or otherwise subject to materials recovery activities. Assignment of a particular condition code or placement in one of DOD's demilitarization accounts is not an indicator of whether an item is a waste, since many of these materials are subject to recovering, reusing, and recycling activities. (See actions associated with the Federal Hazardous Materials Transportation Law of 1998). Unit leaders—

- Train military personnel on proper procedures for the transportation, storage, handling, and return of military munitions.
- Ensure accountability for all munitions.
- Report all problems with damaged or malfunctioning munitions through the chain of command and the issuing/turn-in facility.

NATIONAL ENVIRONMENTAL POLICY ACT OF 1969

A-36. The NEPA affects virtually every proposed action on military installations. Installations pay particular attention to actions that may present a danger to the health, safety, or welfare of civilian and military personnel or cause irreparable harm to animal or plant life. The act requires federal agencies to consider the environmental impacts of their actions during planning and decisionmaking.

A-37. Installations document these considerations while ensuring public involvement in the planning process. Only those actions categorically excluded from NEPA documentation requirements are exempt. (See appendix B, Section II, of 32 CFR 651 for a list of categorical exclusions). EO 12114 extends the application of the act philosophy to major federal actions in foreign nations. No impact to any resource shall be implemented until an environmental assessment or an environmental impact statement is completed according to the NEPA document. Unit leaders—

- Identify areas of environmental concern.
- Identify mission-related environmental risks.
- Identify potential effects of environmental factors on missions and operations.
- Discuss environmental risk in training meetings and briefings.
- Identify alternative training scenarios and techniques.
- Consult installation environmental office personnel regarding requirements for NEPA documentation.

NATIONAL HISTORIC PRESERVATION ACT OF 1966

A-38. The National Historic Preservation Act requires federal agencies to consider the effects of their actions on cultural and historical resources, such as with regard to construction, leases, land transactions, and base realignment and closure. It seeks to safeguard against the loss of irreplaceable historical properties, especially those located on federal land. Many Army facilities are located on historical and archaeological sites, to include prehistoric settlements and 19th century cantonments.

A-39. Unit leaders—

- Identify and recognize possible archaeological and historical artifacts, sites, and structures.
- Plan and conduct training, operations, and logistics activities to avoid damage to archaeological or historical artifacts, sites, or structures.
- Instruct military personnel to leave historical artifacts in place and report newly discovered items to the chain of command.
- Report vandalism, theft, or damage to historical, cultural, or archaeological sites.

NATIVE AMERICAN GRAVES PROTECTION AND REPATRIATION ACT OF 1990

A-40. The Native American Graves Protection and Repatriation Act ensures the protection and rightful disposition of Native American cultural items, including human remains, from federal lands. It establishes a consultation process for the intentional excavation or inadvertent discovery of protected cultural items. Military personnel must immediately report the discovery of Native American remains and artifacts.

A-41. Unit leaders—

- Identify and recognize possible Native American historical artifacts, sites, and remains.
- Plan and conduct training, operations, and logistics activities to avoid damage to Native American historical artifacts, sites, or remains.
- Instruct military personnel to leave Native American historical artifacts, sites, or remains in place and report newly discovered items to the chain of command.
- Report vandalism, theft, or damage of Native American artifacts, sites, or remains.

NOISE CONTROL ACT OF 1972

A-42. Through the Noise Control Act, the President established a national policy to promote an environment free from noise jeopardizing the public health and welfare. The act also regulates noise emissions from commercial equipment, such as transportation and construction equipment. The act exempts noise from military weapons or combat equipment.

A-43. Unit leaders—

- Comply with local and installation noise restrictions.
- Maintain equipment to perform to specifications.
- Check with range control to confirm installation compatible use zone program requirements.

OIL POLLUTION ACT OF 1990

A-44. The Oil Pollution Act is far more comprehensive and stringent than any previous U.S. or international oil pollution liability and prevention law. It is divided into nine titles, focused on oil spills by vessels and facilities. This act serves principally as a response to events such as the grounding of the Exxon Valdez and several subsequent accidents in 1989 and 1990. It establishes a standard for measuring natural resource damage applicable to all actions for such damage.

A-45. In addition, the Oil Pollution Act emphasizes the federal direction of public and private efforts both to avert the threat of an oil spill and to respond to remove oil that has been spilled. The act specifies federal preeminence in undertaking and directing response actions, but preserves state authority over significant aspects of removal activities. Unit leaders—

- Train unit spill prevention/response teams.
- Report all known or suspected spills through the chain of command and according to the unit SOP.
- Comply with the installation spill contingency plan.
- Ensure that the unit has appropriate spill kits and PPE.
- Apply the CRM process to each operation to reduce the probability and severity of potential spills.

PART 651, TITLE 32

A-46. This regulation implements NEPA within the Army, which sets forth Army policies and responsibilities for the early integration of environmental considerations into Army planning and decisionmaking. The NEPA process described in this regulation applies to installations and units. This regulation establishes criteria to determine whether Army actions are covered under categorical exclusion or if an environmental assessment or *environmental impact statement* (**defined as a detailed description of the effects, impacts, or consequences associated with designing, manufacturing, testing, operating, maintaining, and disposing of weapon systems or automated information systems. Under the National Environmental Policy Act, an environmental impact statement is required when cultural resources may be damaged or significantly adversely affected**) is required.

POLLUTION PREVENTION ACT OF 1990

A-47. The Pollution Prevention Act established the national policy that pollution should be prevented or reduced at the source whenever feasible. Preventing pollution offers important economic benefits, because avoiding pollution reduces the need for expensive investments in waste management or cleanup.

A-48. The Pollution Prevention Act is multimedia (in this context, multimedia refers to water, air, and land). Source reduction practices do not focus on treatment and disposal of waste from one media, such as air. Instead, source reduction seeks to eliminate pollutants in all media—water, air, and land.

A-49. Under Section 6602(b) of the Pollution Prevention Act, Congress established a national policy. The policy states the following:

- Pollution should be prevented or reduced at the source whenever feasible.
- Pollution that cannot be prevented should be recycled in an environmentally safe manner whenever feasible.

- Pollution that cannot be prevented or recycled should be treated in an environmentally safe manner whenever feasible.
- Disposal or other release into the environment should be employed only as a last resort and should be conducted in an environmentally safe manner.

A-50. Unit leader actions include complying with all legal requirements by promoting P2 as the preferred means of achieving environmental compliance, protecting human health and the environment by reducing the use of HM to as near zero as possible, and reducing costs by integrating cost-effective P2 practices into all DOD operations and activities, while ensuring performance of DOD's mission.

QUIET COMMUNITIES ACT OF 1978

A-51. The Quiet Communities Act amended the Noise Control Act to allow local communities to develop ordinances controlling unnecessarily loud noises. To minimize contention between installations and surrounding communities, DOD established the installation compatible use zone program. Objectives for this program include the following:

- Assess the environmental impacts of noise produced by proposed actions by both on-post and off-post noise sources.
- Comply with federal regulations.
- Ensure installation mission compatibility with local land use.
- Minimize *environmental noise* (defined as the outdoor noise environment consisting of all noise [including ambient noise] from all sources that extend beyond, but do not include, the workplace) impact through engineering, operational controls, physical location, and architecture.
- Protect the health and welfare of all individuals adjacent to the installation.

A-52. Unit leaders—

- Comply with local and installation noise restrictions.
- Maintain equipment to perform to maintenance specifications.
- Confirm installation compatible use zone program requirements with range control.

RESOURCE CONSERVATION AND RECOVERY ACT OF 1976

A-53. The RCRA (originally the Solid Waste Disposal Act), with amendments, establishes guidelines and standards for HW generation, transportation, treatment, storage, and disposal. All states require RCRA operating permits for HW treatment, storage, and disposal facilities. The act also covers the laws surrounding the disposal of solid waste, to include solid waste management, landfill regulation, recycling, and affirmative procurement.

A-54. RCRA regulations require training for military personnel handling or managing HM. They also require management of underground storage tanks and cleanup of hydrocarbon contamination. Unit leaders—

- Comply with the installation HW management plan.
- Support the installation recycling program (ensuring that Soldiers and Marines understand its importance).
- Remove expended brass, communications wire, concertina, and trip wires from waste (see the Military Munitions Rule).
- Conduct police calls to collect and dispose of solid waste (trash).
- Dispose of kitchen waste only as authorized and prohibit garbage burning/burying.
- Ensure that the unit SOP covers HM/HW, including spill contingencies.
- Collect and turn in HM/HW according to local and installation procedures, both in garrison and in the field.
- Clean up, report, and document hazardous spills properly.
- Transport HW according to local and installation procedures.

- Conduct maintenance and allow the use of HM only after military personnel have been properly trained.
- Ensure that the unit environmental officer is properly trained and that the training is documented.
- Maintain a current HM inventory and an MSDS for every HM in the unit. Provide a copy of the HM inventory to the fire department or installation environmental management office.

SAFE DRINKING WATER ACT OF 1974

A-55. The Safe Drinking Water Act regulates drinking water quality by basing assessments of water quality on levels of pollutants present in the water. Water supply facility managers analyze treated water regularly. If water quality is below standards, water supply providers must notify their customers.

A-56. Unit leaders—

- Enforce the installation water conservation plan.
- Brief military personnel on the impact of polluting water sources.
- Employ P2 practices.
- Report all concerns regarding water quality through the chain of command.

SIKES ACT OF 1985

A-57. The Sikes Act, as amended in November 1997, requires the development and implementation of integrated natural resource management plans on installations where the Secretary of the Army determines significant natural resources exist. Integrated natural resource management plans are comprehensive plans that assist the installation commanders in their efforts to conserve and rehabilitate natural resources consistent with the use of military installations to ensure the preparedness of the armed forces. Installation integrated natural resource management plans reflect a cooperative and mutual agreement between the installation commander, the regional office of the United States Fish and Wildlife Service, and the agency designated by the host state.

A-58. Unit leaders—

- Enforce range control and installation environmental regulations.
- Avoid actions that could harm protected animals and their habitat on the installation and any off-post training areas.
- Recognize threatened and endangered species' habitats and avoid them during training, operations, and logistics activities.
- Mark environmentally sensitive areas as restricted movement areas during field training.
- Consult with the environmental office for other local requirements relating to fish and wildlife.
- Avoid damage to marked wildlife food plots and watering areas.
- Comply with the installation endangered species management plan.
- Participate in the planning, development, and implementation of the installation integrated natural resource management plan.

TOXIC SUBSTANCES CONTROL ACT OF 1976

A-59. The Toxic Substances Control Act places restrictions on certain chemical substances. These restrictions seek to limit human and environmental exposure to highly toxic substances, including chlorofluorocarbons (CFCs), polychlorinated biphenyls (PCBs), and asbestos. The act requires chemical testing of substances entering the environment and regulates the release of these chemicals.

A-60. Unit leaders—

- Report any suspected asbestos-containing material or PCBs to the installation environmental management office.
- Train all military personnel performing maintenance on any air conditioning system on proper procedures for the use, recovery, recycling, or disposal of refrigerants.

STATE AND LOCAL LAWS

A-61. Each state maintains its own regulatory organization charged with developing and implementing environmental regulations. Many state regulations parallel federal environmental regulations and are often more stringent.

A-62. Local laws and ordinances address the concerns of the local communities. Generally, they are based on federal and state laws. However, each municipality or community may place restrictions that are more stringent on certain activities, such as noise restrictions during certain hours of the day.

LAWS, REGULATIONS, TREATIES, AND DEPARTMENT OF DEFENSE INSTRUCTIONS RELATING TO FORCE PROJECTION OPERATIONS

A-63. Specific guidelines govern the operations conducted by our military forces. These guidelines include both specified and implied tasks relating to environmental considerations. Identifying and understanding these tasks and requirements will assist commanders in executing operations in a manner that protects Soldier and Marine health and the environment, while also protecting commanders from liability for environmental damage or violation of the LOW.

FINAL GOVERNING STANDARDS

A-64. The U.S. military is committed to actively addressing environmental quality issues in relation to neighboring communities and assuring that consideration of the environment is an integral part of all decisions. Installations and units OCONUS that are not subject to federal environmental regulations promulgated by EPA will comply, in areas where an FGS/SOFA is not published, with the OEBGD, AR 200-1, and 32 CFR 651. In countries where an FGS/SOFA are published, they will be used according to the executive agent of that country.

A-65. DOD Publication 4715.05-G provides criteria, standards, and management practices for environmental compliance at DOD installations overseas. It provides the baseline information and standards from which all FGS for individual nations are devised.

CHAIRMAN OF THE JOINT CHIEFS OF STAFF INSTRUCTION 5810.01C

A-66. This instruction establishes joint policy, assigns responsibilities, and provides guidance regarding the LOW obligation of the United States. It supports Department of Defense Directive (DODD) 5100.77, which provides policy guidance and assigns responsibility within DOD for a program to ensure compliance with the LOW.

DEPARTMENT OF DEFENSE DIRECTIVE 4715.1E

A-67. This directive emphasizes the following DOD policies. Additionally, it includes general guidance for supporting international activities consistent with national security policy relating to environmental security programs. DODD 4715.1E—

- Demonstrates environmental leadership by considering environmental issues along with other relevant issues.
- Ensures full compliance with all environmental statutes.
- Protects and restores environmental quality.
- Prevents adverse impacts to the environment.

DEPARTMENT OF DEFENSE DIRECTIVE 6050.7

A-68. DODD 6050.7 (enacted in 1974 and certified as current in 2004) provides policy and procedures to enable DOD officials to be informed and take environmental considerations into account when authorizing or approving certain major federal actions that significantly harm the environment at OCONUS locations. Its sole objective is to establish internal procedures to achieve this purpose, and nothing in it shall be construed to create a cause of action.

DEPARTMENT OF DEFENSE DIRECTIVE 6490.2E

A-69. DODD 6490.2E (formerly Comprehensive Medical Surveillance) establishes policy and assigns responsibility for routine, comprehensive health surveillance of all military Soldiers and Marines during active federal service. It also designates the Secretary of the Army as DOD executive agent for the Defense Medical Surveillance System and DOD Serum Repository according to DODD 5101.1.

DEPARTMENT OF DEFENSE INSTRUCTION 6490.03

A-70. DODI 6490.03 (formerly DODI 6490.03) implements policy and replaces—

- Assistant Secretary of Defense for Health Affairs, policy memorandum, Human Immunodeficiency Virus Interval Testing, 29 March 2004.
- Under Secretary of Defense for Personnel and Readiness memorandum, Enhanced Postdeployment Health Assessments, 22 April 2003.
- Assistant Secretary of Defense for Health Affairs memorandum, Policy for Use of Force Health Protection Prescription Products, 24 April 2003.
- Under Secretary of Defense for Personnel and Readiness memorandum, Improved Occupational and Environmental Health Surveillance Reporting and Archiving.

A-71. It assigns responsibilities for deployment health activities under DODD 6490.2E. Lastly, DODI 6490.03 implements policies and prescribes procedures for deployment health activities for joint and Service-specific deployments to monitor, assess, and prevent disease and nonbattle injury; to control or reduce occupational and environmental health risks; to document and link occupational and environmental health exposures with deployed personnel, including exposures to CBRNE-warfare agents; and to record the daily locations of deployed personnel.

DEPARTMENT OF DEFENSE INSTRUCTION 4715.5

A-72. DODI 4715.5 (enacted in 1996) establishes policy, assigns responsibilities, and prescribes procedures for establishing the implementing environmental guidance and standards to ensure environmental protection at DOD facilities and installations in foreign countries. This instruction applies to the actions of DOD components at installations OCONUS, its territories, and possessions.

DEPARTMENT OF DEFENSE INSTRUCTION 4715.8

A-73. This instruction (enacted in 1998) establishes policy, assigns responsibilities, and prescribes procedures for the remediation of environmental contamination on DOD installations and facilities or caused by DOD actions OCONUS. This instruction is for the internal management of DOD and does not create any independent right enforceable against DOD; the United States; or their officers, agents, or employees. It authorizes the cleanups that the United States is obligated by international agreement to perform and contamination that is known to present imminent and substantial endangerment to human health and safety caused by current operations.

EXECUTIVE ORDER 12114

A-74. EO 12114 addresses the environmental effects of major federal actions abroad. It establishes procedures so that federal agencies in foreign countries and global communities can consider the effects of their actions on the environment. The Department of State supervises and coordinates these efforts overseas. The objective of this program is to provide information to decisionmakers, increase awareness and interest in environmental concerns, and encourage environmental cooperation with foreign nations.

INTERNATIONAL LAWS AND TREATIES

A-75. Commanders must consult the SJA for specific advice on international laws or conventions. The following international laws and treaties may affect military operations:

- Biological Diversity Convention.
- International Tropical Timber Agreement.
- International Convention for the Prevention of Pollution From Ships.
- Convention on International Trade in Endangered Species.
- Basel Convention (HW).
- Nitrogen Oxide Protocol (air pollution).
- London Dumping Convention (marine pollution from ships dumping wastes generated on land).
- Montreal Protocol (ozone-depleting substances).
- Kyoto Accord (greenhouse gases).

A-76. U.S. armed forces are obligated to abide by the provisions of treaties and conventions to which the United States is bound. In addition, countries that U.S. forces operate in, with, or through may be bound by treaties that the United States has not ratified. These treaties can impact military operations in several ways. The Basel Convention on the Control of Transboundary Movements of Hazardous Wastes and Their Disposal, for example, could limit HW disposal options available to a deployed force. While at this time the treaty has not been ratified by the Senate, the United States is still a signatory to it. Whether bound by a treaty or not, its mere existence may affect operations. Examples from Bosnia-Herzegovina and other locations have confirmed this situation.

A-77. International treaties that govern armed conflict also affect U.S. military forces. One such treaty is the Convention on the Prohibition of Military or Any Other Hostile Use of Environmental Modification. This treaty prohibits any military use of engineer modification and any technique for changing the dynamics, composition, or structure of the environment through the deliberate manipulation of natural processes.

Appendix B

Environmental Annex to Joint Plans and Orders

The following annex lists typical environmental considerations for joint OPLAN, concept plan, and OPORD development and execution. For larger Army units (brigade and division), the format will provide a guide for finding necessary information for developing their own orders. For divisions and corps operating as JTFs, the format provides an example for developing a similar annex. This appendix includes the format for annex L to joint OPORDs/OPLANs in figure B-1, page B-2. Ensure that current examples are verified with these current references. Each Service uses its own format for similar appendixes/annexes. Unit orders and plans follow individual Service formatting conventions. Army orders normally include environmental considerations in the coordinating instructions (paragraph 3) if not in a separate appendix (see appendix C). When specific command procedures dictate, staff officers include some environmental considerations in logistics and medical annexes. All operations must comply with federal law to the extent possible. This example assumes an overseas deployment in which the vast majority of federal environmental law is not applicable. Plans for training or operations in the U.S. must conform to federal and state laws.

CLASSIFICATION

ENVIRONMENTAL STANDING OPERATING PROCEDURES

Issuing Headquarters

Location

Date

ANNEX L TO XXX OPLAN XXXX-XX

ENVIRONMENTAL CONSIDERATIONS

References.

    a.   JP 3-34. *Joint Engineer Operations*. 12 February 2007.

    b.   DODD 6050.7. *Environmental Effects Abroad of Major Department of Defense Actions*. 31 March 1979.

    c.   Joint Staff Instruction (JSI) 3830.01B. *Environmental Engineering Effects of DOD Actions*. 1 May 1998.

    d.   DODI 4715.5. *Management of Environmental Compliance of Overseas Installations*. 22 April 1996.

    e.   DODI 4715.8. *Environmental Remediation for DOD Activities Overseas*. 2 February 1998.

    f.   Applicable Country-Specific FGS.

    g.   DOD OEBGD.

1.   **Situation**.

    a.   **Purpose**. State the purpose of this annex, the relationship between the environmental considerations, and the supported OPLAN, concept plan, or functional plan.

    b.   **Assumptions**. State the assumptions affecting environmental planning/compliance from the supported OPLAN, concept plan, or functional plan.

    c.   **Limiting Factors**. Outline limitations that are due to lack of foreign access, time, operations security, foreign nation rules or sensitivities, public affairs (foreign and domestic), legal considerations, and resources.

2.   **Mission**. State clearly and concisely the "essential" tasks to be accomplished with regard to the purpose of this annex as it relates to the overall mission stated in the basic plan. The mission statement should address the questions: who, what, when, where, and why.

3.   **Execution**.

    a.   Concept of Operations. Summarize the commander's concept of environmental issues and actions required to support the OPLAN, concept plan, or functional plan. Identify issues and actions which should be addressed during all phases of the operation.

        (1)   Compliance Requirements. State regulatory, legal, and foreign nation compliance requirements based on whether an operation is a combatant operation (in which many requirements are not applicable) or a noncombatant operation.

        (2)   Phased Compliance. Describe in general terms the different environmental concerns in the supported OPLAN, concept plan, or functional plan during different phases of the operation.

CLASSIFICATION

Figure B-1. Sample environmental considerations annex (annex L)

CLASSIFICATION

      (3)   Mission Support. Identify those environmental planning factors which, although not mandated as a matter of law or regulation, will support successful execution of the OPLAN, concept plan, or functional plan in all phases and protect the health and safety of U.S. and allied forces and noncombatants. As a minimum, address certification of local water sources by medical field units, solid and liquid waste management, HM management, flora and fauna protection, archaeological and historical preservation, and spill response.

    b.   Tasks. Identify inter-Service responsibilities of subunified, joint task force, and component commanders for environmental support. Key elements include, but are not limited to, the formulation of a JEMB, individual component responsibilities for the tasks in paragraph 3.a(3) above, environmental planning, and staff training.

    c.   Coordinating Instructions. Outline key coordination that must be accomplished. Place particular emphasis on coordination requirements with higher headquarters, Office of the Secretary of Defense, and other federal agencies. Where applicable, this section should define procedures for transboundary shipment of HM and HW, disposal of HW, and any potential conflicts with the foreign nation.

4.   **Administration and Logistics**.

    a.   Logistics. Address any necessary guidance for administering the environmental effort by the combatant commander. Provide guidance for logistic support for environmental support and compliance when such support is outside the scope of the component responsibilities and resources.

    b.   Reports. Specify the format and instructions for any required reports.

    c.   Joint Environmental Management Board. The JEMB is a temporary board activated to establish policies, procedures, priorities, conflict resolution, and overall direction for environmental management in the theater.

t/

General

Commander

Appendixes:

1. Environmental Assessment.

2. Environmental Assessment Exemptions.

3. JEMB.

OFFICIAL:

s/

t/

Major General

Director, J-4

CLASSIFICATION

Figure B-1. Sample environmental considerations annex (annex L) (continued)

CLASSIFICATION

Issuing Headquarters

Location

Date

APPENDIX 1 TO ANNEX L TO XXX OPLAN XXXX-XX

ENVIRONMENTAL ASSESSMENTS

References.

    a.   JP 3-34. *Joint Engineer Operations.* 12 February 2007.

    b.   DODD 6050.7. *Environmental Effects Abroad of Major Department of Defense Actions.* 31 March 1979.

    c.   JSI 3830.01B. *Environmental Engineering Effects of DOD Actions.* 1 May 1998.

    d.   DODI 4715.5. *Management of Environmental Compliance of Overseas Installations.* 22 April 1996.

    e.   DODI 4715.8. *Environmental Remediation for DOD Activities Overseas.* 2 February 1998.

    f.   Applicable Country-Specific FGS.

    g.   DOD OEBGD.

1.   **Purpose.** State the regulatory or legal requirement for conducting an environmental assessment in conjunction with the supported operation.

2.   **Description of the Action.** State whether an exemption applies to the proposed action, including whether the proposed operation is a "major" action which does "significant harm to the environment or a global resource." If no exemption is being invoked, state the type of assessment being prepared (environmental impact statement, environmental study, or environmental review).

3.   **Exemption or Exclusion.** Describe the basis for exemption. Determine and document its applicability to the operation or seek approval from a higher authority.

4.   **Analysis of Options or Alternatives.** If an environmental report, environmental study, or environmental impact statement is required or federal law in conjunction with an operation, document the actions and/or alternatives that were considered in the planning of the supported operations to minimize the environmental impacts.

5.   **Environmental Setting of the Operation.** Describe the following: (a) general environmental condition of the operational area, (b) vegetation, (c) climate, (d) wildlife, (e) archaeological and historical sites, (f) water quality, and (g) air quality.

6.   **Environmental Impact of the Operation.** Describe the impact on (a) topography, (b) vegetation, (c) water quality, (d) air quality, (e) ecology, (f) archaeological and historical sites, (g) wildlife, (h) the socio-economic and political end state, (i) land use, (j) safety and occupational health, and (k) HM and HW.

7.   **Mitigation and Monitoring Requirements.** Describe actions and assign responsibilities for mitigation and monitoring of environmental impacts of the supported operation.

8.   **Compliance Responsibilities.** State applicability and responsibility for implementation of the OEBGD or FGS during the post hostilities phase.

CLASSIFICATION

Figure B-1. Sample environmental considerations annex (annex L) (continued)

CLASSIFICATION

Issuing Headquarters

Location

Date

APPENDIX 2 TO ANNEX L to XXXX OPLAN XXXX-XX

ENVIRONMENTAL ASSESSMENT EXEMPTIONS

References.

    a.   DODD 6050.7. *Environmental Effects Abroad of Major Department of Defense Actions.* 31 March 1979.

    b.   JSI 3830.01B. *Environmental Engineering Effects of DOD Actions.* 1 May 1998.

1.   **Purpose.** State the basis for invoking or requesting an exclusion or exemption from environmental assessment for the supported operation.

2.   **Background.** State facts identified in the planning process that support an exemption from the requirement for environmental assessment documentation.

3.   **Discussion.** Provide factual rationale for invoking exemption. Assign responsibility for making the exemption determination.

4.   **Determination.** Identify and document the authority making the exemption determination.

CLASSIFICATION

Figure B-1. Sample environmental considerations annex (annex L) (continued)

CLASSIFICATION

Issuing Headquarters

Location

Date

PLANNING GUIDANCE FOR APPENDIX 3 TO ANNEX L

JOINT ENVIRONMENTAL MANAGEMENT BOARD

1. **Purpose**. Describe the composition and function of the JEMB.

2. **General**.

   a. The JEMB is a temporary board which may be activated by the combined joint task force.

   b. The JEMB establishes policies, procedures, policies, and overall direction for environmental management requirements in the theater.

   c. If appropriate, it may assume responsibility for the preparation of annex L, Environmental Considerations.

   d. Joint task force engineer has overall staff responsibility for the JEMB.

3. **Organization**. Upon notification of the joint task force engineer, the JEMB will meet at the joint task force headquarters. The composition of the JEMB will vary depending on the nature of the contingency, the joint task force, and the other forces and agencies involved. It may include representatives of all Services involved, along with the judge advocate general, surgeon, PAO, Defense Logistics Agency/DRMO, American Embassy, United States Agency for International Development, real estate, contracting, safety, and CA.

4. **Procedures**.

   a. As required by the joint task force mission, the JEMB will be activated under the authority of the combined joint task force by the joint task force engineer.

   b. The JEMB meeting locations and physical arrangements will be coordinated, executed, and announced by the joint task force environmental engineer.

   c. JEMB meetings will be chaired by the joint task force engineer.

   d. Members of the JEMB must be empowered as decisionmakers for their organizations.

   e. JEMB decisions will strive for unanimity. In the absence of unanimity, a majority of voting members will decide the issue. The chairman will vote only in the case of a tie.

   f. JEMB decisions will be forwarded to the joint task force Chief of Staff for final approval.

   g. Reclamas of JEMB actions are to be forwarded to the joint task force Chief of Staff.

   h. The joint task force environmental engineer is responsible for preparing the meeting agenda and read-ahead materials, maintaining the minutes of all JEMB meetings, preparing appropriate documentation of all JEMB actions, coordinating the final approval of JEMB actions, and dissemination of approved JEMB actions.

CLASSIFICATION

Figure B-1. Sample environmental considerations annex (annex L) (continued)

Appendix C

Environmental Appendix to the Engineering Annex for Army Operation Plans and Operation Orders

The following annex lists typical environmental considerations for Army OPLAN, concept plan, and OPORD development and execution. For small units (battalions and companies), the format will provide a guide for finding necessary information for developing their own orders. For larger units (brigade and division), the format provides an example for developing a similar appendix. Ensure that current examples are verified with these current references. Army orders normally include environmental considerations in the coordinating instructions (paragraph 3) if not included in a separate appendix within the engineer annex. When specific command procedures dictate, staff officers include some environmental considerations in logistics and medical annexes. All operations must comply with federal law to the extent possible. This example assumes an overseas deployment in which the vast majority of federal environmental law is not applicable. Plans for training or operations in the U.S. must conform to federal and state laws. Tab A of the sample appendix 5 to annex G in Figure C-1 implements the requirement of EO 12114 to conduct environmental assessments, in the form of the EBS, before taking actions that would significantly harm the environment of a foreign nation or the global commons. DODD 6050.7, which implements EO 12114, defines the environmental impact statement, environmental statement, and ECR directed in this tab.

CLASSIFICATION

Copy ___ of ___ copies
Issuing Headquarters
Place of Issue
Date-Time Group of Signature
Message Reference Number

APPENDIX 5 (ENVIRONMENTAL CONSIDERATIONS) TO ANNEX G (ENGINEERING) TO 54th MECHANIZED DIVISION OPLAN 99-7 (U)

References:

    a. JP 3-34. *Joint Engineer Operations*. 12 February 2007.

    b. JSN 3820.01E. *Environmental Engineering Effects of DODA*. 30 September 2008.

    c. DODI 4715.5. *Management of Environmental Compliance at Overseas Installations*. 22 April 1996.

    d. DODI 4715.8. *Environmental Remediation Policy for DOD Activities Overseas*. 2 February 1998.

    e. Applicable country-specific FGS.

    f. DOD OEBGD, or in-theater equivalent, 1 May 2007.

    g. Foreign nation agreements, local operating standards if different from FGS, command special instructions, SOPs, policies, guidance for environmental considerations, or references pertaining to significant environmental factors in the AO.

    h. Unit SOPs.

1. SITUATION.

    a. Enemy forces. Refer to an OPORD or to an environmental annex/appendix to an OPORD. State any environmental factors or conditions that could adversely affect the successful completion of the mission, and/or the health or welfare of friendly forces and the indigenous population. Environmental threats can be natural, collateral, accidental, or caused by actions of the population or enemy forces. (*This operation depends on our ability to provide water for both our forces and the indigenous population through desalinization plants drawing water from the Gulf…the enemy has large amounts of chemical munitions. Special care must be taken when destroying enemy munition dumps to ensure chemical munitions are not being detonated…due to the extremely high water table in the area, special care and considerations must be taken in the siting of landfills and the collection of all waste products…*)

CLASSIFICATION

Figure C-1. Sample appendix 5 (environmental) to annex G (engineering)

CLASSIFICATION

(1) Terrain. List all critical terrain aspects that impact functional area operations.

(2) Weather. List all critical weather aspects that impact functional area operations.

(3) Enemy functional area capability and/or activity:

(a) List known and templated significant environmental hazards. If the information is large and specific enough, this list may become an overlay.

(b) List significant enemy capabilities to use environmental manipulation as a means to impede friendly forces or jeopardize long-term objectives. *(Enemy may release oil directly into the Gulf…Enemy may set oil wells afire to cover their retreat…)*

(c) State the expected employment of enemy functional area assets based on the most probable course of action. *(Enemy will not be effected by international opinion…they will use all means at their disposal to include releasing oil directly into the gulf and setting oil wells afire in an orgy of destruction…)*

(4) Limiting factors. Outline limitations that are due to lack of foreign access, time, operations security, foreign nation rules or sensitivities, public affairs (foreign and domestic), legal considerations, and resources. *(Operations by 54th Mechanized Division will inherently have an environmental impact. Environmental considerations require early integration in the planning process and will be accomplished in conjunction with other planning and the risk management process. The environmental protection level will vary as levels of risk are anticipated to be lower and the correspondingly environmental efforts more comprehensive in proportion to the distance from the combat zone. This appendix does not address munitions storage/disposal, CBRNE activities, or activities on naval ships at sea.)*

b. Friendly forces. Refer to an OPORD or to an annex to an OPORD. State the concept of environmental operations for the higher headquarters. This concept covers relationships between environmental considerations and the supported OPORD, OPLAN, concept plan, or support plan.

c. Attachments and detachments. Refer to an OPORD or an annex to an OPORD (annex L if it is a JOPES OPORD). Identify special environmental teams or personnel.

2. MISSION. State the commander's concept for environmental actions. This concept answers the who, what, when where, how, and why of the relationship between environmental considerations and the supported OPORD, OPLAN, concept plan, or functional plan. Normally, the mission will be to protect, as much as practicable, the health and welfare of U.S. personnel and the indigenous population from environmental threats during the conduct of the operation; to reduce long-term, adverse impact on the economy and public health; and to reduce U.S. costs and liabilities at the completion of the operation.

CLASSIFICATION

Figure C-1. Sample appendix 5 (environmental) to annex G (engineering) (continued)

CLASSIFICATION

3. EXECUTION.

a. Scheme of environmental operations. Summarize the commander's concept of environmental actions required to support the OPLAN, OPORD, or concept plan. Identify issues and actions that should be addressed during all phases of the operation. Identify the desired environmental end state.

(1) Operational effect on the environment. List critical resources that should be protected during the operation, such as forests, croplands, or water- and sewage-treatment facilities. Describe factors to be considered by subordinate unit commanders when making collateral damage decisions.

(2) Environmental resource effect on the operation. List any environmental conditions or factors that could impede successful completion of the operational mission or jeopardize the desired end state. Identify possible targets of environmental sabotage or terrorism.

(3) Compliance requirements. State regulatory, legal, and foreign nation compliance requirements that will apply and under what conditions they may be applicable (combat versus nonhostile, stability operation, or support operation; geographical differences; or event-triggered changes).

(4) Phased compliance. Describe in general terms the major environmental concerns and requirements during different phases of the operation. Specify transition tasks and measures and the appropriate initiating control measures.

b. *Tasks to subordinate units. It will be unusual to have an entry here. If it is important enough to task a given maneuver element to accomplish an environmental task, this tasking must be identified in paragraph 3b of the base order. An example is the tasking of specific units (in conjunction with the surgeon or CBRN officer) to perform environmental reconnaissance missions. If only placed here it is likely to be overlooked by the tasked unit. If including tasks to subordinate units:*

(1) List functional area tasks that specific maneuver elements must accomplish and that the base OPORD does not contain.

(2) List functional area tasks the functional area units supporting maneuver elements must accomplish only as necessary to ensure unity of effort.

c. Coordinating instructions. Outline key coordination that must be accomplished by two or more units and not routinely covered in unit SOPs. Pay particular attention to coordination requirements with higher headquarters, the Office of the Secretary of Defense, and other federal agencies. Unit responsibilities and requirements may vary according to location, activity, or phase of the operation; attach a matrix that specifies various levels of environmental protection. Environmental responsibilities of the surgeon and the logistics officer may be included here if not incorporated in their respective annexes.

CLASSIFICATION

Figure C-1. Sample appendix 5 (environmental) to annex G (engineering) (continued)

CLASSIFICATION

(1) Environmental reconnaissance. Identify general responsibilities here.

(2) Environmental vulnerabilities. Specify general responsibilities for intelligence collection, identification, and response planning for environmental threats to mission success.

(3) Environmental assessments. List conditions under which environmental assessments may be required, conditions when assessments may be sensible even when not required by law or order, and responsibilities for conducting and approving assessments (See tab A and tab B).

(4) Occupation of base camps and rear assembly areas. *(Occupation of base camps or rear assembly areas, and subsequent operations, will be accomplished incorporating environmental considerations whenever feasible and commensurate with the operational situation.)*

(a) An initial EBS (see tab A) will be conducted to determine the preexisting condition of the site and its ecological resources. Direct the conduct of ECRs based on the duration of stay at a given site (to give interim snapshot condition reports) and in response to environmental incidents.

(b) Before departure or abandonment, units will ensure the performance of a final EBS (see tab A) to document the condition of the site, to include water sources, soil, flora, archaeological/ historical facilities, air quality, and other environmental conditions. Document the location of latrines, hazardous waste sites, landfills, hospitals, maintenance activities, POL storage, and any other environmentally sensitive activities.

(5) Facilities.

(a) Environmental baseline surveys. Specify conditions, formats, responsibilities, and reporting of initial EBS, final EBS, and any interim ECRs (see enclosure 1, enclosure 2, and tab C).

(b) Operating procedures. Provide guidance for environmental considerations and services in established facilities.

(c) Closure. Specify closure activities, such as documentation of the location of latrines, HW sites, landfills, hospitals, maintenance activities, POL storage, and other environmentally sensitive activities. Publication of these procedures may be delayed until a more appropriate phase of the operation.

(6) Construction. When planning and conducting general engineering operations, military designers should consider the project's effect on the environment, as well as the applicable U.S. and foreign nation agreements and applicable environmental laws and regulations. *(Soil erosion/runoff control procedures and other common sense procedures will be applied to the maximum extent possible in any case.)*

(7) Claims. *(Under the provisions of Article XXIII of the United States – Republic of Korea SOFA, claims by local national individuals or organizations for damages arising from spills will be handled through established claims procedures.)*

CLASSIFICATION

Figure C-1. Sample appendix 5 (environmental) to annex G (engineering) (continued)

CLASSIFICATION

4. SERVICE SUPPORT.

a. Identify those environmental planning factors that, although not mandated as law or regulation, will support successful execution of the OPLAN, OPORD, concept plan, or functional plan in all phases and protect the health and safety of U.S. forces, allied forces, and noncombatants. As a minimum, address certification of local water sources by medical field units, solid and liquid waste management, HM management, flora and fauna protection, archaeological and historical preservation, and spill response. Disposal of solid and liquid waste will depend upon the location and surrounding environment of the disposal area. The intent is to minimize the environmental impact and to limit potential contamination to the holding site.

(1) Development, use, and protection of potable water sources. Certification of water sources include special considerations for the protection of surface water, groundwater, and water in distribution systems; location and special protection requirements for water and wastewater (gray water, see below) treatment facilities; disposal of effluents from showers and laundry facilities; disposal of brine water (or wastewater) from reverse osmosis water purification unit operations. In CONUS, training exercises require a permit to discharge reverse osmosis water purification unit brine into a water source. Returning brine (or wastewater) directly to the source, untreated, also violates the OEBGD. *(Water will be obtained or processed from approved sources. Water quality certifications will be accomplished according with procedures outlined in the 54th Mechanized Division field SOP. Operational and support elements will not contaminate potable water resources.)*

(2) Solid and liquid waste management. *(Disposal of solid and liquid wastes will depend on location and surrounding environment of the disposal area. The intent is to minimize the environmental impact and to limit potential contamination to the holding site.)*

(a) Solid waste. Requirements include disposal of solid waste (includes sludge); approval process for the use of landfills or incinerators; and protection of solid waste transportation, transfer, and disposal facilities. *(Solid waste will be removed and disposed of at ministry of environment-approved facilities via wartime foreign nation support agreements. In the absence of foreign nation support, solid waste should be incinerated as the preferred method of disposal. Alternatively, burial of waste is acceptable and will employ the characteristics of landfill operations. Trenches will be perpendicular to the prevailing winds, deep enough to contain the long-term waste stream expected and to execute a daily cover of not less than 6 inches of earth, with a final cover of not less than 30 inches. Any trench will be properly marked when closed.)*

(b) Human waste. Handle storage and disposal of human waste in a way that best supports the mission and is most protective of human health. This factor is particularly significant in densely populated areas where basic public health services may be disrupted and standard field sanitation procedures are inadequate. *(Existing sanitary latrines, sewers, and treatment plants should be used to the maximum extent possible. If such facilities have exceeded their capacity or do not exist, human waste will be disposed of according to the operation and the situation encountered. The preferred methods of disposal in order of precedence are sanitary wastewater disposal systems, portable latrines, and slit trenches. Expeditionary sewage collection and disposal will be sited and operated to minimize environmental impact according to unit field sanitation procedures. If possible, do not conduct open burning upwind of populated areas. As a minimum, all slit trenches will be covered with not less than 24 inches of earth fill [12 inches of compacted fill level to the ground surface, and 12 inches of mound fill] before departure from the site. A sign showing the date of closure and the words "Closed Latrine" will be posted at each closed site.)*

Figure C-1. Sample appendix 5 (environmental) to annex G (engineering) (continued)

CLASSIFICATION

(c) Gray water. *(At locations that lack sewage treatment facilities, the preferred method of handling gray water will be by collection and proper disposal via wartime foreign nation support. In the event these preferred options are not achievable during contingency operations or wartime, effluents from showers/bathing facilities will be located downstream of water sources, both civilian and military. Most rivers in the Republic of Korea supply water to Korean populations, and gray water discharges into central waters are prohibited. Construction of temporary drainage facilities must ensure proper drainage of gray water runoff that precludes pooling. Measures will be taken to prevent creation of pest breeding sites.)*

(3) Medical waste. This section includes procedures and locations for storage and disposal of medical waste under normal and emergency conditions, as well as the responsibilities and procedures for approval of disposal methods. *(Disposal of medical waste will be according to guidelines established by the XX [United States] Corps Surgeon. Should facilities be unavailable for permanent disposal, suitable temporary disposal should be accomplished through the use of a suitably labeled, segregated containment area. Wastes will be held in sealed containers or another appropriate manner that minimizes the release of biological contamination into the environment. A record will be made of the type, quantity, and location of the containment area. A copy of the report will be forwarded to the XX [United States] Corps Staff Engineer Section and the surgeon.)*

(4) HM/HW management.

(a) HW management. This section includes procedures and locations for the storage and disposal of HW under normal and emergency conditions, operations of the DRMO or approved contractor facilities, and the recording of abandoned HW sites. *(HW will be collected, packaged, and transferred to the Defense Logistics Agency/DRMO when feasible according to guidelines established by the XX [United States] Corps G-4.) (If the operational situation dictates abandonment of HM/HW, consolidate, contain, and record the location of the items, type of items, and any other information that will facilitate future recovery operations. Forward a copy of the report to both the XX [United States] Corps Staff Engineer Section and G-4.)*

(b) HM management. *(HMs will be stored, transported, and used according to established procedures and in a manner that precludes improper human or ecological exposure. To the extent practical, consolidation and reutilization will be applied to reduce the amount of HM expended and waste generated.)*

(c) Abandonment. *(If the operational situation dictates abandonment of hazardous material/waste; consolidate, contain, and record the location of the items, type of items, and any other information that will assist future recovery operations. Forward a copy of the report to both the XX [United States] Corps Staff Engineer Section and G-4.)*

(d) Spill prevention/control procedures. *(Commanders will maintain spill-prevention/control plans with battalion-level spill response teams, according to the 54th Mechanized Division field SOP. Units will take immediate action to contain the spill, clean up the site to the limit of their capability, mark the site, and report the spill through their chain of command to the XX [United States] Corps Staff Engineer Section, PAO, and G-4. The spill report should be in basic ECR format [see tab B] and at a minimum contain the location, type, and quantity of contaminant[s], status of the cleanup, and an estimate of additional resources required to complete the cleanup.)*

CLASSIFICATION

Figure C-1. Sample appendix 5 (environmental) to annex G (engineering) (continued)

CLASSIFICATION

    (5)   Ecosystem protection. Protect special flora and fauna, wetlands, forests, and croplands and seek approval for the clearing of large areas and approved methods and chemicals, if any, for clearing. *(The requirement to clear fields of fire [as well as limited clearance for health, safety, and troop welfare] may cause the destruction of ecosystems. Destruction and clearing of areas in excess of 100 acres requires the approval of the Commander, XX [United States] Corps.)*

    (6)   Air and noise emissions. Give special consideration to preventing air and noise emissions—normally confined to theater rear areas or to security, support, or humanitarian missions. *(Generators will be operated only in the reduced sound signature mode as defined in division field SOP...Movement of tracked vehicles outside of designated assembly areas, from 0001-2400 on Sundays during this exercise, is prohibited without permission of the Commander, XX [United States] Corps.)*

    (7)   Archaeological and historical preservation. State the requirements to minimize damage to historical sites and buildings, monuments, and works of art. A separate overlay may be required. *(Operational activities that adversely impact on archaeological and historical sites and buildings are to be minimized. If damage occurs, a report of circumstances will be made through operational channels to XX [United States] Corps CA and the PAO.)*

    b. Logistics. Address any necessary guidance for administering the environmental effort by the commander. Provide guidance for logistic support to environmental support and compliance.

    (1)   HM management. Specify unique control measures used in supply, storage, transportation, and retrograde to reduce and regulate the use of HM.

    (2)   Environmental considerations and services locations. Provide, when appropriate, the location of landfills, incinerators, HW collection facilities, water and wastewater treatment plants, watershed protection areas, ecologically sensitive areas, contaminated areas, potentially dangerous industrial facilities, and other points of environmental sensitivity or interest to the command. Include cultural resources if not noted elsewhere.

5. COMMAND AND SIGNAL.

    a. Command. Identify the executive agent for environmental functions in each command post location. Specify responsibilities and levels for issuing guidance and waivers.

    b. Signal. List environmental reporting instructions not specified in unit SOPs; identify the required reports, formats, times, and distribution lists.

                  NAME (An appendix can be signed by either the commander or primary staff officer.)
                  RANK

CLASSIFICATION

Figure C-1. Sample appendix 5 (environmental) to annex G (engineering) (continued)

CLASSIFICATION

Tabs:

   A. Environmental Assessments.

   B. Environmental Assessment Exemptions.

   C. Environmental Baseline Survey.

   D. Base Camp Closure Standards. (To be published)

   E. Electronic Environmental Report Message Formats.

CLASSIFICATION

Figure C-1. Sample appendix 5 (environmental) to annex G (engineering) (continued)

CLASSIFICATION

TAB A (ENVIRONMENTAL ASSESSMENTS) TO APPENDIX 5 (ENVIRONMENTAL CONSIDERATIONS) TO ANNEX G (ENGINEERING) TO 54TH MECHANIZED DIVIVISION OPLAN 99-7 (U)

References:

    a. DODD 6050.7. *Environmental Effects Abroad of Major Department of Defense Actions.* 31 March 1979.

    b. JSN 3820.01E. *Environmental Engineering Effects of DOD Actions.* 30 September 2008.

    c. JP 3-34. *Joint Engineer Operations.* 12 February 2007.

    d. DODD 6050.16. *Policy for Establishing and Implementing Environmental Standards at Overseas Installations.* 20 September 1991.

    e. Applicable country-specific FGS.

    f. DOD OEBGD, or in-theater equivalent, 1 May 2007.

    g. Engineer Support Plan in AOR.

1. **Purpose.** State the regulatory, legal, troop protection, financial, or other reason for conducting an environmental assessment in conjunction with the supported operation.

2. **Background.** State the purpose and concept of the operation and a brief explanation of the relationship of environmental assessments to the successful completion of the operational mission.

3. **Description of the Actions.** State the types of assessments and the conditions under which actions are required. When "major actions" are included in the operation, indicate whether an exemption applies (Tab B of this appendix). If no exemption is being invoked, state the type of assessment(s) to be prepared: environmental impact statement, environmental statement, or environmental report. Indicate requirements for a facility EBS.

4. **Exemption or Exclusion.** Describe the basis for exemption (Tab B of this appendix). Finally, determine and document the applicability to the operation. Seek approval from a higher authority according to Reference A if applicability is not clearly stated.

5. **Analysis of Options or Alternatives.** If an environmental report, environmental statement, or environmental impact statement is required, document the actions and alternatives that were considered in planning the supported operation to minimize environmental impact.

CLASSIFICATION

Figure C-1. Sample appendix 5 (environmental) to annex G (engineering) (continued)

CLASSIFICATION

6. **Environmental Setting of the Operation.** (This and the following paragraphs are useful for scoping/tiering analyses.) Describe or provide references for the description of the general environmental conditions of the operational area, including (a) vegetation, (b) climate, (c) wildlife, (d) archaeological and historical sites, (e) water quality, and (f) air quality.

7. **Environmental Impact of the Operation.** Describe the impact on the topography, vegetation, water quality, air quality, ecosystem functioning, archaeological and historical sites, wildlife, socioeconomic and political end state, land use, safety and public and occupational health, and HM and HW use and disposal.

8. **Mitigation and Monitoring.**

(a) Requirements. Describe actions and assign responsibilities for mitigation and monitoring of environmental impacts of the supported operation.

(b) Compliance Responsibilities. State applicability and responsibility for implementation of the OEBGD or FGS during the posthostilities phase.

CLASSIFICATION

Figure C-1. Sample appendix 5 (environmental) to annex G (engineering) (continued)

CLASSIFICATION

TAB B (ENVIRONMENTAL ASSESSMENT EXEMPTIONS) TO APPENDIX 5 (ENVIRONMENTAL CONSIDERATIONS) TO ANNEX G (ENGINEERING) TO 54TH MECHANIZED DIVISION OPLAN 99-7 (U)

References:

    a.   DODD 6050.7. *Environmental Effects Abroad of Major Department of Defense Actions.* 31 March 1979.

    b.   JSN 3820.01E. *Environmental Engineering Effects of DOD Actions.* 30 September 2008.

1. **Purpose.** State the basis for invoking or requesting an exclusion or exemption from environmental assessment for the supported operation.

2. **Background.** State facts identified in the planning process that support an exemption from the requirement of environmental analysis and documentation.

3. **Discussion.** Provide factual rationale for invoking an exemption. Assign responsibility for making exemption determination.

4. **Determination.** Identify and document the authority making the exemption determination.

CLASSIFICATION

Figure C-1. Sample appendix 5 (environmental) to annex G (engineering) (continued)

CLASSIFICATION

TAB C (ENVIRONMENTAL BASELINE SURVEYS) TO APPENDIX 5 (ENVIRONMENTAL CONSIDERATIONS) TO ANNEX G (ENGINEERING) TO 54TH MECHANIZED DIVISION OPLAN 99-7 (U)

References:

a. DODD 6050.7. *Environmental Effects Abroad of Major Department of Defense Actions*. 31 March 1979.

b. JSN 3820.01E. *Environmental Engineering Effects of DOD Actions*. 30 September 2008.

1. **Purpose.** The primary purpose of an EBS is to identify environmental, health, and safety conditions that pose a potential health threat to military personnel and civilians that occupy properties used by the United States military in the TO. The secondary purpose is to document environmental conditions at the initial occupancy of property to prevent the United States from receiving unfounded claims for past environmental damages.

2. **EBS Requirement.** State the requirement for performing an EBS, the time by which the initial EBS is to be completed, and the responsibilities for conducting and reporting.

3. **Applicability.** Describe conditions under which the EBS is required or may be waived.

4. **Description.** EBSs are divided into initial and closure investigations. The initial investigation is designed to provide an initial overview of the property using real-time field sampling. The initial investigation is updated when there are indications of the potential for significant environmental or health hazard and involves a more comprehensive analysis designed to quantify an identified hazard. Comprehensive analysis requires more time when it uses more specialized equipment that may not be available to all survey teams. The closure EBS is a part of base camp closure standards, but is not limited to base camps (logistics areas, communications sites, airfields, and staging areas). To effectively complete the closure report, it is essential to reference the initial EBS (and update if applicable) and the log of periodic ECRs that have been completed on the particular site/area. The ECR is completed on a periodic basis to document conditions at the site/area, as well as any time a potentially significant environmental event occurs. See enclosure 2 of this tab for an example. This description identifies the protocol to be used in conducting both the initial and closure EBSs. This may include a checklist from a theater regulation or environmental compliance assessment or some other means of guidance. Also address the frequency of ECRs and what constitutes a "significant environmental event."

5. **Support.** List military or contractual support for conducting an EBS. This list may include training for unit officers, preventive medicine personnel, chemical reconnaissance platoons, Logistics Civil Augmentation Program, and USACE support.

6. **Reporting.** Describe report formats, reporting chain, and disposition.

Enclosures:

1. EBS.

2. ECR.

3. Maps, photographs, and digital data.

CLASSIFICATION

Figure C-1. Sample appendix 5 (environmental) to annex G (engineering) (continued)

CLASSIFICATION

ENCLOSURE 1 (ENVIRONMENTAL BASELINE SURVEY) TO TAB C (ENVIRONMENTAL BASELINE SURVEYS) TO APPENDIX 5 (ENVIRONMENTAL CONSIDERATIONS) TO ANNEX G (ENGINEERING) TO 54TH MECHANIZED DIVISION OPLAN 99-7 (U)

References:

a. DODD 6050.7. *Environmental Effects Abroad of Major DOD Actions.* 31 March 1979.

b. JSN 3820.01E. *Environmental Engineering Effects of DOD Actions.* 30 September 2008.

c. DODD 6050.16. Policy for Establishing and Implementing Environmental Standards at Overseas Installations. 20 September 1991.

d. Other applicable environmental laws and regulations.

e. Command guidance references.

f. For a closure EBS, the initial EBS (and any applicable update) and any ECRs are also reference documents.

1. **Site/Property Location.** List the legal address and 6-digit military grid location or latitude and longitude.

2. **General Site Setting.** Note whether the site was visually observed or identified from interviews or record reviews. For an updated initial EBS or a closure EBS, the site should always be visually observed.

a. The methodology used and limitations encountered during the initial (or updated) site reconnaissance or the closure inspection. Describe the method used to reconnoiter the property; for example, the use of grid patterns or other systematic approach. List and describe any limitations encountered during the reconnaissance, such as physical obstructions, bodies of water, pavement, weather, or uncooperative occupants.

b. The current uses of the property. Be as specific as possible.

c. The past uses of the property. List all known past property uses. If a past use is likely to have involved the use, treatment, storage, disposal, or generation of HMs or petroleum products, include a detailed description or indicators of this use. A closure EBS includes information obtained from ECRs as well.

d. Current uses of adjoining properties. Be as specific as possible.

e. Past uses of adjoining properties. If a past use is likely to have indicated recognized adverse environmental conditions, include a detailed description.

CLASSIFICATION

Figure C-1. Sample appendix 5 (environmental) to annex G (engineering) (continued)

CLASSIFICATION

f. Current or past uses of the surrounding areas. List general types of past uses, such as residential, agricultural, or industrial. Limit surroundings to that which can be seen or would clearly affect the area, such as upstream on a waterway.

g. Geologic, hydrogeologic, hydrologic, or topographic conditions. List the conditions and give a general description of the topography in the area. If indicated, analyze the likelihood of contaminant migration on or to the property through the soil or groundwater from the adjacent properties or the surrounding areas.

h. General description of structures. List the buildings and their locations, size, basic construction type, stories, and approximate age.

i.   Roads. List all public thoroughfares adjoining the property and describe all roads, streets, parking areas, and walkways.

j. Water supply. List and differentiate all sources of potable and nonpotable water.

k. Sewage disposal system. Describe sewage disposal systems on the property and their general condition and approximate age.

3. **Interior and Exterior Observations.** To the extent visually/physically observed or identified from interviews or record reviews (list actual source).

a. HM and petroleum products. Describe uses and types of products used on the property and the approximate amount and storage conditions. Indicate if treatment, storage, disposal, or generation occurred on the property.

b. Storage tanks. Describe size, location, condition, and approximate age of all above- and belowground storage tanks.

c. Odors. Describe any noticeable odors and their source.

d. Pools of liquid. Note all surface water and describe all pools or sumps that contain water or other liquids that may contain HM.

e. Drums. Describe all drums and their conditions. If they are known to contain no HM, list contents only.

f. Hazardous substances and petroleum products. Describe all products to include type, amount, and manner/condition of storage.

g. Unidentified substance containers. Describe any open or damaged containers suspected of containing HM or petroleum products.

h. PCBs. Include a description of electrical or hydraulic equipment likely to contain PCBs.

CLASSIFICATION

Figure C-1. Sample appendix 5 (environmental) to annex G (engineering) (continued)

CLASSIFICATION

i. Interior observations of the following:

(1) Heating and cooling systems. Describe, to include the fuel source and amount on hand.

(2) Stains and corrosion. Describe stains on floors, walls, and ceilings.

(3) Drains and sumps. Describe floor drains and sumps.

j. Exterior observations of the following:

(1) Pits, ponds, and lagoons. Describe the pit, pond, or lagoon, especially if it may have been used for HW disposal or waste treatment. Include a discussion and description of any on adjacent or adjoining properties as well.

(2) Stained soil or pavement. Describe any stained soil or pavement.

(3) Stressed vegetation. Describe any stressed vegetation and probable cause.

(4) Solid waste. Describe any filled, graded, or mounded areas that would suggest the disposal of trash or solid waste.

(5) Wastewater. Describe every discharge of a liquid into a stream or ditch that is adjacent to the property.

(6) Wells. Locate and describe all wells (monitoring, potable, dry, irrigation, injection, or abandoned) on the property.

(7) Septic systems. List indications or the existence of on-site septic systems or cesspools.

(8) Ambient air quality. Smog, smoke, and odors from industrial facilities and many HW products can be detected easily. Terrain can also affect air quality. Mountains and canyons can cause temperature inversions, which impact air quality. Setting up base camps with heating units and vehicles in an area prone to temperature inversions can cause poor air quality. Prevailing winds should also be considered.

(9) Unexploded explosive ordnance. Identify and ensure clearance before occupation.

4. **Deletions and Deviations.** Describe all deviations or deletions from the protocol (checklist) used or the environmental standards currently in use by the command. Discuss each one individually and in detail.

5. **Findings and Conclusions Statement.** List the protocol used for the survey, exceptions to the protocol, and any evidence of recognized adverse environmental conditions.

6. **Qualification Statement.** List the qualifications and duty position(s) of the individual(s) preparing the EBS.

CLASSIFICATION

Figure C-1. Sample appendix 5 (environmental) to annex G (engineering) (continued)

CLASSIFICATION

ENCLOSURE 2 (ENVIRONMENTAL CONDITIONS REPORT) TO TAB C (ENVIRONMENTAL BASELINE SURVEYS) TO APPENDIX 5 (ENVIRONMENTAL CONSIDERATIONS) TO ANNEX G (ENGINEERING) TO 54TH MECHANIZED DIVISION OPLAN 99-7 (U)

References:

  a. DODD 6050.7. *Environmental Effects Abroad of Major DOD Actions*. 31 March 1979.

  b. JSN 3820.01E. *Environmental Engineering Effects of DOD Actions*. 30 September 2008.

  c. DODD 6050.16. Policy for Establishing and Implementing Environmental Standards at Overseas Installations. 20 September 1991.

  d. Other applicable environmental laws and regulations, OPORD, and unit SOP.

  e. Site specific EBS (if applicable).

  f. Electronic Environmental Message Formats in tab E.

1. **Site/Incident Location**. List the legal address, 6-digit military grid location, latitude and longitude of the incident location, or reference the applicable EBS to link the ECR to a given site. Refer to the electronic environmental message formats at tab E. (The ECR functions as a situation report [SITREP], or interim report, for a given site. The frequency of ECR reports is a higher headquarters decision but supports the need to document the condition of a given site over time [interim snapshots], as well as helping to ensure that an appropriate environmental focus is being maintained at a given site. The basic format of the ECR may also be used when reporting an incident, such as a POL spill not related to a given EBS or site location.)

2. **Site/Incident Description and Background**. Give a brief description of the site (installation), including its related EBS/historical use(s) or the circumstances surrounding the incident. For an incident at a location not covered by an EBS, it is critical to provide the same sort of information contained in a standard accident report.

3. **Map/Description of the Incident Location**. If the ECR is related to a site covered by an EBS, this entry is able to relate to the information already provided in the EBS (a baseline document). If the ECR defines a location where an incident has occurred that is not covered by an EBS, the description needs to be adequate to direct a follow-on element to the site. In this respect, it is similar to the graves registration report if the incident occurs during a tactical operation where time precludes remaining at the site.

4. **Summary of Environmental Conditions**. List the environmental event(s) at the site/location. All spills should be inventoried. If the ECR is a periodic report for a given site, significant events (such as major spills) should have been reported using the basic ECR format. In this case, simply reference any significant incident report ECRs that may have occurred at the given site over the time frame that the periodic ECR covers. Also provide a "snapshot" report of the types of HW/HM that are stored at the site. Describe minor spills and other events that have occurred over the time frame in question in basic terms, including quantities and the method(s) used to clean the site.

CLASSIFICATION

Figure C-1. Sample appendix 5 (environmental) to annex G (engineering) (continued)

CLASSIFICATION

Example: Four gallons of waste oil spilled at the hazardous waste accumulation site located northwest of the maintenance building at 1600 hours on 16 December 2000. The 22d Military Police Battalion contained the spill with assistance by White & Jones by 1725 hours. About 3 cubic yards of contaminated soil was taken to the White & Jones HW disposal area in Juvonia.

Example: Raw sewage ran from a pump house behind the main warehouse (shown on map) for an estimated 3 days during the initial stages of occupying the camp in early June 2000. The problem was identified on 13 June and corrected when the pump was repaired on 14 June.

Example: A fuel tanker overturned at the road intersection vicinity NV 123456 (see map) at 092000 November 2000 during the road march to Bigtown. Immediate mitigation included spill containment by the employment of all available spill kits with the unit. Higher headquarters was immediately notified. An estimated 4,000 gallons of jet petroleum-8 spilled at that site. The vehicle has been righted, and excavation of the site will begin at first light, 10 November.

5. **Interior and Exterior Observations**. These entries should be viewed as an abbreviated version of the information that would be found in an EBS. Items should only be addressed if they differ from the last ECR or vary from the initial EBS.

6. **Findings and Determinations With Qualification Statement**. A statement similar to the following should appear in this paragraph of the ECR:

According to _____ Reg _____, I have considered whether or not significant environmental impacts will occur as a result of turnover/return of this site (base camp or logistics area) and have determined that (include one of the following statements):

      a. Turnover of this base camp area will not result in environmental impacts significant enough to warrant additional environmental analysis.

OR

      b. Turnover of this base camp area will result in environmental impacts significant enough to warrant additional environmental analysis. Environmental actions or projects must continue after transfer of the base camp area because of substantial (imminent) threat to human health or safety. The impacts of concern are (list impacts):

      (If the report is due to an incident not connected to a specific site/installation, this paragraph is an assessment by the commander/individual on the scene.)

John Q. Jones
MAJ, QM
Mayor, Camp Swampy

CLASSIFICATION

Figure C-1. Sample appendix 5 (environmental) to annex G (engineering) (continued)

CLASSIFICATION

TAB E (ELECTRONIC ENVIRONMENTAL MESSAGE FORMATS) TO APPENDIX 5 (ENVIRONMENTAL CONSIDERATIONS) TO ANNEX G (ENGINEERING) TO 54TH MECHANIZED DIVISION OPLAN 99-7 (U)

References: FM 6-99.2. *U.S. Army Reports and Message Formats*. 30 May 2007.

Environmental Condition Report
REPORT NUMBER: E035

GENERAL INSTRUCTIONS: Use to send periodic information (interim snapshots) of the environmental status of specific sites (assembly areas, base camps, logistical support areas, and medical facilities) where hazards are likely to occur, which can result in significant, immediate and/or long-term effects on the natural environment and/or health of friendly forces and noncombatants. Send in accordance with unit SOPs and commander's direction.

LINE 1—DATE AND TIME _____ (Date-time group [DTG])

LINE 2—UNIT _____ (Unit making report)

LINE 3—LOCATION _____ (Universal traverse mercator [UTM] or 6-digit grid coordinate with military grid reference system (MGRS) grid zone designator of site/incident)

LINE 4—DESCRIPTION _____ (Description of site/incident)

LINE 5—CHANGES _____ (Changes from last ECR or EBS)

LINE 6—HAZARDS_____ (Hazards to natural environment, friendly forces, and/or civilian personnel)

LINE 7—ACTIONS _____ (Summary of actions to minimize hazards/remedial effects)

LINE 8—UNIT POC_____ (Reporting unit point of contact)

LINE 9—ASSISTANCE _____ (Assistance required/requested)

LINE 10—REFERENCE _____ (Site-specific EBS, if required)

LINE 11—NARRATIVE _____ (Free text for additional information required for clarification of report)

LINE 12—AUTHENTICATION_____ (Report authentication)

CLASSIFICATION

Figure C-1. Sample appendix 5 (environmental) to annex G (engineering) (continued)

CLASSIFICATION

2. ( ) <u>Electronic Spill Report Message Format</u>.

TITLE: SPILL REPORT
(Not currently shown in FM 6-99.2)

GENERAL INSTRUCTIONS: Used to send timely information or status of an oil, hazardous material, or hazardous waste spill that could have immediate environmental and/or health effects. Sent in accordance with SOP and commander's direction.
NOTE: Spill reporting and reportable quantities are mandated by federal and local law.

LINE 1—DATE AND TIME _____ (DTG)

LINE 2—UNIT _____ (Unit making report)

LINE 3—DATE/TIME _____ (DTG of spill discovery)

LINE 4—MATERIAL _____ (Material spilled)

LINE 5—QUANTITY _____ (Quantity of spilled material)

LINE 6—LOCATION _____ (UTM or 6-digit grid coordinate with MGRS grid zone designator of spill)

LINE 7—CAUSE _____ (Cause and supervising unit)

LINE 8—SIZE _____ (Size of affected area)

LINE 9—DAMAGE _____ (Damage to the natural environment, if required)

LINE 10—HAZARDS _____ (Hazards to natural environment, friendly forces, and/or civilian personnel)

LINE 11—ACTIONS _____ (Summary of actions taken)

LINE 12—UNIT POC _____ (Supervising unit POC)

LINE 13—ASSISTANCE _____ (Assistance required/requested)

LINE 14—NARRATIVE _____ (Free text for additional information required for clarification of report)

LINE 15—AUTHENTICATION _____ (Report authentication)

CLASSIFICATION

Figure C-1. Sample appendix 5 (environmental) to annex G (engineering) (continued)

Appendix D

Environmentally Related Risk Assessment

CRM is the process of identifying and controlling hazards to conserve combat power and resources. Risk decisions should be based on awareness rather than mechanical habit. Leaders should act with a keen appreciation for the essential factors making each situation unique, rather than reacting with a conditioned response. Commanders consider U.S. government civilians and contract support personnel in the CRM process. Regardless of enemy actions, hazards may exist in areas with no direct enemy contact and in areas outside enemy influence.

OVERVIEW

D-1. Risk decisions are the commander's responsibility. Such decisions are normally based on the next higher commander's guidance in determining an acceptable level of risk for the mission. Except in extreme circumstances, risk decisions should be made at the lowest possible level.

D-2. Both leaders and staff manage risk. Staff members continually look for hazards associated with their areas of expertise; then they recommend controls to reduce risks. Hazards and their resulting risks may vary as circumstances change and as experience is gained. Leaders and individual military personnel serve as assessors for ever-changing hazards, such as those associated with the environment (weather; visibility; and contaminated air, water, and soil), equipment readiness, individual and unit experience, and fatigue. Leaders should advise the chain of command on risk and risk reduction measures.

COMPOSITE RISK MANAGEMENT PROCESS AND ENVIRONMENTAL CONSIDERATIONS

D-3. The CRM process is the process of identifying, assessing, and controlling environmental risk arising from operational factors and making decisions that balance that environmental risk with mission benefits. This description integrates CRM into the MDMP. FM 5-19 outlines the multi-Service CRM process and provides the framework for integrated CRM as a routine part of planning, preparing, and executing operational missions and everyday tasks. Assessing environmentally related risks is part of the total CRM process. These steps identify specific environmental considerations that a commander and his staff must follow:

- Step 1. Identify (environmental) hazards.
- Step 2. Assess (environmental) hazards.
- Step 3. Develop controls and make decisions.
- Step 4. Implement controls.
- Step 5. Supervise and evaluate.

D-4. Knowledge of environmental factors is key to planning and decisionmaking. With this knowledge, leaders quantify risks, detect problem areas, reduce the risk of injury or death, reduce property damage, and ensure compliance with environmental laws and regulations. Leaders should conduct risk assessments using DA Form 7566 (Composite Risk Management Worksheet) before initiating any training, operations, or logistical activities.

D-5. Figure D-1, page D-2, shows a completed sample of DA Form 7566. Items 1 through 4c contain general information. Item 5 lists the tasks associated with the mission or task. Steps 1 through 5 in the following paragraphs explain how to fill in items 6 through 12.

COMPOSITE RISK MANAGEMENT WORKSHEET

For use of this form, see FM 5-19; the proponent agency is TRADOC.

1. MSNTASK		2a. DTG BEGIN	2b. DTG END	3. DATE PREPARED (YYYYMMDD)
586 Engineer Company Convoy		01 0600 R Jun XX	TBD	20060520

4. PREPARED BY		
a. LAST NAME	b. RANK	c. POSITION
Doe, John D.	1LT	Executive Officer

5. SUBTASK	6. HAZARDS	7. INITIAL RISK LEVEL	8. CONTROLS	9. RESIDUAL RISK LEVEL	10. HOW TO IMPLEMENT	11. HOW TO SUPERVISE (WHO)	12. WAS CONTROL EFFEC- TIVE?
Conduct convoy operations.	Vehicle breakdowns and accidents causing spills of hazardous materials, fuel spill.	M	Train all operators and crew personnel to take appropriate action in case of spill; protect themselves; notify chain of command; confine spill.	L	Soldiers review SOP, command environmental program; train drivers before convoy;check spill equipment	Convoy commander, vehicle commander, platoon leadership.	
	Spills during fuel stops	M	Provide spill equipment.	L	Soldiers review SOP, command environmental program; platoon leader will check each spill kit.	Platoon leader.	
	Maneuver damage from off-road movement.	M	Brief all drivers to stay on primary and secondary roads; identify all sensitive areas and habitat along route; conduct map and route recon prior to movement.	L	Soldiers review SOP, command environmental program; provide drivers strip map of route.	Platoon leader; vehicle commander.	

Additional space for entries in Items 5 through 11 is provided on Page 2.

13. OVERALL RISK LEVEL AFTER CONTROLS ARE IMPLEMENTED (Check one)

☒ LOW ☐ MODERATE ☐ HIGH ☐ EXTREMELY HIGH

14. RISK DECISION AUTHORITY			
a. LAST NAME	b. RANK	c. DUTY POSITION	d. SIGNATURE
J. R. Risk	CPT	Commander	SIGNED

DA FORM 7566, APR 2005

Page 1 of 2
APD PE v2.00

Figure D-1. Sample completed risk management worksheet

STEP 1. IDENTIFY ENVIRONMENTAL HAZARDS

D-6. Leaders identify environmental hazards during the mission analysis (see figure D-1, item 6). Environmental hazards include all activities that may pollute, create negative noise-related effects, degrade archaeological/cultural resources, or negatively affect habitats of threatened or endangered species. Geospatial engineering can help the staff visualize and assess those hazards associated with the physical environment. Table D-1 lists common environmental hazards identified by environmental media areas.

Table D-1. Common environmental hazards

Element	Hazard
Air	• Equipment exhaust • Convoy dust • Range fires • Open-air burning • Pyrotechnics/smoke pots/smoke grenades • Parts-washer emissions • Paint emissions • Air-conditioner/refrigeration CFCs • HM/HW release
Archaeological/Cultural	• Sensitive area maneuver • Sensitive areas digging • Artifact disturbance or removal • Demolition/munitions effects • HM/HW spills • Sonic booms/prop wash
Noise	• Low-flying aircraft (helicopters) • Demolition/munitions effects • Nighttime operations • Operations near post/camp boundaries and civilian populace • Vehicle convoys/maneuvers • Large-scale exercises
Threatened/ Endangered Species	• Sensitive area maneuver • Demolition/munitions effects, especially during breeding seasons • Individual species disturbance or habitat • HM/HW spills or releases • Poor field sanitation • Improper cutting of vegetation • Coral reef damage
Soil (Terrain)	• Maneuver area overuse • Demolition/munitions effects • Range fires • Poor field sanitation • Poor maneuver damage control • Erosion • Troop construction effects • Refueling operations • HM/HW spills • Ecologically sensitive areas (such as wetlands and tundra) maneuver

Table D-1. Common environmental hazards (continued)

Element	Hazard
Water	• Refueling operations near water sources • HM/HW spills • Erosion and unchecked drainage • Amphibious/water-crossing operations • Troop construction effects • Poor field sanitation • Vehicle washing at unapproved sites

STEP 2. ASSESS ENVIRONMENTAL HAZARDS

D-7. Risk assessment is a three-stage process used to determine the risk of potential harm to the environment. Leaders consider two factors—probability and severity. Probability is the frequency with which an environmental hazard is likely to occur. Severity is the effect a hazard will have on the environment. Probability and severity are estimates requiring individual judgment and a working knowledge of the CRM process and its terminology. Table D-2 defines the five degrees of probability for a hazard; and table D-3 defines the four degrees of severity.

Table D-2. Hazard probability chart

(A) Frequent: Occurs very often, continuously experienced	
Single item	Occurs very often in service life; expected to occur several times over the duration of a specific mission or operation; always occurs
Fleet or inventory of items	Occurs continuously during a specific mission or operation or over a service life
Individual Soldier or Marine	Occurs very often in career; expected to occur several times during mission or operation; always occurs
All Soldiers and Marines exposed	Occurs continuously during a specific mission or operation
(B) Likely: Occurs several times	
Single item	Occurs several times in service life; expected to occur during a specific mission or operation
Fleet or inventory of items	Occurs at a high rate, but experienced intermittently (regular intervals, generally often)
Individual Soldier or Marine	Occurs several times in career; expected to occur during a specific mission or operation
All Soldiers and Marines exposed	Occurs at a high rate, but experienced intermittently
(C) Occasional: Occurs sporadically	
Single item	Occurs sometime in service life; may occur with equal frequency during a specific mission or operation
Fleet or inventory of items	Occurs several times in service life
Individual Soldier or Marine	Occurs sometime in career; may occur during a specific mission or operation, but not often
All Soldiers and Marines exposed	Occurs sporadically (irregularly, sparsely, or sometimes)

Table D-2. Hazard probability chart (continued)

(D) Seldom: Remotely possible; could occur at some time	
Single item	Occurs in service life, but only remotely possible; not expected to occur during a specific mission or operation
Fleet or inventory of items	Occurs as isolated incidents; possible to occur sometime in service life but rarely; usually does not occur
Individual Soldier or Marine	Occurs as isolated incident during a career; remotely possible but not expected to occur during a specific mission or operation
All Soldiers and Marines exposed	Occurs rarely within exposed population as isolated incidents
(E) Unlikely: Can assume will not occur, but not impossible	
Single item	Occurrence not impossible; but may assume will almost never occur in service life; may assume will not occur during a specific mission or operation
Fleet or inventory of items	Occurs very rarely (almost never or is improbable); incidents may occur over service life
Individual Soldier or Marine	Occurrence not impossible, but may assume will not occur in career or during a specific mission or operation
All Soldiers and Marines exposed	Occurs very rarely, but not impossible

Table D-3. Hazard severity chart

Type	Description
Catastrophic (I)	• Loss of ability to accomplish the mission or mission failure • Death or permanent total disability (accident risk) • Loss of major or mission-critical system or equipment • Major property (facility) damage; severe environmental damage • Mission-critical security failure • Unacceptable collateral damage
Critical (II)	• Significantly (severely) degraded mission capability or unit readiness • Permanent partial disability • Temporary total disability exceeding 3 months (accident risk) • Extensive (major) damage to equipment or systems • Significant damage to property or the environment • Security failure • Significant collateral damage
Marginal (III)	• Degraded mission capability or unit readiness • Minor damage to equipment or systems, property, or the environment • Lost day due to injury or illness, not exceeding 3 months (accident risk) • Minor damage to property or the environment
Negligible (IV)	• Little or no adverse impact on mission capability • First aid or minor medical treatment (accident risk) • Slight equipment or system damage but fully functional and serviceable • Little or no property or environmental damage

Stage 1

D-8. A leader assesses the probability of each hazard. For each hazard (item 6 of DA Form 7566) identified, he would determine—

- A vehicle accident or breakdown causing a fuel/HM spill would seldom happen. This assessment is based on experience and the information provided in table D-2, page D-4.
- Spills during refueling stops may occasionally be expected. This is based on his judgment and the information provided in table D-2.
- Maneuver damage from off-road movement could happen frequently. This is based on his working knowledge and the information provided in table D-2.

Stage 2

D-9. A leader assesses the severity of each hazard identified. Definitions for the degree of severity are not absolutes; they are more conditional and are related to mission variables. A leader must use his experience, judgment, lessons learned, and SMEs to help determine the degrees of severity.

D-10. A leader uses the determinations from Stage 1 with the severity caused by an occurrence in Stage 2 to determine the overall risk of each hazard. From the information in figure D-1, page D-2, a leader would determine—

- A vehicle accident or breakdown causing a fuel/HM spill could be significant and cause major damage to the environment. The severity would be critical. This is based on experience and the information provided in table D-3, page D-5.
- Spills during refueling stops could cause minor damage to the environment. The severity would be marginal. This is based on his judgment and the information provided in table D-3.
- Maneuver damage from off-road movement would cause little or no environmental damage. The severity would be negligible. This is based on his working knowledge and the information provided in table D-3.

Stage 3

D-11. First, a leader determines the risk level of each hazard. Next, using the defined degrees of probability and severity and the risk assessment matrix (see table D-4), the overall environmentally related risk level is determined.

Table D-4. Risk assessment matrix

Severity	Probability				
	Frequent (A)	Likely (B)	Occasional (C)	Seldom (D)	Unlikely (E)
Catastrophic (I)	E	E	H	H	M
Critical (II)	E	H	H	M	L
Marginal (III)	H	M	M	L	L
Negligible (IV)	M	L	L	L	L

Risk Categories

Extremely High (E)

Mission failure if hazardous incidents occur during mission; a frequent or likely probability of catastrophic loss (IA or IB) or frequent probability of critical loss (IIA) occurs.

High (H)

Significantly degraded mission capabilities in terms of required mission standard, failing to accomplish all aspects of the mission, or not completing the mission to standard (if hazards occur during mission); occasional to seldom probability of catastrophic loss (IC or ID); a likely to occasional probability of a critical loss occurring (IIB or IIC) with materials, frequent probability of marginal (IIIA) losses.

Moderate (M)

Expected degraded mission capabilities in terms of required mission standard; reduced mission capability (if hazards occur during mission); unlikely probability of catastrophic loss (IE). The probability of a critical loss occurring is seldom (IID). Marginal losses occur with a probability of no more often than likely (IIIB or IIIC). Negligible (IVA) losses are a frequent probability.

Low (L)

Expected losses have little or no impact on accomplishing the mission. The probability of critical loss is unlikely (IIE), while that of marginal loss is no more often than seldom (IIID through IIIE).

D-12. For the hazards identified in table D-1, page D-3, a leader would determine—

- Vehicle accidents and breakdowns causing fuel/HM spills would seldom happen; but if they did, the severity could be critical. Based on this information and table D-4 (severity row, critical; probability column, seldom), he determines the overall assessment to be moderate.
- Spills during refueling stops will happen occasionally; when they do, the severity will be marginal. Based on this information and table D-4 (severity row, marginal; probability column, occasional), he determines the overall assessment to be moderate.
- Maneuver damage from vehicle off-road movement will happen frequently. The damage caused by this movement would be negligible. Based on this information and table D-4 (severity row, negligible; probability column, frequent), he determines the overall assessment to be moderate.

D-13. These determinations are then entered on the assessments in item 7 of DA Form 7566.

STEP 3. DEVELOP ENVIRONMENTAL CONTROLS AND MAKE DECISIONS

D-14. Controls eliminate or reduce the probability or severity of each hazard, thereby lowering the overall risk. Controls may consist of one of the categories listed in table D-5, page D-8, which also lists examples.

Table D-5. Environmentally related controls

Control Type	Environmentally Related Examples
Educational	• Conducting unit environmental awareness training • Conducting an environmental briefing before deployment • Performing tasks to environmental standards • Reviewing environmental considerations in AARs • Reading unit environmental SOPs and policies • Conducting spill prevention training • Publishing an environmental annex/appendix to the OPORD/OPLAN
Physical	• Providing spill prevention equipment • Establishing a field trash collection point and procedures • Establishing a field satellite accumulation point and procedures • Policing field locations • Practicing good field sanitation • Filling in fighting positions • Posting signs and warnings for off-limits areas
Avoidance	• Maneuvering around historical/cultural sites • Establishing refueling and maintenance areas away from wetlands and drainage areas • Crossing streams at approved sites • Preventing pollution • Limiting noise in habitats of endangered and threatened species • Avoiding refueling over water sources • Curtailing live vegetation use for camouflage

D-15. Many environmental risk controls are simply extensions of good management, housekeeping, operations security, and leadership practices. Risk reduction controls may include rehearsals, change of venue, establishment of procedures, and increased supervision. Using the information from table D-5, a leader completes item 8 on DA Form 7566.

D-16. Once all practicable risk control measures are in place, some risk will always remain. Based on the controls that he develops, a leader reassesses the hazards using the procedures from step 2. Once he determines the residual risk for each hazard, he completes item 9 on DA Form 7566. Based on the highest residual risk determination in item 9, this becomes the overall mission/task risk and is checked in block 13. The residual risk requires the commander's attention, and he will decide whether or not to accept the risk. The commander may direct his subordinates to consider additional controls or a change in the COA.

STEP 4. IMPLEMENT ENVIRONMENTAL CONTROLS

D-17. Implementing controls requires informing all subordinates of the risk control measures. To do this, a leader defines the controls by completing item 10 of DA Form 7566. He should state the way in which each control will be implemented and assign responsibility for the implementation by completing item 11 on DA Form 7566. For example, if the control measures are for a fuel spill hazard, a leader ensures that operators are properly trained to dispense fuel and that appropriate spill equipment is available. Then he must ensure that these controls are in place before an operation.

D-18. A leader must anticipate environmental requirements and incorporate them as part of his long-, short-, and near-term planning. The key to success is identifying the who, what, where, when, and how aspects of each control. This information should be entered on DA Form 7566.

STEP 5. SUPERVISE AND EVALUATE

D-19. Leaders continuously monitor controls throughout an operation to ensure their effectiveness and to modify them as required. To this end, leaders—

- Make on-the-spot corrections and evaluate individual and collective performances.
- Hold those in charge accountable.
- Require performance of all tasks to applicable environmental standards.
- Ensure that the AAR process includes an evaluation of environmentally related hazards, controls, Soldier and Marine performance, and leader supervision.
- Ensure that environmental lessons learned are developed for use in future operations.

D-20. Each control identified and implemented must be evaluated (item 12 on DA Form 7566) to determine if the control was adequate for the associated risk. This evaluation should include feedback provided to the Soldiers and Marines associated with the risk.

SUMMARY

D-21. The ability of a leader to identify hazards is key. A reality in today's missions is that the aspect of a hazard can change rapidly. Items of little initial risk can quickly become major threats due to unforeseen natural or man-made events. Leaders must be aware of this possibility. Complacency concerning existing controls in rapidly changing situations should be viewed as a hazard itself.

D-22. Completing the risk assessment alone, while failing to identify effective controls, usually results in a go or no-go decision based on the initial risk. If risk assessment does not accurately identify hazards and determine the level of residual risk, a leader is likely to make a risk decision based on incomplete or inaccurate information. If the risk assessment places missions in a routine, low-risk category, the commander may not be informed of a risk decision, resulting in a risk level that could imperil his higher commander's intent and other organizations. The CRM process is intended to provide reasonable controls to support mission accomplishment.

This page intentionally left blank.

Appendix E

Environmental Baseline Survey

The EBS is a multidiscipline site survey. It is conducted during the initial stage of any Service or joint operational deployment and followed by a closeout survey when a site is returned to the foreign nation or when joint forces depart the site. The EBS documents existing deployment area environmental conditions (to include cultural), determines the likelihood for present and past site contamination (such as hazardous substances, petroleum products, and derivatives), and identifies potential vulnerabilities (to include occupational and environmental health risks). The closeout survey defines the conditions existing at the time of departure from a site and documents any changes/variations in conditions from the EBS. Surveys accomplished in conjunction with operational deployments that do not involve training or exercises (contingency/expeditionary operations) should be completed to the extent practicable, consistent with operational requirements for all occupations exceeding 30 days. In cases where less than 30 days of occupation are expected, an environmental assessment should still be conducted to support Servicemember FHP. The EBS is generally performed in conjunction with an EHSA.

PREPARATION AND IMPLEMENTATION OF THE SURVEY

E-1. This appendix provides guidance for the preparation of the EBS. Environmental reconnaissance (see FM 3-34.170/MCWP 3-17.4) is conducted to collect the information necessary for the EBS. The reconnaissance is typically focused by information requirements identified by environmental staff planners researching the potential AO. An EBS is typically performed by or with support from general engineer elements, including an on-site visit by environmental specialists as soon as the situation permits. However, engineer reconnaissance teams may need to perform an initial site assessment prior to an EBS with or without assistance from general engineers. While this appendix provides guidance to the general engineer and environmental specialist for completing a detailed EBS, including the site survey, it can also guide the engineer reconnaissance team conducting an initial assessment to begin development of the EBS.

PREPARATION

E-2. The EBS addressed in this manual is focused for use during contingency/expeditionary operations where other established foreign nation agreements or arrangements for a base camp site may not exist. (See FM 3-34.400 for specific planning considerations). Guidance should be provided in annex L of the joint OPORD/OPLAN to direct the conduct of surveys, especially in those situations where specific foreign nation agreements or arrangements may not exist or a foreign nation government may not be operating. It may also come from appendix 5 (Environmental Considerations) to annex G (Engineering) of an OPORD/OPLAN. Through the use of the EBS, Services can maintain situational awareness, maximize combat power, and reduce and/or eliminate the negative effects of occupational health and environmental exposures.

E-3. The primary purposes of an EBS are: (1) the protection of Service personnel (eliminating, minimizing, or mitigating environmental health risks to Servicemembers); (2) sustainability determination of a designated location (includes encroachment considerations and potential requirements to increase the population of Servicemembers or actions performed at a site); (3) sensitivities involved with cultural or architectural considerations; (4) and minimizing any potential U.S. liability for the condition of a site at the time U.S. forces depart. Environmental specialists initiate EBS planning and preparation during the initial planning stages of any military operation through deliberate information gathering and staff estimates. These specialists include, but are not limited to, engineer and medical expertise that incorporate medical intelligence and geospatial information in the planning process. While containing some considerations of FHP, the EBS is not a complete medical assessment and so is always linked to the conduct of the EHSA and ideally accomplished in direct conjunction with this document and process.

E-4. Researching the AO and the specific potential sites that the operational commander will want to inhabit and use for base camps, airfields, logistic sites, and other relatively permanent locations in an AO are part of the staff planning process. This includes map reconnaissance with supporting geospatial products, review of medical information and intelligence about a site, and any other information obtainable (historical or current information) about proposed locations during the planning process. The respective staff estimates by the engineer, surgeon, logistician, joint staff/component/brigade or battalion civil-military operations officer (J-9/G-9/S-9) (with CA support), and others must include this assessment as a part of their normal planning process to evaluate all relevant environmental considerations. The preparation work performed at this point is not considered an EBS, but rather the preparation work to minimize the likelihood of choosing poor sites from an environmental and FHP viewpoint. If adequate information is not available on likely sites to be used, this information becomes information requirements that are fed into the IPB. Some of these may be critical enough to be considered a PIR. All of this assessment process is a part of the predeployment work required to ultimately create EBSs for each specific site, but does not in itself create an EBS. A physical visit of each site by environmental specialists is required for an EBS to be completed. Similarly, while research and preparation are completed to be able to perform a site closeout, a physical survey is required for one to be accomplished.

E-5. The preventive aspects present through the planning of required EBSs serve as a force multiplier and mission enabler through the early identification of environmental, health, and safety conditions that may pose potential health threats to military personnel and civilians that occupy designated areas within the theater of operations. They also assist in making recommendations on a particular site by taking into consideration suitability (to include both natural and cultural considerations) and sustainability determinations for that site. It is critical to obtain an assessment of projected/sustained use for a site and a projected duration of use for a given site from the operational planners. The engineer staff officer is directly involved and uses this information in the engineer support plan and integrates this information into staff planning.

IMPLEMENTATION

E-6. Estimates from the planning process are confirmed or adjusted based on physical site inspection during the EBS. An EBS is conducted for any base camp or similar site that will be in existence for more than 30 days. Ideally, the EBS will be accomplished in conjunction with an EHSA. This survey (and potential preceding assessment) conducted during contingency/expeditionary operations documents environmental conditions before (or immediately after) the occupation of any base camp or related site. This serves to protect Servicemembers by documenting property suitability as well as prevent the United States from receiving unfounded claims for past environmental damage.

E-7. While damage claims are the primary focus for many of the other EBSs performed by the DOD, it is of secondary importance in supporting the operational commander during contingency operations. When ultimately departing from a site, a closure survey is completed using the same basic format as the EBS to provide comparative information documenting the change in conditions over the life of occupation of that site by Servicemembers.

E-8. The importance of a standardized multi-Service format should be apparent. This format is intended to include adequate minimal medical considerations in the case where an EHSA is not able to be conducted in conjunction with the EBS. While each situation/site will be unique, the format for the EBS is intended to provide the standardized multi-Service framework for completion of the physical survey/assessment. Additional applicable references and tools are also listed with this template. See table E-1, page E-4.

E-9. In between the time frame of the EBS and the closure report is a requirement to periodically conduct inspections of the base camp or other similar facility to ensure that environmental considerations are being actively incorporated in the life of the site. This report is called an ECR and is focused on how well the commander of that site is applying relevant and directed environmental considerations. ECRs will be conducted for as long as the site is occupied and not less than on a quarterly basis to measure the environmental health/status of the base camp or similar site. These are ideally linked to medical survey efforts to both combine their effect and to minimize their administrative effects on the command. A standardized template is included as figure E-1, page E-6.

ENVIRONMENTAL BASELINE SURVEY CONTENT

E-10. Ideally, an EBS will be prepared to the fullest extent possible for each site to document environmental and environmental health conditions prior to the time of Servicemember arrival. This snapshot provides immediate information to the commander and creates a baseline record of conditions at that time. At some point, it is also likely that a closure report will be completed, but this is not the focus of the commander occupying the site. The EBS investigation is designed to provide the commander and his staff with an overview of the designated location/site using real-time field sampling, historical information, and readily available intelligence. Information sources include—

- IPB.
- Current reconnaissance reports of a given location/site.
- Intelligence reports.
- Digital information sources (National Geospatial-Intelligence Agency, Armed Forces Medical Intelligence Center, Defense Intelligence Agency, and others).
- Other geospatial information and products.

E-11. Deliberate information gathering and research for environmentally specific and historical information must be part of the investigative process in the execution of the EBS. This will include interviews with personnel having knowledge of the designated location to gain historical information about a site if possible. In some cases this may be performed by real estate personnel before a site is ever occupied.

E-12. A physical site inspection is performed by environmental specialists to obtain firsthand visual and physical information pertaining to the property to identify recognized environmental conditions and characteristics. The linkage of environmental and occupational health hazards are integrated as a part of the inspection. These inspections include the information categories contained in the EBS format. As a minimum, this inspection should include—

- Physical description and condition. Note the condition and location of facilities/improvements (if applicable), including the presence of buildings and other structures. Also record sites of known contamination within or immediately adjacent to the property boundaries and, if possible, try to determine the contaminant(s) of concern and the media affected. Include information, if available, on any remediation efforts and sampling conducted.
- Historical use(s) and user(s). Identify any visual and physical indications of past use(s) that may have impacted the property through the use, treatment, storage, disposal, or generation of hazardous substances or petroleum products. Include a list of past owners, occupants, and past uses of the property where available.
- Adjacent land use. The general type of property usage (such as residential, commercial, or industrial) should be documented. Identify any visual and physical indications (such as soil staining or stressed vegetations) of current and past land use practices that may be indicative of a contaminant release.
- Soil type and land cover. Note the soil type and general types of vegetation present on the property. Include in this paragraph any observations of stressed vegetation and potential causes (such as hazardous substances or petroleum product release, lack of irrigation, or high-traffic area).

● Hydrologic and geologic features. In this portion, include hydrologic features important to drainage, such as creeks, ditches, and riverbeds.

● Water supply. Identify any sources of potable water on the property as well as an estimated associated capacity. Note the presence of water facilities, such as pump stations, storage tanks, system age and condition, and its components. In addition, document any wastewater or other liquids discharging from the property into a drain, ditch, stream, or on or adjacent to the location/property.

Table E-1. Environmental baseline survey format

1. Cover page for EBS	3.2.1. Current use of site
1.1. Title will be "Environmental Baseline Survey"	3.2.2. Historical use of site
1.2. Location identification	3.3. Use of adjoining properties
1.2.1. This identification will indicate the location's recognized name or similar means of identification, i.e., *Logistics Staging Area Doe*	3.3.1. Current use of adjoining properties
	3.3.2. Historical use of adjoining properties
1.2.2. Name of city, township, or AO for the location of the site	4. Site description
	4.1. Location. General description of the site location that will include the following information:
1.3. Identification of lead surveyor	4.1.1. Detailed description of the site location
1.3.1. Organization/agency with responsibility for conducting EBS	4.1.2. Organization designated for occupation of the site
1.3.2. Standard name line of project leader	4.1.3. Grid location of the area
1.3.3. Period of survey	4.1.4. Map series
1.3.3.1. Start date of survey	4.2. Site and vicinity characteristics
1.3.3.2. End date of survey	4.2.1. Physical setting
1.3.4. DSN telephone number (if available)	4.2.2. Topography
2. Executive summary (separate page)	4.2.3. Geology
2.1. Findings. Written to provide users of the EBS a broad overview of the findings regarding the designated location where the EBS was conducted. Discuss specific PIRs addressed/evaluated in the EBS	4.2.4. Soils
	4.2.5. Vegetation
	4.2.6. Hydrology
	4.2.7. Raw materials
2.2. Recommendations. General recommendations to be considered by users of the EBS that notes any controls or actions that should be addressed. Recommendations must be supported by findings during the execution of the EBS	4.3. Detailed Site Description
	4.3.1. Structures
	4.3.2. Roads
	4.3.3. Drinking Water Sources
	4.3.4. Waste disposal
2.3. Notes. General comments regarding sampling, additional testing conducted, and related items considered during the development of the recommendations in line 2.2	4.3.5. Other improvements
	4.4. Use of site
	5. Information sources and supporting documents
3. Introduction	
3.1. Provide purpose of the EBS, include PIRs to be addressed	
3.2. Limitations of assessment in the execution of the EBS	

Table E-1. Environmental baseline survey format (continued)

6. Information from site reconnaissance
  6.1. Background of location upon identification for occupation
  6.2. Detailed analysis of information gathered in that includes (but not limited to):
    6.2.1. Presence of animals or other vectors such as insects (for example, mosquitoes and sand flies)
    6.2.2. Potential radioactive sources (present or past)
    6.2.3. Hazards and health risks
      6.2.3.1. Site specific
      6.2.3.2. Offset site
    6.2.4. Environmental hazards
      6.2.4.1. Site specific
      6.2.4.2. Offset site
    6.2.5. Waste disposal
      6.2.5.1. Current status
      6.2.5.2. Historical perspective
      6.2.5.3. Planned Improvements or changes
    6.2.6. Agricultural implications
      6.2.6.1. Site specific
      6.2.6.2. Offset site
    6.2.7. Identified environmental and environmental health hazards
      6.2.7.1. Historical
      6.2.7.2. Present
      6.2.7.3. Potential future
    6.2.8. Site assessment, to include detailed walk-through with building and infrastructure assessments
	7. Environmental and environmental health sampling data
	  7.1. Sampling and analysis plan(s), to include justification for number, type, and location of samples collected, as well as analysis to be performed on the samples collected. Sampling should be identified as either confirmation or delineation
	  7.2. Sampling results analysis, to include a summary table of sampling results
	  7.3. Environmental health site assessment summary (if applicable)
	8. Findings and conclusions
	  8.1. Identification of environmental conditions that have the potential for significant impacts to health or mission
	  8.2. Detailed concerns
	9. Recommendations
	  9.1. Usability
	  9.2. Further investigation and additional assessments required to fully address concerns
	  9.3. Identify and recommend controls to address concerns where applicable

SUSTAINED SITE SURVEYS

E-13. The primary purpose of a base camp is mission support, synchronized with the overall military mission of the deployed force. To execute mission support, a base camp must provide force protection to deployed forces, resource management of critical infrastructure, training opportunities for deployed forces and permanent party, and maintenance of the facilities. Included in that mission support is the continued application of environmental considerations, to include the critical aspects of FHP. This includes periodic, sustained site surveys/assessments similar to those performed by an installation staff. The ECR (see figure E-1, page E-6) assists with that requirement.

CLASSIFICATION

ENVIRONMENTAL CONDITIONS REPORT [ECR]

References:

a. DODD 6050.7, "Environmental Effects Abroad of Major Department of Defense Actions," 31 March 1979.

b. JSN 3820.01E, "Environmental Engineering Effects of DOD Actions," 30 September 2008.

c. DODD 6050.16, "Policy for Establishing and Implementing Environmental Standards at Overseas Installations," 20 September 1991.

d. Other applicable environmental laws and regulations, OPORD, and unit SOP.

e. Site specific EBS (if applicable).

1. Site/Incident Location. List the legal address and 6-digit military grid location or latitude and longitude of the incident location or reference the applicable EBS to link the ECR to a given site. Refer to the electronic environmental message formats at Tab E. (The ECR functions as a situation report, or interim report, for a given site. The frequency of ECR reports is a higher headquarters' decision but supports the need to document the condition of a given site over time [interim snapshots], as well as helping to ensure that an appropriate environmental focus is being maintained at a given site. The basic format of the ECR may also be used when reporting an incident, such as a POL spill, not related to a given EBS or site location).

2. Site/Incident Description and Background. Give a brief description of the site (installation), including its related EBS/historical use(s) or the circumstances surrounding the incident. For an incident at a location not covered by an EBS, it is critical to provide the same sort of information contained in a standard accident report.

3. Map/Description of the Incident Location. If the ECR is related to a site covered by an EBS, this entry is able to relate to the information already provided in the EBS (a baseline document). If the ECR defines a location where an incident has occurred that is not covered by an EBS, the description needs to be adequate to direct a follow-on element to the site. In this respect, it is similar to the graves-registration report if the incident occurs during a tactical operation where time precludes remaining at the site.

4. Summary of Environmental Conditions. List the environmental event(s) at the site/location. All spills should be inventoried. If the ECR is a periodic report for a given site, significant events, such as major spills, should have been reported using the basic ECR format. In this case, simply reference any significant incident report ECRs that may have occurred at the given site over the time frame that the periodic ECR covers. Also provide a "snapshot" report of the types of HW/HM that are stored at the site. Describe minor spills and other events that have occurred over the time frame in question in basic terms, including quantities and the method(s) used to clean the site.

Example: Four gallons of waste oil spilled at the hazardous waste accumulation site located northwest of the maintenance building (shown on map) at 1600 hours on 16 December 2000. The 22nd Military Police Battalion (MP Bn), contained the spill with assistance by White & Jones, by 1725 hours. About 3 cubic yards of contaminated soil was taken to the White & Jones HW disposal area in Juvonia.

CLASSIFICATION

Figure E-1. ECR format

CLASSIFICATION

Example: Raw sewage ran from a pump house behind the main warehouse (shown on map) for an estimated 3 days during the initial stages of occupying the camp in early June 2000. The problem was identified on 13 June and corrected when the pump was repaired on 14 June.

Example: A fuel tanker overturned at the road intersection vicinity NV 123456 (see map) at 092000 November 2000 during the road march to Bigtown. Immediate mitigation included spill containment by the employment of all available spill kits with the unit. Higher HQ was immediately notified. An estimated 4000 gallons of jet petroleum (JP)-8 spilled at that site. The vehicle has been righted, and excavation of the site will begin at first light, 10 November.

5. <u>Interior and Exterior Observations</u>. These entries should be viewed as an abbreviated version of the information that would be found in an EBS. Items should only be addressed if they differ from the last ECR or vary from the initial EBS.

6. <u>Findings and Determinations with Qualification Statement</u>. A statement similar to the following should appear in this paragraph of the ECR:

According to _____ Reg _____, I have considered whether or not significant environmental impacts will occur as a result of turnover/return of this site (base camp, logistics area) and have determined that (include one of the following statements):

a. Turnover of this base camp area will not result in environmental impacts significant enough to warrant additional environmental analysis.

OR

b. Turnover of this base camp area will result in environmental impacts significant enough to warrant additional environmental analysis. Environmental actions or projects must continue after transfer of the base camp area because of substantial (imminent) threat to human health or safety. The impacts of concern are (list impacts):

(If the report is due to an incident not connected to a specific site/installation, this paragraph is an assessment by the commander/individual on the scene).

> John Q. Jones
> MAJ, QM
> Mayor, Camp Swampy

CLASSIFICATION

Figure E-1. ECR format (continued)

This page intentionally left blank.

Appendix F

Hazardous Material/Hazardous Waste Management Procedures for Field Operations

This appendix provides guidance for assisting units in the proper management of HM/HW during operations. Proper management practices will safeguard the health of military personnel and protect the environment. Additionally, these measures will ease logistical burdens and produce cost savings through HW minimization and P2. They are intended to assist military personnel in the development of unit and operation-specific SOPs for HM/HW management in any AO. Although this appendix focuses on maneuver brigade and battalion operations, the information provided may be adapted to company- and platoon-size units during any operation.

REFERENCES

F-1.   Key references for HM/HW handling are as follows:
- 29 CFR and 40 CFR.
- Applicable laws and regulations regarding HM usage and waste management (consult your higher headquarters or supporting environmental management office).
- OPLANs and OPORDs.
- TM 38-410.
- Unit SOPs.
- USACHPPM TG-217.

RESPONSIBILITIES

F-2.   Many commodities used by the military are hazardous or contain HMs with special requirements for storage and handling. The dangers posed by these items may be serious, and personnel should be aware of the domestic and international laws and regulations associated with them. These laws and regulations place special emphasis on communicating the hazards associated with these products, as exposure may result in serious personal injury, permanent disabilities, and even death. Property and the environment may also be damaged or destroyed. It is imperative that all military personnel recognize and understand the hazards associated with these commodities.

HAZARDOUS MATERIAL/HAZARDOUS WASTE MANAGEMENT PROGRAM

F-3.   Proper management of HM/HW during operations is critical to the protection of human health and the environment. Without a management program backed by command emphasis, military personnel, and the environment are at risk of potential exposure to HM/HW.

IMPORTANCE OF HAZARDOUS MATERIAL/HAZARDOUS WASTE MANAGEMENT

F-4. Severe injuries or irreparable environmental damage could result from improper HM/HW management. In addition to protecting human health and the environment, proper management of HM/HW produces cost savings through HW minimization and P2. A portion of the funds used for cleanup procedures due to mismanagement of HM/HW may impact unit training budgets and military readiness.

HAZARDOUS MATERIAL/HAZARDOUS WASTE MANAGEMENT PLANS

F-5. The key to a successful management program lies in planning and informing. HM/HW management plans should be specific for the given operation, and commanders must place an emphasis on the program to ensure that all personnel are aware of the requirements. Plans may be altered based on the mission or tactical situation, but informing the command of proper procedures is critical in maintaining a successful program.

KEY ASPECTS OF HAZARDOUS MATERIAL/HAZARDOUS WASTE MANAGEMENT

F-6. Several important aspects exist in HM/HW management. At a minimum, personnel must know how to properly handle, transport, and store HM and how to properly collect and dispose of HW. Proficiency in these management practices will ensure that neither personal safety nor the environment is jeopardized during operations.

SPILL RESPONSE PLANS

F-7. Emergency HM/HW spill response plans must be prepared before any operation. These plans should address all aspects of spill response, to include site-specific response procedures and spill response equipment requirements for each major HM/HW operation. They should be distributed throughout the unit before any operation.

HAZARDOUS MATERIAL/HAZARDOUS WASTE FIELD PROCEDURES

F-8. Using the correct procedures for HM/HW handling is critical to protection measures and environmental protection. Field environment operations, whether during training or deployment, present additional hazards to the management of HM. Proper measures—including enforcement of the use of PPE and proper procedures for the handling, storing, and transporting of HM/HW—must be developed and implemented. See the following vignette.

Issue

Field expedient HW accumulation sites pose environmental and safety risks.

Discussion

The DRMO Forward Support Team–Europe established two main HW accumulation sites and nine feeder sites in Iraq for storing large volumes of waste oil generated in-country. Mission variables dictated that the inherent risks of convoy operations in the hostile environment were high, requiring commanders to reduce the frequency of HW convoys or to discontinue transport altogether. Commanders were forced to set up their own HW accumulation site inside their base camps.

These areas had problems associated with—

- HWs that were not segregated.
- Lack of secondary containment.
- Leaders that did not provide proper supervision on the sites.
- Sites that were situated too close to camp perimeters—creating a protection issue. (Sites are a potential target for hand grenades and IEDs.)
- Actions that put the health and safety of Soldiers and Marines at risk.

Techniques and Procedures

- Commanders must ensure that personnel are trained in the handling of HM/HW before setting up a base camp HW accumulation site.
- Leaders must familiarize themselves with the combatant command's (command authority) requirements for managing HW in-theater and ensure compliance.
- Trained personnel and leaders must supervise site operations and Soldiers and Marines to ensure proper handling and management of HW.
- When setting up an HW accumulation site, units must—
  - Identify a manager for the HW accumulation site.
  - Identify the types of HW materials present.
  - Specify the authorized amounts of HW collected.
  - Segregate the HWs.
  - Locate the HW accumulation site at a safe distance from troop bedding/duty areas and perimeters (a minimum of 50 feet).
  - Maintain adequate storage and proper collection containers on hand.
  - Provide electrical grounding for containers.
  - Label the containers.
  - Maintain MSDSs on hand for each item.
  - Set up an emergency wash/decontamination site.
  - Plan for adequate secondary containment.
  - Plan for spills and maintain appropriate PPE and spill kits readily available.
  - Secure the HW accumulation site.
  - Supervise all activities within the HW accumulation site.

Note. The fence is the perimeter around the HW accumulation site, not the base camp perimeter.

HAZARDOUS MATERIAL/HAZARDOUS WASTE HANDLING

F-9. The most important aspect of HM/HW handling is in identifying the hazard(s) associated with each individual chemical. Once appropriate hazards are identified, steps may be taken to minimize personnel and environmental exposure. Hazardous characteristics may be found on the MSDS for each chemical.

F-10. MSDSs provide critical information for safeguarding human health and protecting the environment. They include information on the hazardous characteristic(s) of the chemical, the appropriate PPE, spill response procedures, signs and symptoms of overexposure, and first aid procedures. MSDSs may be obtained through the unit supply channels and should be maintained at the following operations: HM storage and HW accumulation sites, tactical-refueling operations, maintenance operations, and medical treatment facilities. It is important to note that MSDSs are material and manufacturer-specific, which means that each chemical brand name contains a different MSDS. HW managers should ensure that appropriate MSDSs are available during operations.

F-11. Primary operations requiring the use of PPE include the transportation and accumulation of HM/HW, tactical-refueling operations, and maintenance operations. In the event that MSDSs are not available and cannot be obtained during an operation, a field expedient PPE should be used to help protect personnel when handling HM/HW or in the event of a spill. Table F-1 lists national stock numbers (NSNs) for PPE commonly used when handling HM/HW in a field environment.

Table F-1. Personal protective equipment

NSN	Description
Aprons	
8415-01-189-6228	Rubber material, acid-resistant
8415-01-100-7742	Plastic material, oil-resistant, and waterproof
Gloves	
8415-00-266-8673	Synthetic rubber, acid- and alkali-resistant
8415-00-266-8675	Synthetic rubber, acid- and alkali-resistant
8415-01-138-2497	Butyl rubber, acid- and alkali-resistant
8415-01-138-2498	Butyl rubber, acid- and alkali-resistant
Safety Goggles	
4240-00-052-3776	Molded plastic flexible frame with clear plastic lenses and adjustable headband
4240-01-055-2310	Lightweight goggles with vinyl resin frame and saddle-type nose bridge
4240-01-292-2818	Polycarbonate plastic lens with a molded plastic frame (may be worn over most prescription glasses)

HAZARDOUS WASTE COLLECTION

F-12. HW should be collected at the point of generation. The key to proper collection is in segregating, containerizing, and labeling the waste. HW managers should coordinate with brigade and battalion S-4s to ensure that all units have the resources needed for proper collection. Units establish HW accumulation sites to temporarily store HW until arrangements can be made to remove it. Each waste stream needs to have its own container. Containers need to be inspected for dents, leaks, and corrosion; should be labeled; and should be kept closed when not being filled. HW containers should be removed from the site as soon as possible after being filled to 85 percent capacity. Secondary containment needs to be established, and the site needs to be protected from damage (such as accidental spills, vehicle accidents, and weather effects) and possible hostile actions (such as a mortar attack). HW accumulation sites should be located away from troop billeting areas and should be located to avoid potential contamination of water sources (such as storm drains, drainage ditches, and water courses).

WASTE SEGREGATION

F-13. Generators of HW must ensure that waste streams remain segregated. Improper segregation of HW streams at the point of generation could result in an incompatible waste mixture, posing a significant health risk. In addition, a mixture of HW and non-HW (such as general trash) must be managed and disposed of as HW, drastically increasing HW disposal costs. Proper segregation at the point of generation will simplify the overall management process, protect human health and the environment, reduce disposal costs, and enhance the potential for recycling the HW.

CONTAINERIZING HAZARDOUS WASTE

F-14. HW must be collected in appropriate containers. The best type of container is the original container (if it is capable of being closed) in which the material was shipped in before being rendered a waste. If the original container is not available or the waste volume exceeds the capacity of the original container, use any container compatible with the waste stream. When filling a container, ensure that adequate headspace remains to allow for expansion of the material (3 to 4 inches in a 55-gallon drum, 1.5 to 2 inches in a 5-gallon can, and 1 inch in a 1-gallon can). Only nonsparking tools should be used when containerizing a reactive or flammable waste.

HAZARDOUS MATERIAL/HAZARDOUS WASTE TRANSPORTATION PROCEDURES

F-15. HM/HW should be transported only in approved vehicles. These vehicles should contain appropriate placards and manifests for the materials being transported. In addition, drivers must be certified to transport hazardous cargo. Certification training may be coordinated through the supporting transportation unit. The supporting transportation unit can also provide site-specific information or waive certain requirements, based on the tactical situation encountered during the operation.

EMERGENCY EQUIPMENT

F-16. Personnel transporting hazardous cargo should be supplied with the required PPE. In addition to PPE, each vehicle approved for HM/HW transport must be supplied with a spill response plan and the appropriate spill response equipment.

F-17. Units should be prepared to respond to emergency operations. The unit should maintain—

- Spill kits. Based on unit mission and the type of HM/HW used, spill kits provide containment and cleanup should an accidental spill occur.
- Fire extinguisher. Each storage area containing flammable materials or waste is supplied with an ABC-type (monoammonium phosphate) fire extinguisher.
- Emergency eyewashes. Potable water must be readily available for emergency eye washing. This will help in providing first aid measures on-site in the event of a leak or spill.
- PPE. Two sets of the PPE are readily available at each storage area. Reference the MSDSs for the required PPE.
- Spill response. A spill response plan and spill response equipment are readily available at each accumulation area.

HAZARDOUS MATERIAL/HAZARDOUS WASTE STORAGE

F-18. As a rule, an HW accumulation site is considered a storage area when it contains more than 55 gallons of HM/HW. HW accumulation sites are temporary sites where HW may be stored for up to 90 days. Storage sites should be identified during the predeployment phase of the operation or as soon as the unit establishes its operating area. Set up HM/HW storage areas at least 15 meters (50 feet) downwind and down gradient of personnel billeting and dining facility operations. Eight-digit grid coordinates and inventories of the storage areas should be maintained in the event that the unit must rapidly evacuate the area.

F-19. HW accumulation site areas must be properly secured within the unit's AO to prevent unauthorized access from both U.S. and foreign nation personnel. The material stored may be considered valuable to the local population and scavengers. Concertina wire may be necessary to properly secure the storage area.

F-20. HW accumulation sites must be segregated into the following four general categories or sections:

- Reactives.
- Flammables/ignitables.
- Corrosives.
- Toxics.

F-21. Further segregation may be required based on the compatibility of individual materials (reference MSDSs for each material to identify appropriate storage sections). Each storage section must be separated by a distance of 6 feet or a physical barrier to prevent incompatible materials from mixing and producing an adverse chemical reaction or toxic fumes. A recommended storage segregation chart for materials commonly used during operations is shown in table F-2. Containers holding reactive or flammable materials or waste should be grounded during storage, and only nonsparking tools should be used when handling these containers.

SECONDARY CONTAINMENT

F-22. Secondary containment is designed to protect human health and the environment in the event of a leak or spill. Proper secondary containment includes hardstands, tarps, plastic liners, and sandbags. For storage of materials on a hardstand, ensure that the containers are placed on a pallet with a sandbag perimeter for containment of spilled liquids. If a hardstand is not available, place all materials within each category on a tarp or plastic liner with sandbags surrounding the containers. Secondary containment should be large enough to contain 10 percent of the overall volume or 100 percent of the volume of the largest container of HM/HW stored, whichever is larger. An additional tarp or plastic liner should be available to cover the tops of the containers during adverse weather conditions.

CONTAINERS

F-23. All containers must be kept closed and maintained in good condition at all times. Supervisors should not permit open funnels or tubes to be attached to containers. Rusty or residue-covered containers are unacceptable.

STORAGE OF FUEL CANS

F-24. Five-gallon fuel cans are usually scattered throughout a unit during operations. They should be consolidated within each company or platoon AO, placed on a tarp or piece of plywood, and surrounded by a soil berm or sandbags for secondary containment, if possible. This will prevent spills from adversely affecting personnel or the environment. When filling fuel cans, personnel must ensure that 1.5 to 2 inches of headspace remains to allow for vapor expansion.

Table F-2. Storage segregation chart

Material/Waste	Hazardous Characteristic(s)
Storage Section A (Reactives)	
Chlorination kits–reactive	Empty aerosol cans are reactive in a fire
Approved decontaminates	Possible reaction with other decontaminants or chemicals
Storage Section B (Flammables)	
Chemical agent resistant coating–toxic	Paint flammable and toxic
Cleaning compounds	Flammable and toxic
Deicing agents	Flammable
Fuels	Flammable
Lacquers/varnishes	Flammable, irritant, and noxious
Paints	Flammable and noxious
Paint thinners	Flammable and noxious
Parts cleaners	Flammable and toxic
Sealants	Flammable and toxic
Solvents	Flammable, irritant, and toxic
Windshield cleaners	Flammable
Storage Section C (Corrosives)	
Antifreeze	Irritant and noxious
Carbon remover	Irritant and toxic
Paint strippers	Corrosive and noxious
Radiator leak compounds	Irritant
Weapons cleaners	Irritant and toxic
Storage Section D (Toxins)	
Grease	Noxious
Lubricants	Noxious
Oils	Noxious
Oil contaminated solids	Noxious
Paint primers	Toxic
Storage Section E (Additional Storage Section)	
Battery acid	Corrosive and toxic
Dry batteries	Reactive in a fire

BATTERY STORAGE

F-25. An activity that includes battery storage *must* provide fire suppression equipment. In addition, storage areas and equipment must be approved by the local fire department. A point of contact must also be provided to the local fire department. TM 38-410 and TB 43-0134 outline the requirements to—

- Protect bulk storage of batteries with sprinklers.
- Keep batteries cool, dry, and away from open flame, heat, and combustibles and in a well-ventilated area with temperatures not to exceed 130 degrees Fahrenheit (54 degrees Celsius). Refrigeration is not necessary.
- Do not mix new and used batteries because it is difficult to distinguish between them. Many next generation batteries contain state of charge indicators.
- Segregate storage from other HM and other battery chemistries. It is critical that lead acid batteries be kept away from nickel cadmium or nickel metal hydride batteries.
- Protect batteries against being damaged, crushed, punctured, or short-circuited.
- Do not smoke or eat in battery storage areas.
- Store batteries separately from other HM.
- Use open flame devices only under proper supervision and with adequate safeguards.
- Do not accumulate nonhazardous solid waste batteries.
- Do not store batteries collected for turn-in to the DRMO more than 90 days.
- Ensure that fire extinguishers are available. Use an AB-type (water) fire extinguisher to fight fires involving small quantities of batteries.

RECORDKEEPING

F-26. Detailed HW records start at the accumulation site. A log should be kept of the type of waste received, the quantity received, the date received, and information on the unit that generated the waste. This log should be kept at all accumulation areas at brigade and battalion level. The unit HW manager is responsible for completing the appropriate turn-in documentation and applicable local forms. These should be completed once the waste is retrograded from the maneuver battalion accumulation areas to the brigade storage area. The unit should prepare a plan for the closure of HW accumulation sites. This plan should detail the way in which all waste and waste residues will be removed from the accumulation areas when they are no longer needed or in use.

INSPECTIONS

F-27. HW managers should conduct daily inspections of HM/HW accumulation areas. They will ensure that all requirements described above are met and that containers are in good condition.

HAZARDOUS WASTE DISPOSAL

F-28. Two primary disposal options for HW exist that can be implemented in any joint operations area (JOA): disposal through an approved contractor or retrograding HW back to CONUS. Units must not incinerate or bury any HW unless explicitly approved by both U.S. and foreign nation authorities. Commanders must determine the most viable means of approved HW disposal before entering the JOA by contacting their higher headquarters/supporting DRMO.

SUPPLY ACTIONS

F-29. Supply officers should maintain a system to monitor the amount of HM on hand to ensure that units are not stockpiling HMs. Excess HM storage may lead to unnecessary personal or environmental exposure. Supply and logistics personnel should coordinate among themselves and with the various environmental agencies to identify available alternative products, which can reduce the overall HW production.

TACTICAL-REFUELING OPERATIONS

F-30. POL personnel should conduct tactical-refueling operations at a designated logistics release point. Conducting tactical-refueling operations in a unit's AO should be avoided due to safety hazards associated with maneuvering a fuel tanker or heavy, expanded-mobility tactical truck (HEMTT) and conducting grounding operations at each vehicle. POL personnel should conduct actual refueling whenever possible.

F-31. During refueling operations, secondary containment (such as large drip pans) should be placed under the vehicle and under the fuel hoses. When refueling 5-gallon fuel cans, the cans should be placed inside the drip pans used for secondary containment. This will prevent small-volume fuel spills from accumulating and contaminating the soil. The spilled fuel should be transferred to a labeled 5-gallon waste fuel container and disposed of as HW. Ensure that proper emergency equipment is present during all refueling operations.

FIELD MAINTENANCE OPERATIONS

F-32. Maintenance operations should be conducted on a hardstand, tarp, or plastic liner, if available. Maintenance personnel will be required to supply their own PPE, spill response equipment, potable water for emergency eye washing, and liquid waste. All wheeled vehicles should contain drip pans, and all tracked vehicles should contain belly plates. Collected fluids must be placed in appropriate waste containers and disposed of as HW. Each company-size unit must maintain one labeled 5-gallon container for drip pan waste.

F-33. All drained fluids must either be returned to the vehicle or placed in an appropriate waste container for recycling or disposal as an HW. Maintenance areas should be supplied with two labeled 55-gallon liquid-waste containers for each of the following waste streams: used oil, waste fuel, waste antifreeze, and POL-contaminated solids. HW managers can coordinate the proper set up of accumulation site and the turn-in of waste containers and acquire empty 55-gallon liquid-HW containers from the appropriate support platoon.

DINING FACILITY OPERATIONS

F-34. Dining facility personnel may use M-2 burners, which operate on motor gasoline, during operations. Major safety and environmental issues include fuel storage, filling, and lighting operations.

F-35. Whether using motor gasoline or diesel fuel, filling operations should be conducted on a tarp or plastic liner with a soil berm or sandbag perimeter for secondary containment in the event of a spill. Spilled fuel must be collected immediately using an absorbent material. The used absorbent material should be placed in a plastic bag and disposed of as HW.

F-36. Lighting operations must be conducted at least 50 feet away from fuel storage and M-2 burner filling operations. Lighting operations should be conducted on open soil so that any residual fuel will freely burn during the operation.

OPERATION OF HEATERS, GENERATORS, AND LIGHT SETS

F-37. Personnel who use field heaters must ensure that the fuel supply (usually a 5-gallon fuel can) possesses secondary containment in the event of a leak or spill. The best way to provide this secondary containment is to elevate the fuel supply on a tripod or the back of a vehicle and place a drip pan under the fuel hose to collect any spilled fuel. The overflow fuel line should also have secondary containment, and all leaking fuel lines must be repaired or replaced. Collected fluids must be placed in appropriate waste containers and disposed of as HW. Each company-size unit should maintain one labeled 5-gallon container for waste fuel from the operation of heaters.

F-38. Generators and light sets must be operated in a manner protecting the environment from potential contamination. To provide this protection, operate generators on a piece of plywood and completely surround the generator with a soil berm or sandbag perimeter. This will prevent leaking fuel from contaminating the surrounding soil. Another alternative is to operate generators on a trailer and ensure that all spilled fuel is collected and placed in appropriate waste containers; each company-size unit should maintain one labeled 5-gallon container for waste fuel from the operation of generators. In addition, personnel should conduct preventive maintenance checks and ensure that all leaking generators are repaired or replaced.

SPILL RESPONSE

F-39. While good HM/HW management practices will minimize the chance of spills and thereby avoid the additional effort required to clean up any incidents, accidents will still happen. When they do, it is imperative that personnel are trained and prepared to mitigate the damage and to clean up the spills.

SPILL RESPONSE PLAN

F-40. A spill response plan must be available for each operation. The following major operations should have a copy of this plan: tactical refueling, maintenance, and HM/HW accumulation and transportation. The plan should address, at a minimum, site-specific response procedures and spill response equipment requirements for each major operation.

SPILL RESPONSE PROCEDURES

F-41. In the event of an HM/HW spill, the procedures listed below must be implemented immediately by trained personnel within the unit. Personal safety must never be compromised during the response. Should the situation exceed unit capabilities, evacuate the area, inform the chain of command, and contact the local HM spill response team or range control. Emergency telephone numbers or radio frequencies should be obtained and distributed throughout the unit as necessary before the operation begins. Personnel—

- Protect themselves. Use the required PPE for the spilled material specified in the MSDS and evacuate all nonessential personnel from the immediate area.
- Stop the flow. The flow of HM/HW must be stopped at the source to control the spill. This may be as simple as placing the container upright or closing a valve. In the event of a spill of flammable material, use only nonsparking tools and ensure that metal-to-metal contact is avoided.
- Contain the spill. Proper containment includes placing drip pans where the material contacts the soil, placing soil berms or sandbags around the contaminated area, and placing absorbent material in the area of the spill. The purpose of this step is to prevent the spread of contamination.
- Report the spill. Notify the chain of command and unit HW manager immediately.
- Clean the spill. Equipment used to clean a spill must be chosen carefully. Use only nonsparking tools if the material is flammable or explosive. For corrosive materials, use equipment that will not corrode or deteriorate (for example, nonmetallic equipment). Collect used absorbent and contaminated soil in plastic bags and transfer the bags into a labeled sturdy container to be disposed of as HW.
- Replace spill response equipment. Obtain replacement spill response equipment through the unit supply channels to ensure that personnel can properly respond in the event of another spill.

SPILL RESPONSE EQUIPMENT

F-42. Spill response equipment is essential to protecting the environment in the event of an HM/HW spill. The type and amount of spill response equipment needed depends on the operation. Units may also need to acquire hydrophobic-absorbent materials for operations conducted in areas susceptible to large amounts of precipitation. Spill response equipment required for specific operations is discussed in the following paragraphs.

Tactical-Refueling Operations

F-43. Tactical-refueling operations are limited to the handling of fuel products, such as diesel and motor gasoline. The extent of the operations and load-carrying capabilities of fuel tankers and HEMTTs restricts the amount and type of spill response equipment needed. In the event of a major spill during refueling operations, personnel primarily need two nonsparking picks and two nonsparking shovels to excavate contaminated soil and several large plastic bags to contain the excavated soil for disposal as HW. Approximately 10 pounds of absorbent and several small plastic bags are sufficient to respond to small-volume spills on a hardstand. Nonsparking tools should also be readily available. Additional resources may be obtained through supply channels as required.

Field Maintenance Operations

F-44. Field maintenance operations deal with all Class III items. Repeated small-volume spills are indicative of field maintenance operations. Approximately 25 pounds of absorbent, two nonsparking shovels, two brooms, and several small plastic bags for contaminated absorbent are sufficient to maintain field maintenance operations during operations. Additional resources may be obtained through supply channels, as required.

Hazardous Material/Hazardous Waste Accumulation

F-45. HM/HW storage operations deal with all Class III items. Leaking containers and small-volume spills are indicative of field HM/HW accumulation operations. Approximately 15 pounds of absorbent, two nonsparking shovels, two brooms, and several small plastic bags for contaminated absorbent are needed at each storage area. Additional resources may be obtained through supply channels as required.

Hazardous Material/Hazardous Waste Transportation

F-46. HM/HW transportation operations deal with several classes of supply in different size containers. Leaking containers and small-volume spills are indicative of HW transportation operations; however, the potential exists for large-volume spills in the event of an accident. Each approved vehicle for HM/HW transportation should maintain approximately 25 pounds of absorbent, two picks, two nonsparking shovels, one broom, and several small and large plastic bags for contaminated soil. Additional resources may be obtained through supply channels if deemed necessary.

This page intentionally left blank.

Appendix G

Base Camp Operations

This appendix provides guidelines for integrating environmental considerations into base camp operations. The increase in the number of expeditions and contingency operations has lead to an increased requirement for military personnel to operate from base camp facilities. The establishment of base camps and the occupation of existing facilities (such as ports and airfields) require extensive integration of environmental considerations. These sites, which may approach the size of small cities, can require a tremendous allocation of resources. In addition, they generate wastes in quantities similar to small cities, but without the existing infrastructure to support it. Planning for base camp operations must begin as early as possible in the operation, including in the establishment of environmental guidelines, oversight authority, site selection, and camp operating procedures. Refer to FM 3-34.400 for additional information.

BASE CAMP OVERSIGHT AND PLANNING

G-1. Senior commands may establish a base camp coordination agency/JEMB to assist in the conduct of operations. While these agencies perform separate functions, their coordination is important to ensure consistent operations. The base camp coordination agency establishes the standards for and coordinates the location, construction, and occupancy of base camps and installations. The JEMB establishes and coordinates policy for environmental matters. While sometimes referred to as a "temporary" board, the JEMB is a requirement as long as there are base camps and similar sites to manage. The JEMB may even be created during the planning phase to support the integration of environmental considerations into the planning process. Chaired by the senior engineer or a member of his staff, the JEMB includes primary staff membership (such as legal, medical, and CA) expertise to round out input for all environmental considerations. By working together, these two agencies may complement each other's efforts.

G-2. Base camp planning is typically initiated at a joint level and is a function of the collaboration between operators and logisticians as they attempt to define the number, the size, and the locations of potential base camps to support a deployment and the questions related to the standards (construction and other) that will be applied to each base camp. Staff assessments are collated by the engineer and fed into the base camp planning process. For each site, a base camp development site plan is developed with a supporting base camp development plan. The base camp development plan is a set of interrelated documents that record the planning process for laying out, determining the scope, and initiating implementing actions for the base camp.

Site Selection

G-3. The selection of base camp and installation sites is critical to the integration of environmental considerations. While the tactical situation may often dictate the locations, whenever possible environmental considerations need to be integrated into the decision process. Units must avoid areas that may contain contamination, such as industrial facilities and other areas that include or are adjacent to landfills or other health hazards. In addition, military personnel should not be billeted in structures such as ammunition bunkers or aircraft hangers for extended periods of time to avoid exposure to TIC/TIM hazards. Some areas of consideration in site selection include—

- Presence of TIC/TIM or HM/HW hazards (including asbestos and PCBs).
- Industrial facilities in the area that may subject personnel to contaminants.
- Potential for dust or noise.

- Landfills and waste dumps.
- Drainage (both into and from the site).
- Proximity to civilian populations.
- Adequate space for HM/HW and POL storage and protection.
- Adequate space for latrine and gray water facilities.
- Existing environmental infrastructure, such as water and sewer.
- Overall safety of structures on the site.
- Proximity to areas of standing water that may spread illness.
- Possible endangered species or critical habitats.
- Presence of historical, cultural, or religious sites.
- Interference with the normal routine of the local civilians.

G-4. Although not all of these criteria may be met, a good balance of factors will help to ensure the protection of the environment and the health of Soldiers and Marines. As always, the tactical mission and the requirements of protection will also weigh heavily on any base camp locations. The EBS is an important part of determining site suitability.

Environmental Baseline Surveys

G-5. An EBS (see Appendix E) should be conducted within 30 days of site occupation. This survey helps to address three primary issues: the identification of risk factors, the determination of initial site conditions, and assistance in base camp or installation layout. Environmental and safety risks to the health of Soldiers, Marines, and local civilians may be determined by investigating the site. This helps determine the overall site suitability for occupation. Factors such as evidence of environmental contamination, landfills, and surrounding land/industrial uses may impact site suitability. Determining initial site conditions also helps when comparing the closeout EBS; this prevents liability to U.S. forces for damage or contamination that may have been present before site occupation. The existing infrastructure and the surrounding area are surveyed to help planners determine the best locations (from an environmental and health standpoint) for force beddown, maintenance, sanitation, HM/HW and POL storage, and motor pool locations.

G-6. The survey requires personnel with the necessary training and expertise to identify potential hazards and may require the taking of various air, soil, and water samples. It will be helpful to determine previous site usage, hazards on the site, and the potential for hazards generated from areas surrounding the site. Hazards are those generated as a result of military operations and include both those presented to personnel occupying the site and to the surrounding civilian population.

Environmental Health Site Assessment

G-7. An EHSA is conducted to determine whether environmental contaminants from current or prior land use, disease vectors, or other environmental health conditions that could pose health risks to deployed personnel exist at the deployment sites. Additionally, it also identifies industrial facility operations and commodities near the site that could, if damaged or destroyed, release contaminants harmful to personnel. An EHSA is generally conducted in conjunction with an EBS, since the two documents support each other. While the EBS is generally more visual and engineer-related, the EHSA is more analytical (including a greater variety and detail of sampling), with a greater focus on health hazards.

Environmental, Safety, and Occupational Health

G-8. Environmental, safety, and occupational health (ESOH) standards should be addressed from a safety and environmental standpoint. Initial site selection, structure use, and repair estimates must include ESOH factors. These include items such as electrical systems; water systems; ventilation; air quality; slip, trip, and fall hazards; structural integrity; PPE; and the use of existing industrial infrastructure, such as overhead lifts, chain hoists, and cable systems.

BASE CAMP LAYOUT

G-9. While all base camps are unique in their layout due to variables (such as terrain, use, size, and type of tenant units), certain relationships between base camp layout and environmental considerations tend to be constant. Considerations with regard to base camp layout include—

- Locating POL and HM/HW storage areas and motor pools away from billeting areas and drainage features.
- Locating latrines and gray water disposal areas away from dining facilities, food storage areas, and water distribution points.
- Locating landfills and burn pits downwind from the camp or from billeting areas when possible.
- Avoiding locating billeting areas in low-lying areas or adjacent to standing water.

BASE CAMP OPERATIONS

G-10. The operation of base camps and other installations (such as airfields, ports, internment/resettlement facilities, and enemy prisoner of war camps) requires the integration of environmental considerations. Commanders and staffs must identify and use all available knowledge, including reachback capabilities to CONUS, to assist in meeting these challenges. Certain areas of base camp operation require particular attention to avoid environmental impacts and to protect Soldier, Marine, and civilian health and quality of life. Environmental considerations in the development and operation of these sites include the following:

- Field sanitation.
- HM/HW storage, transportation, disposal, and safeguarding.
- Spill response and reporting.
- Potential for base camp or mission expansion.
- POL storage and safeguarding.
- Solid waste disposal sites or waste removal.
- Dust abatement.
- Burn pit locations and operation.
- Latrine and shower facility locations.
- Gray water disposal or removal.
- Mess facility locations.
- Establishment of guidance and policy on ESOH standards.
- Medical and infectious waste storage and disposal.
- Protection against disease vectors (such as rodents and insects).
- Guidelines for pesticide use.
- Motor pool locations.
- Wash rack locations and operation.
- Drainage.

FIELD SANITATION

G-11. The baseline FHP concern for field commanders is in field sanitation. This is directly linked to preventive medicine, which each commander may directly affect as a resident unit of a base camp. For information on unit-focused protective/preventive measures, see FM 4-25.12 and FM 21-10. Most of these measures should be captured in unit SOPs, and the transition to applying them to base camp standards should be virtually seamless in its application. As standards on the base camp improve, some of these considerations will be alleviated by improvements in camp facilities.

HAZARDOUS MATERIAL/HAZARDOUS WASTE MANAGEMENT

G-12. Controlling and managing HM/HW protects the water, the soil, and the air of a base camp from harmful levels of contamination. The military uses large quantities of HMs, such as fuels, paints, batteries, pesticides, and solvents. Often, these compounds contain acids, metals, and other toxins. The military work environment is at least as conducive to HM/HW spills as is the standard workplace. Given these conditions, U.S. military forces must take extra precautions to ensure that they minimize environmental contamination by hazardous substances. Even low-level exposure to HM may adversely affect the health of Soldiers and Marines. This is one of the first environmental protection issues that should be addressed at base camps. Its FHP aspects cause it to be of critical importance to the base camp commander and the units living there. Appendix F provides additional guidance on HM/HW operations.

PETROLEUM, OIL, AND LUBRICANTS OPERATIONS

G-13. Refueling of vehicles and containers always raises the level of risk that spills will occur. Because refueling operations are a necessity for base camps and the units associated with them, commanders must make them a priority. Spills have significant implications for safety, FHP, and environmental protection—especially the potential effect on water supplies. Because of these realities, POL operations are a focus area for base camps, even in their initial stages of development. In addition, these operations may have a potentially damaging effect to the inhabitants of the base camp. Planning for spills and spill response should already be a part of unit SOPs, and Soldiers and Marines should generally follow these basic procedures in conjunction with base camp guidance. See Appendix F for additional information on POL procedures and spill response.

DUST SUPPRESSION

G-14. Dust created by operations presents both a health hazard and hazard to equipment. Unfortunately, clearing large areas for motor pools, helicopter landing pads, roads, and billeting areas creates significant dust hazards. Various techniques, such as placing larger aggregate paving areas (when feasible), ensuring that vegetative strips remain in place, and applying various chemical dust palliatives help to suppress dust. GTA 05-08-018 and TM 5-830-3 provide additional supporting information.

BASE CAMP SUSTAINMENT

G-15. From an environmental considerations view, sustainment includes periodic inspections of conditions in the form of the ECR and various medical reports in support of FHP. This will support the base camp staff in a similar way to the support provided to an installation commander and staff.

G-16. The longer U.S. forces operate a base camp, the more likely it is that efforts will be made to increase quality of life for the Soldiers and Marines living there. This could occur in a variety of areas. One of the areas that may be impacted is environmental considerations. The reestablishment of a foreign nation government and the ensuing establishment of an FGS for that nation may also affect environmental standards. Compliance requirements may make the adjustment to these standards a requirement rather than a commander's decision.

BASE CAMP CLOSURE

G-17. The closure of a base camp is a part of the initial planning process that identified the need for a given base camp and provided an estimate for its duration. The environmental considerations included in the initial planning must attempt to factor in the end state of a base camp and the requirement to ultimately return the real estate and facilities to a local government. In some cases, restoration involving the removal of pollution and contaminants from the environment may be required. An EBS is included in the process of closure to provide the final snapshot of conditions for documentation. Together with the initial EBS/EHSA and subsequent ECRs/medical inspections, the final EBS provides a picture of the environmental life of a base camp, which may be used to deal with claims against the government (or directed remediation) or to address questions of FHP after the site is no longer occupied by Soldiers and Marines. Areas of environmental concern in the closure of base camps include—

- Removing HM/HW and POL stockpiles.
- Removing soil contaminated by HM/HW or POL.
- Filling in fighting positions and bunkers and removing tactical and communications wires.
- Closing and marking landfills and latrines.

ENVIRONMENTAL PROGRAM GOALS AND IMPACTS

G-18. Environmental program areas provide the framework for all programs on an installation to support environmental protection. To a degree, these are also used to support base camps. Although these program areas focus on installation use, they are also relevant for base camps, especially those with a long life where the base camp approaches the standards associated with installations.

G-19. Military programs protecting the environment correspond to legal requirements to protect air, land, water, human health, and natural and cultural resources. Portions of these programs will almost certainly be brought forward to affect life on a base camp. To the degree that they do, table G-1 summarizes program goals and their impacts.

Table G-1. Typical environmental program areas and goals/impacts

Program Area	Goal	Military Impact
Air	Control emissions	POL storage, energy production, waste disposal, smoke operations, fugitive dust
Asbestos management	Minimize release of and exposure to asbestos	Building acquisition, site demolition, vehicle repair costs
Cultural resource management	Protect historical and cultural heritage	Restricted buildings, additional costs for building renovations
HM management	Prevent pollution, comply with HM regulations	Procurement, base camp storage and inventory management, turn-in programs for HM
HW and solid waste management	Minimize waste generation	Training in segregation, recycling, and substitution
P2	Reduce pollution and waste generation	Turn-in procedures for reusable items, recycling
Spill prevention and response	Prevent and respond to spills	Base camp and unit spill plans
Water resource management	Conserve and protect water sources	Erosion control, storm water control, vehicle drip pans, wash racks

G-20. In general, at the battalion level or below, these program requirements are integrated into existing unit programs and procedures. They need not be addressed as separate environmental programs. However, commanders should coordinate with appropriate base camp environmental staff (and the base camp coordination agency and base camp assistance/assessment team) to determine their application.

This page intentionally left blank.

Appendix H

Environmental Officer

AR 200-1 defines an environmental officer/Marine Corps environmental compliance coordinator as an individual assigned to an organization or unit to accomplish environmental compliance requirements on behalf of the commander, director, or supervisor. The designated person also coordinates with supporting installation environmental staff for requirements clarification and assistance. The commander determines organizational levels and the required grade suitable for environmental officers. Environmental officers are generally required at battalion and unit (company, battery, or troop) level. In garrison directorates, they are generally required at the division level (branch level if the organization generates HW).

ENVIRONMENTAL OFFICER

H-1. Environmental compliance is the unconditional obedience to international, foreign nation, federal, state, and local environmental rules, regulations, and guidelines that affect current operations. In units including a staff officer with similar responsibilities, the environmental officer will usually be given this additional duty. In company-size units, this duty will generally translate to an additional duty.

H-2. The environmental officer manages environmental issues within the unit and ensures environmental compliance. He also coordinates through the respective chain of command with the supporting installation environmental staff to clarify requirements and obtain assistance. The vignette on page H-4 further illustrates the requirement to coordinate with the installation environmental staff.

H-3. While this position of responsibility is not a formal staff position, the environmental officer is critical to the commander's environmental program. The environmental officer—

- Advises the unit on environmental compliance during training, operations, and logistics functions.
- Advises and updates the commander on the unit's environmental consideration integration and performance standards.
- Updates and maintains the environmental portion of the SOP.
- Coordinates between the unit and higher/installation headquarters environmental staffs.
- Manages information concerning unit environmental training and certification requirements.
- Conducts unit environmental self-assessments.
- Conducts environmental risk assessments.
- Serves as the SME to the commander on the integration of environmental considerations into OPLANs/OPORDs.

H-4. Table H-1, page H-2, provides information relating to the environmental officer and applicable references, required training, and the point of contact for each duty. The environmental officer must identify and assess the status of compliance with any new regulatory requirements enacted since the last assessment and address any special areas of concern specified by higher headquarters.

Table H-1. Environmental officer duties

Duties	Applicable References	Specific Training	Point of Contact
Advise the commander on environmental considerations affecting unit operations, and provide liaison between the unit, higher headquarters, and supporting environmental management office	• AR 200-1 • MCO P5090.2A		• Chain of command • Supporting environmental management office • SJA office • United States Army Engineer School (USAES), Directorate of Environmental Integration (DEI) <http://www.wood.army.mil/dei> • United States Army Environmental Command (USAEC) <http://aec.army.mil/usaec>
Assess unit environmental management program	• AR 200-1 • Command policies and regulations • MCO P5090.2A	Training in compliance topics applicable to the organization and unit/organizational compliance assessment tools and techniques	• Chain of command • Supporting environmental management office • USAES, DEI • USAEC
Assess unit HW accumulation site	• AR 200-1 • Command policies and regulations • MCO P5090.2A	• Annual training in HW requirements related to the job and measures to take during an emergency • Satellite accumulation point training	• Chain of command • Supporting environmental management office • USAES, DEI • USAEC
Assess unit HM/HW program	• AR 200-1 • Command policies and regulations • FM 3-34.5	• Annual training in HW requirements related to the job and measures to take during an emergency • Annual training in HM requirements of their job and measures to take during an emergency	• Chain of command • Supporting environmental management office • USAES, DEI • USAEC

Table H-1. Environmental officer duties (continued)

Duties	Applicable References	Specific Training	Point of Contact
Assess unit solid waste management program	• AR 200-1 • Command policies and regulations • MCO P5090.2A		• Chain of command • Supporting environmental management office • USAES, DEI • USAEC
Assess unit spill prevention program and P2 program	• AR 200-1 • MCO P5090.2A	Annual training, hours vary	• Chain of command • Supporting environmental management office • USAES, DEI • USAEC
Respond to a spill	• AR 200-1 • Command policies and regulations • MCO P5090.2A	Annual training, hours vary	• Chain of command • Supporting environmental management office • USAES, DEI • USAEC
Assess unit recycling program	• AR 200-1 • MCO P5090.2A		• Chain of command • Supporting environmental management office • USAES, DEI • USAEC
Assess unit training area management procedures (field operations)	• AR 350-19 • Command policies and regulations • Local installation regulations for training area usage	• ITAM briefing • Range safety officer briefing	• Chain of command • Local ITAM coordinator • USAES, DEI • USAEC
Assess environmentally related risks in military operations	• Unit SOP	• Unit-level training • Safety officer training	• Chain of command • Supporting environmental management office • USAES, DEI
Conduct environmental awareness training	• AR 200-1 • Command policies and regulations • MCO P5090.2A • Unit SOP	Ongoing, with use of poster's briefings and written information	• Chain of command • Supporting environmental management office • USAES, DEI

Table H-1. Environmental officer duties (continued)

Duties	Applicable References	Specific Training	Point of Contact
Integrate environmental consideration into unit SOPs, policies and procedures, and OPORDs/ OPLANs	• AR 200-1 • FM 5-0 • Command policies and regulations • MCO P5090.2A • Unit SOP	Command information briefings	• Chain of command • Supporting environmental management office • USAES, DEI

ENVIRONMENTAL OFFICER TRAINING

H-5. The environmental officer will be trained to accomplish assigned duties. Improper training may result in NOVs, fines, and more work (see the vignette for more information about proper training). The training requirements for the environmental officer depend on the environmental issues within the unit and the coordination required through the respective chain of command. Units should consult with their higher headquarters and supporting environmental management office for location-specific training requirements outlined in table H-1.

H-6. Installations (including OCONUS) currently provide installation-specific training programs. Check with the local environmental management office for attendance requirements. The Environmental Compliance Officer's Course (052-E-0036) and other training resources for the unit environmental officer to use are available through the Army's Reimer Training and Doctrine Digital Library at <http://www.train.army.mil>.

Issue

Troop self-help projects result in state environmental fines (asbestos/lead-based paint).

Discussion

State environmental regulatory departments closely scrutinize the demolition projects of older structures on installations. Many of these structures contain asbestos-containing materials and lead-based paint, both of which are known health hazards. Installations are required to notify the state before beginning demolition or renovation projects. All asbestos-containing materials and lead-based paint must be removed by trained personnel. Several installations received NOVs for failure to comply with this requirement. These NOVs were issued to units who disturbed asbestos-containing materials and lead-based paint during self-help projects. State regulators also issued an NOV for Soldiers and Marines discarding asbestos-containing materials items into trash containers.

Techniques and Procedures

Commanders and installation environmental offices must be proactive in promoting asbestos and lead-based paint awareness not only to tenant units but also those units training or conducting mobilization operations on the installation.

Unit leaders must—

* Ensure that the environmental officer contacts the supporting environmental management offices or DPW for all self-help projects.

* Comply with installation-specific regulations and approved self-help project plans to prevent the disturbance, mishandling, or improper disposal of asbestos-containing materials and lead-based paint.

* Attend asbestos and lead-based paint awareness classes conducted by the environmental management office or DPW.

* Supervise Soldiers and Marines conducting self-help projects. Ensure that Soldiers and Marines comply with guidance in the self-help project work plan.

For more information on asbestos and lead-based paint, view the USAEC Web site: <http://aec.army.mil/usaec/>.

This page intentionally left blank.

Appendix I

Sample Command Policy

This appendix provides an example of an environmental policy letter and a unit order for appointing an environmental officer. Figure I-1, page I-2, depicts a commander's environmental policy letter, and figure I-2, page I-3, provides an example of an environmental officer appointment order. Additional policy letters may be required for specific operations within your unit and may be drafted using the basic format of the memorandums in this appendix.

DEPARTMENT OF THE ARMY
100TH COMBAT SUPPORT BATTALION
APO AE 09096

ABCD-UVW-CO   27 March 2006

MEMORANDUM FOR: See Distribution

SUBJECT: 100TH Combat Support Battalion (CSB) Commander's Policy (CP) 8-5, *Command Environmental Program*

1. The mission of the 100th CSB is to support troop units by operating, maintaining, and repairing infrastructure and facilities. This policy implements the 100th CSB Environmental Program to protect and conserve the environment. Our program includes:

   a. Complying with applicable environmental policy, laws, and regulations and ensuring that all base activities are in compliance with environmental regulations and other requirements.
   b. Assessing the 100th CSB and Directorate activities and services continually in an effort to plan for the mitigation or minimization of potentially negative impacts to the environment to assure that our activities do not adversely affect the environment.
   c. Identifying the significant environmental impacts from activities and ensuring that they are considered when establishing objectives and targets in our Environmental Management System.
   d. Ensuring that all activities identify and address pollution prevention opportunities in the 100th CSB, and assist in meeting or exceeding Army goals for pollution prevention.
   e. Integrating environmental considerations into all of our mission procedures and work practices so that environmental awareness and compliance are a routine part of the way we execute 100th CSB activities and services, in both garrison and the field.
   f. Employing environmental management procedures to prevent activities and/or conditions that pose a threat to human health, safety, and the environment.
   g. Cooperating with all HN agencies to further our common environmental objectives.

2. Supervisors will ensure that copies of this policy are posted in maintenance shops, work areas, and offices as appropriate. This policy will be available for public review at the Battalion HQ, Building 600.

3. The contents of this policy will be reviewed and revalidated annually on the anniversary date of its publication. Revalidation will be sent to the 100th CSB Adjutant within two weeks of the anniversary date. Policies requiring revision will be submitted thirty days prior to the anniversary date for the Commander's approval/signature.

4. The point of contact for this policy is MAJ Joseph Dogwood, BN Environmental Officer at DSN 555-9688.

SIGNATURE BLOCK

DISTRIBUTION:
1 – Ea Individual
1 – Unit File
1 – Ea Subordinate Unit

Figure I-1. Sample commander's environmental policy letter

DEPARTMENT OF THE ARMY
100TH COMBAT SUPPORT BATTALION
APO AE 09096

ABCD-UVW-CO   27 March 2006

MEMORANDUM FOR: See Distribution

SUBJECT: Environmental Officer Appointment

1. Effective 27 March 2006, the following individual is appointed as the Environmental Officer for
    the unit indicated:

    MAJ Joseph Dogwood
    423-45-6789
    HQ Company, 100 Combat Support Battalion, APO AE 09096

2. Authority: AR 200-1

3. Purpose: To plan, execute, and monitor all aspects of the Command Environmental Program.

4. Period: Until officially released or relieved.

5. Specific Duties:

    a. Advise the commander on environmental laws and regulations that affect unit operations.
    b. Assess the unit's environmental program to include:
        (1) Unit accumulation sites
        (2) HM/HW program
        (3) Solid waste management program
        (4) Unit spill prevention program
        (5) Unit recycling program
        (6) Unit land management procedures
        (7) Integration of environmental considerations in military operations
    c. Respond to HM/HW spills.
    d. Plan, conduct, and/or supervise environmental awareness training.
    e. Monitor/assess the Command Environmental Program continually.

6. Special Instructions: The Environmental Officer will utilize the Chain of Command, plus any
    specified local notification chain when applicable. The Environmental Officer is responsible
    for implementing the Commander's Environmental Program. The Environmental Officer is
    authorized and encouraged to consult with the Installation/Base Camp Environmental Office
    and SMEs for guidance and assistance in accomplishing these duties.

SIGNATURE BLOCK

DISTRIBUTION:
1 – Ea Individual
1 – Unit File
1 – Ea Subordinate Unit

Figure I-2. Sample environmental officer appointment order

This page intentionally left blank.

Appendix J

Unit Environmental Standing Operating Procedures

This appendix provides an example of an Army unit environmental SOP, outlining the command environmental program within a unit. Unit environmental SOPs are described in figure J-1, page J-2. Figure J-2, page J-16; figure J-3, page J-18; and figure J-4, page J-20, further detail specific unit SOPs. Due to differing state, local, or foreign nation requirements, these SOPs must be modified based on consultation with unit higher headquarters and the installation/base camp environmental staff. This sample unit environmental SOP is divided into six sections (maintenance, supply, CBRN, communication, field mess operations, and operations/training), which correspond to a typical unit organization. Units should extract the information in these sections and incorporate them into the appropriate section of their SOP. Alternatively, a unit may use these samples as a guide to developing a stand-alone environmental SOP. While this approach elevates the visibility and importance of environmental issues and procedures, unit personnel in specific functional areas may overlook the information without adequate command emphasis. The environmental SOP should reflect requirements as they pertain to the unit's daily operations (such as installation or state regulations) and reflect requirements that may be in effect during deployments. The SOP should emphasize sustainable practices and the integration of environmental considerations into daily operations and should be flexible enough to accommodate both garrison and deployment environmental considerations. Additional information for specific requirements during deployments can be found in the mission OPORD/OPLAN or specific base camp SOPs.

APPENDIX ____ TO ANNEX___
ENVIRONMENTAL STANDING OPERATING PROCEDURES

Unit Designation
Mailing Address
Date

1. References.

Installation Environmental SOP, Higher Headquarters Environmental SOP, and AR 200-1.

2. Purpose.

a. This appendix standardizes procedures for environmental compliance with federal, state, local, and HN laws and regulations. Failure to comply may result in the following:

(1) Endangerment of personnel health and safety.

(2) Citations by federal and state regulating agencies.

(3) Civil or military penalties against offenders.

(4) Delay or halt in mission accomplishment.

b. This appendix is applicable to all assigned or attached personnel and governs the environmental aspects of all unit activities.

3. Responsibilities.

a. The commander—

(1) Establishes a unit HM and HW management policy.

(2) Ensures that personnel comply with the provisions of referenced SOPs, regulations, and public law.

(3) Ensures that the environmental compliance officer, the HM/HW coordinator, and senior personnel have received the proper training and that they, in turn, train their subordinates.

(4) Ensures that all personnel who are exposed to HM in the course of their work receive initial training within 90 days of assignment concerning the hazards to which they are exposed and the precautions required to protect themselves in the work environment. These personnel must also receive annual refresher training.

(5) Ensures that all unit personnel receive initial environmental awareness training within 90 days of assignment and refresher training annually thereafter.

(6) Ensures that all unit personnel have received HAZCOM training (OSHA requirement).

(7) Ensures that all environmental training is properly documented and records are filed in the unit operations/training office.

(8) Ensures that a self-inspection program is in effect for the unit.

b. The executive officer—

(1) Serves as the commander's eyes and ears for environmental matters.

(2) Conducts periodic unit self-assessment surveys.

(3) Oversees environmental integration into staff operations.

Figure J-1. Unit environmental SOP

c. The ECO and HW/HM (MOS 9954) Marine—

    (1) Provides advice on environmental compliance to the commander.

    (2) Serves as a link between the unit commander and higher/installation headquarters environmental staff.

    (3) Performs other duties as outlined in chapter 1 of this manual.

d. The maintenance officer—

    (1) Serves as the unit's HM/HW coordinator.

    (2) Serves as the unit's spill response coordinator.

    (3) Ensures accountability for all HM and HW.

    (4) Ensures that HM and HW are stored and disposed of properly.

    (5) Ensures that HM and HW spills are immediately contained and reported to the fire department and the installation's environmental office.

    (6) Reports nonfunctional/inoperative treatment/collection facilities (oil/grease interceptors, floor drains, catch basins, and waste tanks) to the installation's environmental office via the unit's environmental compliance officer.

e. The motor sergeant—

    (1) Establishes and maintains an HW accumulation (HW less than 55 gallons) area with proper separation of incompatible products.

    (2) Inspects HW accumulation areas weekly and documents results.

    (3) Ensures that leaking containers are overpacked and/or the uncontaminated contents containerized in functional containers.

    (4) Ensures that only waste oil is placed in the waste oil tank or drums.

    (5) Ensures that the waste oil tank or drums are pumped out when full or 90 days after previous pumping, whichever occurs first (check with installation environmental coordinator).

    (6) Ensures that the wash rack oil/water separator is clean and serviceable.

    (7) Maintains an inventory log of all stored waste products, to include exact location of each container.

    (8) Labels all HW containers properly as they are put in service and ensures turn-in and delivery to the DRMO or contractor and pick up within 90 days of accumulation start date (coordinate with the environmental management office).

f. The unit supply sergeant—

    (1) Initiates and processes turn-in documents for the turn-in of HM and HW.

    (2) Maintains a suspense file and validates receipt copies of turn-in documents for all scrap, HM, and HW shipped to the DRMO.

g. The prescribed load list clerk—requisitions mercury and lithium batteries with recoverability code "A" only upon turn-in of a like item and quantity.

h. The CBRN NCO—

    (1) Inspects all possible decontaminant solution 2 (DS2) and super tropical bleach (STB) accumulation sites (CONEXes, wall lockers, and POL accumulation area) to ensure that these products have been properly turned over to DOL/supply for consolidated storage.

    (2) If the unit is temporarily in possession of decontamination agents DS2 or STB:

        (a) Ensures that DS2 and STB are stored in separate locations.

Figure J-1. Unit environmental SOP (continued)

(b) Inspects containers monthly for leakage, and records results. Arranges for leakers to be overpacked and turned in to the DRMO.

(3) Properly disposes of CBRNE-related training material that is classified as hazardous according to installation directives and DRMO policies.

i.   Mechanics—

(1) Place HW in properly designated containers.

(2) Never place HW in a dumpster; this is an **illegal** disposal.

(3) Promptly report leaks/spills to the motor sergeant and/or maintenance officer. Report spills directly to the fire department and installation's environmental office, if necessary, to ensure prompt response.

(4) Wear proper protective clothing when handling HM or HW.

(5) Keep HM and HW accumulation containers closed except to add or remove product.

j.   Medics—

(1) Segregate medical waste from nonmedical waste at the point of generation.

(2) Place medical waste in designated containers.

(3) Wear proper protective clothing when handling medical waste.

(4) Store collected medical waste in a secure manner/area.

k.   Individual Soldiers and Marines—

(1) Comply with the unit's environmental requirements and the installation's SOP.

(2) Maintain environmental awareness throughout daily activities.

(3) Provide recommendations to the chain of command on techniques to ensure compliance with environmental regulatory requirements.

(4) Identify the environmental risks associated with individual and team tasks.

(5) Support recycling programs.

(6) Report HM and HW spills **immediately** to (phone number for spill reporting).

(7) Make sound environmental decisions in the absence of a supervisor or specific command guidance by considering the following:

(a) Prior training.

(b) General guidance from the chain of command.

(c) Concept of right and wrong.

(d) Common sense.

(e) Environmental ethic.

Figure J-1. Unit environmental SOP (continued)

4. **Safety**.

a. Material Safety Data Sheet. MSDSs provide critical information for safeguarding human health and protecting the environment. This information includes the hazardous characteristics of the substance, the appropriate PPE, spill response procedures, signs and symptoms of overexposure, and first aid procedures. MSDSs can be obtained through unit supply channels and should be maintained at each location where HM is being used. It is important to note that MSDSs are material- and manufacturer-specific, which means that each <u>brand name</u> of a chemical has a different MSDS.

b. PPE. PPE is the primary means of safeguarding human health when handling HM/HW. The most important aspect when choosing the appropriate PPE for a given operation is the hazardous characteristics of the substance. Always refer to the manufacturer's MSDS before choosing the appropriate PPE. If the prescribed PPE cannot be obtained during a field or contingency operation, field-expedient PPE should be used to help protect Soldiers and Marines when handling HM/HW or in the event of a spill. Leaders ensure that their Soldiers and Marines have the appropriate PPE when exposed to HM/HW during handling. Recommended field-expedient PPE is listed below:

<u>HM/HW stream</u>
1. Fuel products
2. Oil products/lubricants
3. Antifreeze
4. Acid batteries
5. Medical waste
6. Pesticides

<u>Field-expedient PPE</u>
1. Field gloves, goggles, and wet-weather gear
2. Field gloves and goggles
3. Field gloves and goggles
4. Double-lined field gloves, goggles, and wet-weather gear
5. Field gloves, goggles, and wet-weather gear
6. Consult the MSDS and Preventive Medicine

NOTE: Field-expedient PPE should only be used when the required PPE is not available since it does <u>not</u> provide the level of protection recommended by the manufacturer. Additionally, field-expedient PPE that is used to handle HM/HW should not be used for normal operations after being used as PPE.

Figure J-1. Unit environmental SOP (continued)

SECTION 1 - MAINTENANCE

1. **General.**

    a. Select maintenance activity sites so that POL-contaminated water will not enter a storm drain.

    b. Conduct the following activities daily:

        (1) Check the level of used oil in storage tanks. Schedule for tanks to be picked up when 3/4 full.

        (2) Clean all foreign material from drip pans and aboveground oil tank screens.

        (3) Empty refuse barrels when 3/4 full to prevent overflows.

    c. Procure, store, and use only those chemical products specifically authorized by the appropriate TM or lubrication order for the level of maintenance performed.

    d. Keep MSDSs for all chemicals/solvents/materials used in work areas in a file that is readily accessible to personnel who work there. Brief personnel on chemical hazards, protective clothing requirements, first aid, and spill response before they use hazardous chemicals.

    e. Use products that are safe and biodegradable, when possible.

    f. Comply with the Army's oil analysis program as a method of reducing the amount of waste oil produced.

    g. Properly label, segregate, and store HM.

2. **Maintenance Bays.**

    a. Conduct maintenance washing/steam cleaning at the motor pool wash rack—not in the maintenance bay. (Maintenance cleaning in the bays will be authorized only during extended, below freezing temperatures that interfere with the vehicle maintenance mission [applicable only if equipped with an oil/water separator].)

    b. Do not wash heavily soiled and/or oily maintenance bay floors with solvent or other unauthorized material. Clean up oil and fuel with dry sweep or rags only. Collect dry sweep and dirt in nonleaking containers as HW for disposal through the DRMO.

    c. Confine solvent use to solvent washing machines that meet the National Fire Prevention Association's safety regulation standards. Obtain approval for use of solvents, other than mineral spirits, from the installation's environmental office before use.

    d. Ensure that all solvent washing machines have lids that remain closed when not in use.

    e. Do not sweep or dump trash, garbage, nuts, bolts, and other solid waste into floor drains or mix with used dry sweep. Put such items into covered, leak-proof containers. Empty containers into dumpsters, as needed, to prevent spillover.

    f. Place drip pans under points of leakage on vehicles with known seeps and leaks to preclude discharges into wastewater collection systems. Drain all water from drip pans daily and dispose into a sanitary sewer drain protected by an oil separator.

    g. Use the exhaust ventilation system whenever a stationary vehicle is running inside the maintenance bay.

    h. Keep catch buckets in all floor drains that are designed for them. Inspect and empty dry sweep and trash daily. In bays not equipped with oil-water separators, keep floor drains permanently closed if HM/HW are handled or stored there.

    i. Use the exhaust ventilation system whenever a stationary vehicle is running inside the maintenance bay.

Figure J-1. Unit environmental SOP (continued)

3. **Grease Racks/Pits.**

   a. Use approved used oil tanks to collect and subsequently recycle used oil. (Grease racks and maintenance or inspection pits are designed for oil change and vehicle lubrication only.)

   b. Introduce only uncontaminated used motor oil into the used oil tanks. Use separate containers for hydraulic, transmission, and brake fluids. Do <u>not</u> place solvent, fuel, water, antifreeze, dirt, dry sweep, hardware, or trash in used oil tanks.

   c. Dispose of used oil, transmission, and fuel filters in normal trash containers <u>after</u> draining for 24 hours and double bagging in plastic. (Units/installations should purchase equipment for pressing oil from filters and then recycling the metal.)

   d. Mark and position containers for new and used dry sweep at the grease rack to clean up spills or leaks.

   e. Keep floor of the grease rack and the immediate surrounding area free of POL buildup.

4. **Wash Racks.**

   a. Use wash racks for light exterior washing only. Wash extremely soiled vehicles at the installation's central vehicle wash facilities.

   b. Obtain authorization from the installation's environmental office for cleaners used in washing activities, since cleaners will drain into the sanitary sewer. Post readable signs to indicate specific, authorized cleaners, solvents, or soaps.

   c. Do not use portable steam cleaners or clean engines at wash racks. These activities cause the oil to suspend in the water and the separator to function improperly. Only use steam cleaners in designated areas.

   d. Do not pour POL products, solvents, antifreeze, or other regulated substances into wash rack drains.

   e. Position trash containers at wash racks for disposal of refuse generated during the washing process.

   f. Do not sweep dirt and trash resulting from washing vehicles into the wash rack or pile trash along the perimeter. Place trash in proper containers for disposal at the landfill. Report quantities of dirt in excess of what can reasonably be placed in a trash container to the installation for disposal.

   g. To prevent pooling and possible discharge into storm drains, immediately discontinue washing if a wash rack drain becomes clogged. Notify a supervisor to call in a work order request immediately. Maintain wash rack as "out of service" until all necessary repairs are made.

   h. The motor sergeant will do the following on a daily basis:

      (1) Check for leaking water hydrants and report leaks to the DPW or facility engineer work order desk.

      (2) Check for proper policing of the wash rack, and ensure that the area is free of trash, oil-soaked rags, and soil/sand.

      (3) Inspect drains and sand traps to ensure proper operation of the wash rack drainage system. Call the DPW work order section if plugged.

      (4) Inspect oil-water separator for proper operation.

5. **Parts/Material Requisitioning and Storage Areas.**

   a. Requisition the minimum quantity required for mission accomplishment.

   b. Ensure that recoverability codes are used whenever applicable.

   c. Keep a copy of the applicable MSDS for each HM on hand in a binder in the parts storage area.

   d. Label and segregate all HM from nonhazardous items.

Figure J-1. Unit environmental SOP (continued)

e.   Make special indications for any materials that have shelf life considerations.

f.   Consider alternative, nonhazardous substitutes whenever processing a request for HM. Check with the installation's environmental office for suggestions.

6.   **POL Storage Areas.**

a.   Store all POL products with secondary containment. Construct berms 1 1/2 times the volume of the largest container ("must contain the contents of the single largest tank plus sufficient freeboard for precipitation") stored in the storage area to preclude spillage outside the immediate area. Obtain exceptions to this policy from the installation's environmental office.

b.   Store all HM in a location protected from the elements to maintain container integrity (to prevent rusting and protect labels from fading).

c.   Inspect containers and labels weekly for leaks and incomplete/unreadable or out-of-date labels. Stop leaks in containers (overpack the container or place the contents in a nonleaking container). Maintain legible labels to reflect actual container contents.

d.   Maintain an inventory of POL products. Keep MSDSs on hand for any HM present.

e.   Use POL and other HM stock on a first-in, first-out basis.

f.   Do not tip a drum on its side to issue POL products outside the POL storage area. Use transfer pumps (preferred method) for dispensing POL products.

g.   Place a drip box or pan under the supply valve when the drum is tipped on its side. Line boxes and pans with absorbent pads and maintain on a regular basis. Clean up spillage immediately using dry sweep in areas with concrete floors.

h.   Immediately report spills of any quantity that enter the environment (soil, water, or drain) to the unit's environmental compliance officer and the appropriate installation officials. (See tab A.)

i.   Keep used oil free of contamination (water, dry sweep, hardware, trash, solvent, antifreeze), and store only in approved used oil aboveground storage tanks.

j.   Use separate containers to store used brake fluid, solvents, and hydraulic and transmission oils. (Should mixing of waste streams occur, the product becomes "waste contaminated with an unknown substance" and will require analysis by the DRMO before disposal.)

k.   Contact DRMO for pumping or turn-in, whichever applies, when used oil tanks/barrels are 3/4 full. (Units may be required to go through the installation's environmental management office, who will contact the DRMO.)

l.   Discontinue accumulation of used oils if leaks in storage containers are detected. Immediately report leaks to the unit environmental compliance officer and the installation environmental management office.

m.   Obtain approved containers from the DRMO for proper disposal of contaminated dry sweep and other accumulated HW. Clearly mark containers for proper waste disposal.

n.   Dispose of used filters for oil, transmission, and fuel as normal trash after draining for 24 hours and double bagging in plastic. (Units/installations should investigate equipment for pressing oil from filters and then recycling the metal.)

o.   Permanently close all floor drains in maintenance areas where HM/HW are handled or stored and provide for secondary-containment, single-wall containers. Do not store HM near sanitary or storm sewer drains. Immediately report any amount of POL spillage entering a floor or storm drain to the unit's environmental compliance officer and the installation's environmental management office.

Figure J-1. Unit environmental SOP (continued)

p. Place each HM container of 5 gallons or more accumulation capacity in a POL shed or portable secondary-containment device. (If these storage means are not available, the storage area will be bermed to contain 1 1/2 times the largest container volume in the event of a spill.)

7. **Fuel Dispensing and Storage Area.**

a. Two personnel perform the operation when filling any size container with fuel—one will run the pump, and the other will dispense the fuel. This procedure provides adequate manpower, to monitor the pump for leaks and shut off the pump in case of an emergency. It also prevents overfilling the container.

b. Handle fuel contaminated with dirt and water as HW, and dispose through the DRMO.

c. Dispose of oil-contaminated fuel, as a result of fuel cell leaks or other mechanical system failure, as HW through DRMO.

d. Contact the direct support unit for assistance and guidance if tankers or fuel pods must be purged.

8. **Procedures for Accumulation Site.**

Provide accumulation sites for used petroleum products and HW. Place sites aboveground on a nonpermeable, bermed hardstand; label them; and locate them 50 feet or more from any building. Leaking, corroded, or otherwise deteriorated containers must be overpacked in DOT-approved drums. Coordinate with the installation environmental management office for assistance in determining the appropriate overpack containers, labeling/marking requirements, arranging for pick up of used oil, and other HW/HM collection issues.

a. Keep an accumulation log for each used oil or HW container in use. Specify as follows:

(1) Contents.

(2) Date the container was opened.

(3) Date and quantity of each addition to the container.

(4) Name of person adding to the container.

(5) Date container is filled or closed.

(6) Date the container is removed by DRMO.

b. Store used oil and HW according to installation guidelines.

(1) Place all accumulation of HW on a nonpermeable bermed hardstand.

(2) Label and locate the stand 50 feet or more from any building.

(3) Protect the accumulated HW from the elements, including heat and cold.

(4) Provide an enclosure to keep containers free from obscuring snow cover to allow for routine visual inspections in areas prone to heavy snowfall.

(5) Store used greases, solvents, brake fluids, hydraulic fluid, motor oil, and antifreeze in separate containers.

(6) Keep containers (drums, cans, or tanks) closed, except when depositing waste, as a safeguard against spills and to prevent water from entering the containers.

(7) Obtain a replacement through the prescribed load list section or the troop support office if 2 1/2- or 2 3/4-inch threaded caps on 55-gallon drums are missing.

(8) Ensure that secondary containment is provided that is capable of containing 11/2 times the volume of the largest container stored in the storage area.

(9) Do not accumulate HW in an open container; it is a serious violation of HW regulations.

Figure J-1. Unit environmental SOP (continued)

c. Leave the following headspace to prevent overflow due to expansion:

55-gallon drum ....3 to 4 inches.

5-gallon cans...................................1 1/2 to 2 inches.

1-gallon can ....1 inch.

d. Dispose of used oil in an appropriate aboveground container.

(1) Label the storage tank(s) USED OIL ONLY (by type such as motor oil, transmission oil, or hydraulic oil), and make certain personnel are trained to place only used oil in the tanks. If a 55-gallon drum is needed, use NSN 8110-00-823-8121.

(2) Ensure that waste oil tanks are pumped on a regular schedule. Notify the motor sergeant or the unit's HM/HW coordinator if the tank fills up before the scheduled pick up date or the tank is not pumped on schedule.

e. Use vermiculite (NSN 7930-00-269-1272) or absorbent pads to soak up puddles and Safestep (NSN 7930-01-145-5797) or sawdust (NSN 7930-00-633-9849) to clean up hardstands if HM or HW is spilled. Place all contaminated soil and absorbent material in removable head drum(s) (NSN 8110-00-082-2626 or 8110-00-292-8121) and turn in to the DRMO. Notify the installation's environmental office (see tab A).

f. Overpack chemical products and POL contained in leaking, corroded, or otherwise deteriorated containers in approved drums, and dispose of them as HW through the DRMO. Contact the installation's environmental office for assistance in determining the appropriate overpack containers.

(1) To be accepted for turn-in, waste material must be in a safe, nonleaking, durable container.

(a) Overpack leaking containers in steel or plastic removable head overpack drums, available through the supply system.

(b) Pack leaking containers of liquids in absorbent material (NSN 7930-00-269-1272), available at the General Services Administration (GSA) store or through GSA or Defense Logistics Agency catalogs.

(c) Overpack a leaking 55-gallon drum in an 85-gallon drum. Place an absorbent material all around a leaking, overpacked container, to include underneath the container and with the maximum amount possible placed in the space between the overpack container and leaking container. There must be 6 inches of absorbent on the bottom and top of the interior container, with at least 2 inches around the sides (adjust for different-size drums and overpacks).

(d) Overpack leaking containers of nonliquid HW in a serviceable container. Call the installation's environmental office or the DRMO when in doubt as to the type of container to use since many liquids such as battery acid cannot be packed in steel containers.

(2) Contact the installation's environmental office for a loaner if drums are not available for overpacking an emergency spill. Requisition a replacement drum for the installation's environmental office. Used drums are frequently available at the DRMO. Removable head 55-gallon drums (NSN 8110-00-082-2626) should be stocked by installation supply. Ensure that spill kits are procured for handling future spills.

(3) Request assistance from the installation's environmental office on compatibility of waste, packing, and labeling of containers. Maintain this information in the waste-stream file for each waste.

Figure J-1. Unit environmental SOP (continued)

g. Inspect HW weekly. Document results of the Inspection on a log made accessible to state and federal inspectors. Identify description of the waste, location, quantity, date accumulation started, end of 90-day period, date removed to the DRMO or by contractor, remarks (condition of storage area and containers), inspector's printed name, signature, and date of inspection. Coordinate this action with the installation's environmental office.

9. **Vehicle Parking Areas.**

a. Park vehicles only in designated parking areas.

b. Do not discharge any POL product or contaminated soil into or near a storm drain. This is forbidden. Vehicle parking areas drain into storm sewers; storm sewers drain into streams, which lead into the nearest surface-water body.

c. Place drip boxes/pans under all drip points of vehicles with potential for leaking POL.

d. Use dry sweep to clean up POL spills where vehicles are parked, and dispose as HW through the DRMO.

e. Do not wash vehicles on the vehicle parking line. Wash according to paragraph 4 of this SOP.

f. Ensure that no vehicle leaves the motor pool if it leaves a visible, continuous, or intermittent trail of POL on the ground (Class 3 leak).

10. **Disposal of Empty Containers and Hazardous Items.** Include information on turn-in of mufflers and exhaust pipes, brake shoes and clutch plates, fuel tanks, aerosol cans, PCB capacitor and transformers, hydraulic rams and gas cylinders, shock absorbers, oil-saturated wood and pallets, paint and paint containers, solvents and thinners, oils and greases, antifreeze, oily rags, sweeping compound, oil and fuel filters, wash rack soil/sand residue, spill clean up debris and residue, and products with expiration dates.

a. Turn-in procedures. The procedures for turning in HM varies widely due to differing state and local requirements. Seek the assistance of the supporting installation and DRMO for information on filling out and processing the turn-in document.

b. Transport. Transportation of HW is strictly controlled. Check with the supporting installation and DRMO to determine if transport by the unit is allowed.

11. **Refueling Operations.**

a. General.

(1) Conduct tactical refueling operations at a designated logistics resupply point.

(2) Avoid conducting refueling operations in a unit's operations area due to the safety hazards associated with maneuvering a fuel tanker or HEMTT and conducting grounding operations at each vehicle.

(3) Ensure POL section personnel conduct the actual refueling whenever possible.

b. Secondary containment.

(1) Place secondary containment (large drip pans) under the vehicle and under the fuel hoses during refueling operations.

(2) Place 5-gallon fuel cans inside the drip pan when refueling, for secondary containment, preventing small volume fuel spills from accumulating and contaminating the soil.

(3) Transfer spilled fuel to a labeled 5-gallon waste-fuel container, and dispose as HW.

c. Emergency equipment.

(1) Firefighting. Supply each refueling vehicle with a minimum of two fire extinguishers. Set up fire extinguishers on each side of the tanker or HEMTT during refuel operations to expedite emergency response measures. Ensure that vehicles have their basic issue inventory items.

Figure J-1. Unit environmental SOP (continued)

(2) Emergency eyewash. Ensure potable water is readily available for emergency eye washing to provide first aid measures on-site in the event a spill or leak occurs during refueling operations.

(3) PPE. Ensure that each refueling vehicle has two sets of PPE. Reference the MSDS for required PPE, or reference paragraph 4 at the beginning of this SOP for field-expedient PPE. Wear gloves and goggles when conducting refueling operations. Use aprons or wet weather gear to respond to a spill or repair a leak. Ensure that this equipment is available.

(4) Spill response. Ensure that a copy of the spill response plan is readily available during all refueling operations.

12. **Spills.** (See tab A for spill response plan. You should also refer to GTA 05-08-003.)

a. Protect yourself and other personnel, stop the flow, and then contain the spill. Immediately contain and report all spills that have entered or threaten to enter floor or storm drains.

b. Report all spills according to the installation spill contingency plan. Reporting procedures and reportable quantities may vary from installation to installation. The unit's spill response team conducts clean up. Allow light fuel to evaporate into the atmosphere; absorb oil with dry sweep or equivalent. (See tab A.)

c. Report POL spills larger than 1 gallon of heavy oil or 5 gallons of fuel to the installation's fire department. (Check the installation spill contingency plan for any differing local requirements.)

d. Conduct spill cleanup per the spill response plan at tab A. Additional cleanup guidance will be provided when the spill is reported.

e. Maintain (on hand) supplies and equipment (absorbent materials) appropriate for initial containment of the types of spills possible in the unit. Refer to the MSDS associated with each product, or call the HW material section of the DRMO for guidance on the necessary spill response supplies to have on hand. Spill equipment and material will be similar to that contained in tab B.

SECTION 2 - SUPPLY

1. **Requisitioning.** Check with the installation's environmental office for an up-to-date list of HM and guidance on the Army's Hazardous Substance Management System. The Hazardous Substance Management System, with its centralized management and strict inventory control, will reduce the use and disposal of hazardous substances.

a. Requisition the minimum quantity required for mission accomplishment.

b. When processing a request for an HM, consider alternative, nonhazardous substitutes. Check with the installation's environmental office for suggestions.

c. Ensure that recoverability codes are used whenever applicable.

d. Special indications will be made for any materials that have shelf life considerations.

2. **Storage.**

a. Label and segregate all HM from nonhazardous items.

b. Keep a copy of the applicable MSDS for each HM on hand in a binder in the HM supply storage area.

3. **Turn-In/Disposal.** Check with the supporting installation and DRMO for local requirements for turn-in of HW and unused HM.

Figure J-1. Unit environmental SOP (continued)

a. Keep an accumulation log for each HW that is waiting turn-in to DRMO. Identify the date each container was opened, date and quantity of each addition to the container, name of the person adding to the container, date container is filled or closed, and date of turn-in to DRMO.

b. Keep turn-in documents for HM and HW on file for 2 years. Keep HW manifests on file for 50 years.

4. **Paint.**

a. Do not open more than one can of each color of paint at any time.

b. Store paints indoors in a nonflammable material locker or in a POL shed. Store paints by compatibility.

c. Keep paint in original, labeled containers.

d. Maintain an MSDS in the paint locker for each type of paint stored.

e. Turn in any unopened, reusable, excess, or no longer needed paint products to the appropriate material management support activity for redistribution or sale.

f. Store all waste paint and thinners/solvents separate from unused or good paint products.

g. Consult the installation environmental management office and chain of command for proper disposal of all paint.

h. Store and dispose of paint thinners (HM) as directed by the environmental office and the DRMO.

5. **Batteries.**

a. Exchange batteries on a one-for-one basis.

b. Store used batteries separately by type while waiting turn-in; accompany with an accumulation log. Coordinate with your local installation environmental management office to confirm proper labeling requirements.

c. Ensure that there are no leaking batteries; handle carefully, and place leaking batteries in appropriate containers.

d. Keep turn-in documents on file for a period of 2 years.

SECTION 3 - CBRNE

1. **Requisitioning, Storage, and Disposal/Turn-In.** (See section 2.)

a. Process all requisitions and turn-ins through unit supply.

b. Keep a copy of the applicable MSDS for each HM on hand in a binder in the storage area.

c. Store DS2 and STB containers in dry and well-ventilated separate locations.

d. Check daily DS2 and STB containers for leaks or corrosion.

e. Overpack and turn in to DRMO any DS2 and STB container found to be leaking.

f. Properly dispose of out-of-date chemical agent testing kits as HW.

SECTION 4 - COMMUNICATION

1. **Requisitioning, Storage, and Disposal/Turn-In.** (See section 2.)

2. **Batteries.**

a. Issue batteries by exchanging them with used batteries on a one-for-one basis.

b. Immediately turn in used batteries to unit supply for storage while waiting turn-in to DRMO.

Figure J-1. Unit environmental SOP (continued)

SECTION 5 – FIELD MESS OPERATIONS

Field mess personnel use M-2 burners that operate on motor gasoline during field and contingency operations. The major safety and environmental issues are fuel storage, filling, and lighting operations.

1. **Fuel Storage.**

   a. Store 5-gallon fuel cans closed at all times.

   b. Do not attach open funnels or tubes to the containers. Maintain containers in good condition.

   c. Do not use rusty or residue-covered containers. They are unsafe and unacceptable.

2. **Filling Operations.**

   a. Conduct filling operations on a tarp or plastic liner with a soil berm or sandbag perimeter for secondary containment in the event of a spill.

   b. Immediately collect spilled fuel using an absorbent material.

   c. Place used absorbent material in DOT-approved containers, and dispose of as HW.

3. **Lighting Operations.**

   a. Conduct lighting operations at least 50 feet away from fuel storage and M-2 burner filling operations.

   b. Conduct lighting operations on open soil so that any residual fuel will freely burn during the operation.

SECTION 6 - OPERATIONS/TRAINING

1. **Training.**

   a. Provide initial environmental-awareness training to all personnel within 90 days of assignment and annually thereafter.

   b. Train all personnel to accomplish their tasks according to laws and regulations and to respond properly in emergencies.

   c. Train all personnel that have contact with HM or HW within 90 days of assignment and annually thereafter. Ensure that personnel who have not yet received initial environmental training are properly supervised when they work with materials potentially hazardous to themselves or the environment.

   d. Document all environmental training and keep on file in the operations/training office.

   e. Identify quarterly requirements for environmental compliance officer training. Request training allocations from the installation's environmental management office for two personnel (primary and alternate) in the installation's environmental compliance officer course. Request an additional training allocation when either environmental compliance officer is within 90 days of departure.

2. **Risk Assessment.**

   a. Complete an environmental-related risk assessment for all field training of platoon size or larger. (See chapter 2 and appendixes D and E.)

   b. Use checklists, found in Appendix D, for long-range, short-range, and near-term planning, training execution, and training evaluation as an aid in minimizing negative environmental impacts for those areas found to have high risk.

Figure J-1. Unit environmental SOP (continued)

3. **Maneuver Damage.**

    a.   Designate a maneuver damage control officer for each FTX.

    b.   Incorporate maneuver damage considerations into the OPORD for each FTX.

    c.   Brief unit personnel on maneuver damage considerations and minimization measures before each exercise.

    d.   Include maneuver damage as a discussion topic at all AARs.

Tabs:

    A.   Spill Response Plan.

    B.   Spill Equipment and Materials.

    C.   Electronic Message Report Formats.

    D.   Field Procedures.

    E.   Points of Contact for Assistance.

Figure J-1. Unit environmental SOP (continued)

TAB A – SPILL RESPONSE PLAN

1. Immediate Action. A spill is defined as any quantity of petroleum product over 5 gallons (or according to local laws since some states are more stringent than 5 gallons) or any quantity of any other HW. Should a spill occur, the immediate actions are as follows:

    a. Protect yourself and other personnel.

        (1) Evacuate the area, if necessary, due to the type of spill.

        (2) Take personal precautions as detailed on the MSDS for the material spilled.

        (3) Use the proper PPE.

        (4) Extinguish smoking materials and all sources of ignition.

        (5) Turn off power if there is the possibility of fire.

        (6) Ventilate the area.

    b. Stop the flow (do it **safely**).

        (1) Shut off valves, turn drums upright, and use other procedures that will stop the flow, if possible.

        (2) Do not take unnecessary chances, but stop the flow if it is possible without injury or contamination.

        (3) Shower and change clothes as soon as possible if HW contamination occurs.

    c. Contain the spill (**quickly** and **safely**).

        (1) Contain the spill by throwing absorbent, floor sweep, or dirt on it.

        (2) Make dams to keep the spill from spreading further, and do not let it enter storm or sewer drains or other waterways.

        (3) Divert the flow to prevent the spill from entering any water source, including drains, if containment is not possible.

    d. Report the spill immediately.

        (1) Report the spill to the supervisor/superior.

        (2) Sound the alarm or give verbal warning.

        (3) Have another person call the installation's fire department while you continue to assess the size and severity of the spill.

        (4) Immediately report to the unit environmental compliance officer or the installation's environmental office spills of any HM other than a petroleum product, regardless of quantity.

        (5) The senior person in charge makes a copy of the pertinent MSDS for emergency response personnel in the event of a reportable spill.

    e. Clean up the spill.

        (1) Scoop up contaminated material and put it in a container. Mark the container with "Hazardous Waste, Contaminated Absorbent (Dirt)" if the spill occurred on concrete or asphalt and the spill was cleaned up with absorbent or dirt.

        (2) Check with the unit supply sergeant or the DRMO for proper disposal.

    f. Replace spill equipment.

        (1) Immediately after a spill is cleaned up, the spill response team's noncommissioned officer in charge (NCOIC) will account for all tools and supplies. The NCOIC will order replacement consumables (sweeping compound and rags) from unit supply. He will also identify missing property and initiate appropriate action (statement of charges or report of survey) to maintain accountability.

        (2) The spill response team's NCOIC will ensure that spill kit inventories are complete before resealing the drums.

Figure J-2. Tab A – Spill response plan to unit environmental SOPs

g. Maintain a point of contact list for assistance (listed by office, name, telephone number, and building).

    (1) Fire department.

    (2) Installation's environmental management office.

    (3) Unit's environmental compliance officer.

2. Response and Cleanup Instructions.

a. Take the immediate actions in paragraph 1 above.

b. Ensure any PPE specified in the MSDS is properly used.

c. Transfer the fluid to a serviceable container if the container is still leaking fluid.

d. Absorb the remaining spilled liquid with absorbent material. Use only the amount necessary to absorb the spill. Take remedial action if the spill is too large while waiting for the fire department.

e. Clean up the material with a nonsparking shovel or broom and place the residue in a serviceable container with a secure lid.

f. Label the container.

    (1) Label the container—"POL SPILL RESIDUE"—for fuel, oil, or hydraulic fluid spills.

    (2) Label the container—"(Name of Chemical) SPILL RESIDUE - FLAMMABLE"—for flammable liquid spills (including solvents, paints, paint thinners, and alcohol).

    (3) Label the container—"(Name of Acid) SPILL RESIDUE - ACID"—for acid spills.

g. Store the container in the HW storage area while waiting turn-in.

h. Turn in the residue container to the DRMO.

    (1) Label the container—"(Name of Chemical) SPILL RESIDUE - FLAMMABLE"—for flammable liquid spills (including solvents, paints, paint thinners, and alcohol).

    (2) Label the container—"(Name of Acid) SPILL RESIDUE - ACID"—for acid spills.

i. Store the container in the HW storage area while waiting turn-in.

j. Turn in the residue container to the DRMO.

Figure J-2. Tab A – Spill response plan to unit environmental SOPs (continued)

TAB B – SPILL EQUIPMENT AND MATERIALS

Each unit/activity should maintain a spill kit to respond to accidental releases and spills of HM. Below is a list of recommended equipment that should be maintained in the unit/activity spill kit. This list is not all-inclusive and should be expanded depending on the mission of the unit/activity. It is the responsibility of the unit/activity to purchase replacement or additional items to keep the contents of the kit stocked with necessary equipment. Additional kits must be purchased by the unit/activity that needs them, and additional quantities will be based on the likely size or frequency of potential spills.

Hazardous Material/Hazardous Waste Supplies

Containers (DOT or equivalent)

NSN	ITEM
8105-00-848-9631	Bag, polyolefin, 5 millimeters, 36 x 54 inch
8125-00-174-0852	Bottle, plastic, 1 gallon (polyethylene)
8125-00-731-6016	13 gallon
8125-00-888-7069	5 gallon
8110-00-254-5719	Drum, steel, 1 gallon*
8100-00-128-6819	1-gallon steel drum (17C)*
8110-00-254-5722	4-gallon steel drum*
8110-00-282-2520	5-gallon steel drum (17C)*
8110-00-254-5713	Drum, steel, 6 gallon (w/ring)*
8110-01-204-8967	Pail, shipping, steel, 5 gallon (DOT 17C)*
8110-00-519-5618	Drum, steel, 10 gallon (DOT 17C)*
8110-00-753-4643	19-gallon steel drum (17C)*
8110-00-366-6809	30-gallon steel drum (17C)*
8110-00-030-7779	30-gallon steel drum*
8110-00-030-7780	50-gallon steel drum (17C)*
8110-00-823-8121	55-gallon steel drum (17M)*
8110-00-030-9783	Drum, steel 55 gallon (bung & vent) (DOT 17E)*
8110-01-282-7615	Drum, polyethylene, 55 gallon*
8110-01-101-4055	85-gallon steel disposal drum (no lining)*
8110-01-101-4056	85-gallon steel recovery drum (epoxy phenolic lining)*
8110-01-101-4055	Drum, hazardous material*

* Refers to open top containers
For bung container, refer to federal logistics or contract the G-4.

FM 3-34.5/MCRP 4-11B

Figure J-3. Tab B – Spill equipment and materials to unit environmental SOPs

Absorbent

NSN	ITEM
7930-00-269-1272	Clay, ground unit of issue (UI-bag)
1939-01-154-7001	Nonskid absorbent (UI-40 bag skid)
5640-00-801-4176	Insulation, thermal, vermiculite (UI-bag) (packing material)
4235-01-423-1466	4 each, 1 cubic foot bag
4235-01-423-0711	1 each, 1 cubic foot bag
4235-01-423-1463	30 each, 18 x 18 inch pillows
4235-01-423-1467	20 each, 2 inch x 10 foot sock
4235-01-423-1465	10 each, 4 inch x 8 foot booms
4235-01-423-2787	10 inch x 10 foot booms

Spill Prevention

NSN	ITEM
8135-00-579-6491	Plastic sheet, clear
8135-00-579-6492	Plastic sheet, black
4235-01-423-7214	Spill kit
4235-01-423-7221	Spill kit

Figure J-3. Tab B – Spill equipment and materials to unit environmental SOPs (continued)

TAB C – ELECTRONIC MESSAGE REPORT FORMATS

References: FM 6-99.2, "US Army Reports and Message Formats," 30 April 2007.

1. ( ) <u>ECR Format</u>.

TITLE: ENVIRONMENTAL CONDITION REPORT
REPORT NUMBER: E035

GENERAL INSTRUCTIONS: Used to send periodic information (interim snapshots) of the environmental status of specific sites (assembly areas, base camps, logistical support areas, and medical facilities) where hazards are likely to occur and can result in significant, immediate, and/or long-term effects on the natural environment and/or health of friendly forces and noncombatants. Sent according to unit SOP and commander's direction.

LINE 1—DATE AND TIME_____ (DTG)

LINE 2—UNIT _____ (Unit making report)

LINE 3—LOCATION _____ (UTM or 6-digit grid coordinate with MGRS grid zone designator of site/incident)

LINE 4—DESCRIPTION _____ (Description of site/incident)

LINE 5—CHANGES _____ (Changes from last ECR or EBS)

LINE 6—HAZARDS_____ (Hazards to natural environment, friendly forces, and/or civilian personnel)

LINE 7—ACTIONS _____ (Summary of actions to minimize hazards/remedial effects)

LINE 8—UNIT POC _____ (Reporting unit point of contact)

LINE 9—ASSISTANCE _____ (Assistance required/requested)

LINE 10—REFERENCE _____ (Site specific EBS, if required)

LINE 11—NARRATIVE_____ (Free text for additional information required for clarification of report)

LINE 12—AUTHENTICATION_____ (Report authentication)

Figure J-4. Tab C – Electronic message report formats to unit environmental SOPs

3. ( ) <u>Electronic Spill Report Message Format</u>.

TITLE: SPILL REPORT (SPILLREP)
(Not currently in FM 6-99.2)

GENERAL INSTRUCTIONS: Used to send timely information or status of an oil, hazardous material, or hazardous waste spill that could have immediate environmental and/or health effects. Sent according to SOP and commander's direction.
NOTE: Spill reporting and reportable quantities are mandated by federal and local law.

LINE 1—DATE AND TIME _____ (DTG)

LINE 2—UNIT_____ (Unit making report)

LINE 3—DATE/TIME _____ (DTG of spill discovery)

LINE 4—MATERIAL _____ (Material spilled)

LINE 5—QUANTITY_____ (Quantity of spilled material)

LINE 6—LOCATION_____ (UTM or 6-digit grid coordinate with MGRS grid zone designator of spill)

LINE 7—CAUSE_____ (Cause and supervising unit)

LINE 8—SIZE _____ (Size of affected area)

LINE 9—DAMAGE_____(Damage to the natural environment, if required)

LINE 10—HAZARDS _____ (Hazards to natural environment, friendly forces, and/or civilian personnel)

LINE 11—ACTIONS _____ (Summary of actions taken)

LINE 12—UNIT POC _____ (Supervising unit POC)

LINE 13—ASSISTANCE _____ (Assistance required/requested)

LINE 14—NARRATIVE_____(Free text for additional information required for clarification of report)

LINE 15—AUTHENTICATION _____ (Report authentication)

Figure J-4. Tab C – Electronic message report formats to unit environmental SOPs (continued)

This page intentionally left blank.

Appendix K
Material Safety Data Sheets

An MSDS is a summary of information on a given chemical, which identifies the material, its health and physical hazards, its exposure limits, and the precautions involved. An MSDS also describes the hazards of a material and provides information on the way the material may be safely handled, used, and stored. Soldiers and Marines should request a copy of an MSDS when receiving a hazardous chemical from supply and retain it for turn-in purposes. Commanders should periodically review each MSDS pertaining to their unit to ensure a quick response when identifying symptoms and handling emergencies. Commanders must also have one of these forms for every chemical in the Soldier and Marine work area. Each version of an MSDS must be approved by the DOL or G-4. The MSDS does not contain a special format, nor does it include all known data for a given chemical. However, typical components are outlined in 29 CFR 1910. The MSDS can be generated by data and obtained through the Hazardous Material Information Resource System or directly from the product vendor or supplier. Table K-1, page K-2, provides a reference for information found in an MSDS. Table K-2, page K-3, details the chemical hazards portion of the MSDS.

MATERIAL SAFETY DATA SHEET INTRODUCTION

K-1. This information allows a unit to—
- Protect Soldier and Marine health.
- Store materials safely.
- Respond to spills and emergencies quickly and correctly.

K-2. When a material is issued, Soldiers and Marines should ask supply personnel to provide an MSDS. A sample MSDS for motor fuel is shown in figure K-1, pages K-4 through K-9. However, Soldiers and Marines should remember that MSDS forms vary. If an MSDS is unavailable for a particular hazardous substance, contact the installation safety office for assistance.

Table K-1. MSDS guide

Section/Topic	Typical Contents
Section 1–Product and Company Identification	• Product name • Manufacturer's name and address • Trade or common name of product
Section 2–Hazardous Ingredients	• National Institute for Occupational Safety and Health (NIOSH)/Chemical Abstract System Number • Chemical name and percentage • Workers' exposure limits
Section 3–Hazards Identification	• Emergency overview • Potential health effects

Table K-1. MSDS guide (continued)

Section/Topic	Typical Contents
Section 4–First Aid Measures	• Inhalation • Skin • Eyes • Ingestion
Section 5–Firefighting Measures	• Flash point • Flammable limits • Automatic ignition temperature • General hazards • Extinguishing media • Firefighting procedures • Unusual fire and explosion hazards • Hazardous combustion products
Section 6–Environmental Release Measures	Steps to be taken in case material is released or spilled
Section 7–Handling and Storage	Precautions to be taken in handling and storage
Section 8–Exposure Controls/Personal Protection	• Engineering: Recommended respiratory and ventilation • Personal protection: PPE, if needed
Section 9–Physical and Chemical Properties	• Vapor pressure • Vapor density • Specific gravity • Evaporation rate • Solubility in water • Freezing point • Measure of the acidity or alkalinity of a solution (pH) • Appearance and odor • Boiling point • Physical state • Viscosity • Volatile organic compounds
Section 10–Stability and Reactivity	• Stability • Conditions to avoid • Incompatibility (materials to avoid) • Hazardous decomposition or byproducts • Hazardous polymerization • Conditions to avoid
Section 11–Toxicological Information	• Hazardous ingredients • Chemical Abstract System Number

Table K-1. MSDS guide (continued)

Section/Topic	Typical Contents
Section 12–Ecological Information	See figure J-1, page J-4
Section 13–Disposal Considerations	See figure J-1, page J-4
Section 14–Transport Information	• Proper shipping name • Hazard class • Reference • Identification number • Label • Hazard symbols
Section 15–Regulatory Information	See figure K-1, page L-8
Section 16–Other Information	See figure K-1, page L-9

Table K-2. Chemical hazards

Health Hazards	Physical Hazards
• Illness • Acute or chronic health effects • Injury	• Explosion and/or fire • Violent chemical reactions • Other hazardous situations

MATERIAL SAFETY DATA SHEET

SECTION 1 - PRODUCT AND COMPANY IDENTIFICATION

PRODUCT NAME: GASOLINE, UNLEADED

GENERAL USE: Motor fuel

PRODUCT DESCRIPTION: Blend of petroleum distillates, highly flammable. This MSDS covers multiple grades of lead-free and unleaded fuels: regular, premium, extra and oxygenated.

TESORO

MANUFACTURER'S NAME	DATE PREPARED: February 8, 2003	
Tesoro Petroleum Companies, Inc.	SUPERSEDES: April 18, 2002	Page 1 of 6
ADDRESS (NUMBER, STREET, P.O. BOX)	TELEPHONE NUMBER FOR INFORMATION	
300 Concord Plaza Drive	Tesoro Call Center (877) 783-7676	
(CITY, STATE AND ZIP CODE) COUNTRY	EMERGENCY TELEPHONE NUMBER	
San Antonio, TX 78216-6999 USA	Chemtrec (800) 424-9300	
DISTRIBUTOR'S NAME		
Same		
ADDRESS (NUMBER, STREET, P.O. BOX)	TELEPHONE NUMBER FOR INFORMATION	
(CITY, STATE AND ZIP CODE) COUNTRY USA	EMERGENCY TELEPHONE NUMBER	

SECTION 2 - HAZARDOUS INGREDIENTS

HAZARDOUS COMPONENTS	CAS #	% (Sect. 16) (by volume)	OSHA PEL PPM	OSHA PEL MG/M³	ACGIH TWA PPM	ACGIH TWA MG/M³	SARA TITLE III	RQ LBS
Gasoline	8006-61-9	100	300	900	300			
Contains or may contain:								
Toluene (a,b,c,e,f,g)	108-88-3	0 - 35	200		50		Yes	1000
Xylene (mixed) (a,b,c)	1330-20-7	0 - 25	100	435	100		Yes	1000
Pentane	109-66-0	0 - 20	1000	2950	600			
Trimethylbenzenes, mixed isomers (a)	25551-13-7	0 - 4			25		Yes	
Benzene (a,b,o,d,e,f)	71-43-2	0 - 5	1		0.5		Yes	10
Butane	106-97-8	0 - 12	800	1900		800		
Ethylbenzene (a,c)	100-41-4	0 - 5	100	435	125	545	Yes	1000
Heptane	142-82-5	0 - 2	500	2000	400			
Cyclohexane (a,b,c)	110-82-7	0 - 5	300	1050	300		Yes	1000
n-Hexane	110-54-3	0 - 8	500	1800	50	176		
n-Octane	111-65-9	0 - 1	500	2350	300	1400		
Ethanol	64-17-5	0 - 20	1000	1900	1000			
Naphthalene (a,b,c,g)	91-20-3	0 - 1.1	10	50	10		Yes	100
Trimethylbenzene 1,2,4 (a)	95-63-6	0 - 7	25	125			Yes	
Isopentane	78-78-4	0 - 20	not established					
Styrene (a,c,d,e,g)	100-42-5	0 - 4	100		20		Yes	1000
Methyl tert - butyl ether (a)	1634-04-4	0 - 18			40	144	Yes	
Ethyl tert - butyl ether	637-92-3	0 - 21	not established					
Tertiary - Amyl methyl ether	994-05-8	0 - 20	not established					
Alkanes, Cycloalkanes, Alkenes, Aromatic hydrocarbons		balance						

(a,c) See Section 15

(b) Indicates that the Resource Conservation and Recovery Act (RCRA) has determined the waste for this chemical is listed as hazardous and must be handled according to regulations in 40 CFR 260-281.

(d) Indicates substance appears on National Toxicology Program (NTP) list of carcinogens, International Agency for Research on Cancer (IARC) list of carcinogens or is regulated by the Occupational Safety and Health Administration (OSHA) as a possible carcinogen.

(e) Indicates listing in Table Z -, 29 CFR 1910.1000, one of 26 chemicals with substance - specific requirements, value shown is 8-hour Time Weighted Average. See table for acceptable ceiling concentration limits and acceptable maximum peak above the acceptable ceiling concentration.

(f) California Prop 65, Safe Drinking Water and Toxic Enforcement Act of 1986, chemicals known to the state to cause cancer or reproductive toxicity. A person in the course of doing business must warn others who may consume, come into contact with, or otherwise be exposed to this chemical.

(g) Product is listed or defined as a marine pollutant in IMDG Code or 49 CFR 172.101 Appendix B, List of Marine Pollutants and must be classified as an Environmentally Hazardous Substance, Class 9, in addition to any other defined hazards for this product.

Figure K-1. Sample MSDS

MATERIAL SAFETY DATA SHEET

PRODUCT NAME: GASOLINE, UNLEADED
February 8, 2003

SECTION 3 - HAZARDS IDENTIFICATION

EMERGENCY OVERVIEW

Bronze to amber colored liquid, extremely flammable, potentially hazardous vapors. Can cause eye and skin irritation upon contact. Inhalation of vapors can cause anesthetic effect leading to death in poorly ventilated areas. Danger Poison! Harmful if swallowed and/or aspirated into the lungs. Hazard symbols for this product - F, XI, XN Risk Phrases - R11 20 36 38.

POTENTIAL HEALTH EFFECTS

INHALATION: High concentrations are irritating to the respiratory tract; may cause headache, dizziness, nausea, vomiting and malaise. Xylene causes central nervous system effects, anemia, liver and kidney effects, and eye damage after repeated or prolonged exposure to high concentrations.

SKIN: Brief contact may cause slight irritation; prolonged contact may cause moderate irritation or dermatitis. Xylene causes central nervous system effects, anemia, liver and kidney effects, and eye damage after repeated or prolonged exposure to high concentrations.

EYES: High vapor concentration or contact may cause irritation and discomfort.

INGESTION: May result in vomiting; aspiration of vomitus into the lungs must be avoided; DO NOT induce vomiting. Minute amounts aspirated into the lungs can produce severe lung injury, chemical pneumonitis, pulmonary edema or death.

CARCINOGENICITY   NTP? Yes   IARC MONOGRAPH? Yes   OSHA REGULATED? Yes

Gasoline has been classified as a Group 2B carcinogen (possibly carcinogenic to humans) by the International Agency for Research on Cancer (IARC). Contains chemical(s) known to the State of California to cause cancer. Contains benzene, which has been classified as a carcinogen by the National Toxicology Program (NTP), and a Group 1 carcinogen (carcinogenic to humans) by the International Agency for Research on Cancer (IARC). Contains ethylbenzene which has been classified as a Group 2B carcinogen (possibly carcinogenic to humans) by the International Agency for Research on Cancer (IARC).

SECTION 4 - FIRST AID MEASURES

INHALATION: Remove affected person to fresh air; provide oxygen if breathing is difficult; if affected person is not breathing, administer CPR and seek immediate emergency medical attention.

SKIN: Remove contaminated clothing; wash affected area with soap and water; launder contaminated clothing before reuse; if irritation persists, seek medical attention.

EYES: Remove contact lenses. Flush eyes with clear running water for 15 minutes while holding eyelids open; if irritation persists, seek medical attention.

INGESTION: DO NOT induce vomiting; if vomiting occurs spontaneously, keep head below hips to prevent aspiration of liquid into lungs; seek immediate medical attention. Vomiting may be induced only under the supervision of a physician.

SECTION 5 - FIRE FIGHTING MEASURES

FLASH POINT (METHOD USED)	FLAMMABLE LIMITS	LEL: 1.3%		UEL: 7.6%
-45° F (-42.7° C) TCC	AUTOIGNITION TEMPERATURE:	495° F (257° C)	NFPA CLASS:	IA

GENERAL HAZARDS: This product presents an extreme fire hazard. Liquid evaporates very quickly, even at low temperatures, and forms vapor (fumes) which can catch fire and burn with explosive violence. Invisible vapor spreads easily and can be set on fire by many sources such as pilot lights, welding equipment, and electrical motors and switches.

EXTINGUISHING MEDIA
   Carbon dioxide, water fog, dry chemical, chemical foam

FIRE FIGHTING PROCEDURES
   Firefighters must wear full facepiece self - contained breathing apparatus in positive pressure mode. Do not use solid stream of water since stream will scatter and spread fire. Fine water spray can be used to keep fire - exposed containers cool.

UNUSUAL FIRE AND EXPLOSION HAZARDS
   Closed containers can explode due to buildup of pressure when exposed to extreme heat. Do not use direct stream of water on pool fires as product may reignite on water surface. Caution - Material is extremely flammable!

HAZARDOUS COMBUSTION PRODUCTS
   Smoke, fumes, oxides of carbon

Figure K-1. Sample MSDS (continued)

MATERIAL SAFETY DATA SHEET

PRODUCT NAME: GASOLINE, UNLEADED
February 8, 2003
Page 3 of 6

SECTION 6 - ENVIRONMENTAL RELEASE MEASURES

STEPS TO BE TAKEN IN CASE MATERIAL IS RELEASED OR SPILLED: CAUTION - EXTREMELY FLAMMABLE - Evacuate and ventilate area; confine and absorb into absorbent; place material into approved containers for disposal; for spills in excess of allowable limits (RQ) notify the National Response Center (800) 424 - 8802; refer to CERCLA 40 CFR 302 and SARA Title III, Section 313 40 CFR 372 for detailed instructions concerning reporting requirements.

SECTION 7 - HANDLING AND STORAGE

PRECAUTIONS TO BE TAKEN IN HANDLING AND STORAGE: Keep container closed when not in use; protect containers from abuse; protect from extreme temperatures. CAUTION - EXTREMELY FLAMMABLE - keep away from all sources of ignition. "Empty" containers may contain residue which may form explosive vapors. Do not weld or cut near empty container that has not been professionally reconditioned. Use non-sparking tools when opening and closing containers. Maintain well ventilated work areas to minimize exposure when handling this material. Review all operations which have the potential of generating an accumulation of electrostatic charge and/or a flammable atmosphere (including tank and container filling, splash filling, tank cleaning, sampling, gauging, switch loading, filtering, mixing, agitation, and vacuum truck operations) and use appropriate mitigating procedures. Improper filling of portable gasoline containers creates danger of fire. Only dispense gasoline into approved and properly labeled gasoline containers. Always place portable containers on the ground. Be sure pump nozzle is in contact with the container while filling. Do not use a nozzle's lock-open device. Do not fill portable containers that are inside a vehicle or truck/trailer bed.

SECTION 8 - EXPOSURE CONTROLS / PERSONAL PROTECTION

ENGINEERING CONTROLS

The use of local exhaust ventilation is recommended to control emissions near the source. Provide mechanical ventilation of confined spaces. Use explosion-proof ventilation equipment. See Section 2 for Component Exposure Guidelines.

PERSONAL PROTECTION:

RESPIRATORY PROTECTION (SPECIFY TYPE): None required while threshold limits (Section 2) are kept below maximum allowable concentrations; if TWA exceeds limits, NIOSH approved respirator must be worn. Refer to 29 CFR 1910.134 or European Standard EN 149 for complete regulations.

PROTECTIVE GLOVES: Neoprene or nitrile rubber gloves with cuffs.

EYE PROTECTION: Safety goggles with side shields

OTHER PROTECTIVE CLOTHING OR EQUIPMENT: Safety eyewash nearby

WORK / HYGIENIC PRACTICES: Practice safe workplace habits. Minimize body contact with this, as well as all chemicals in general.

SECTION 9 - PHYSICAL AND CHEMICAL PROPERTIES

VAPOR PRESSURE (MM Hg) 5 - 15 PSI @ 100° F	VAPOR DENSITY (AIR = 1) 3.0 - 4.0
SPECIFIC GRAVITY (WATER = 1) 0.700 - 0.800	EVAPORATION RATE (n-Butyl Acetate = 1) < 1
SOLUBILITY IN WATER Negligible	FREEZING POINT Not determined
pH Not applicable	APPEARANCE AND ODOR Bronze to amber liquid, characteristic gasoline odor
BOILING POINT 80 - 430°F (26.0 - 221° C)	PHYSICAL STATE Liquid
VISCOSITY Not specified	VOLATILE ORGANIC COMPOUNDS (Total VOC's) 6.25 lbs / gallon

SECTION 10 - STABILITY AND REACTIVITY

STABILITY	UNSTABLE: STABLE: XXX	CONDITIONS TO AVOID: Extreme temperatures, open flames, sparks
INCOMPATIBILITY (MATERIALS TO AVOID): May react with strong oxidizing agents, such as chlorates, nitrates, peroxides, etc.		
HAZARDOUS DECOMPOSITION OR BYPRODUCTS: Decomposition will not occur if handled and stored properly. In case of a fire, oxides of carbon, hydrocarbons, fumes, and smoke may be produced.		
HAZARDOUS POLYMERIZATION	MAY OCCUR: WILL NOT OCCUR: XXX	CONDITIONS TO AVOID: None

Figure K-1. Sample MSDS (continued)

MATERIAL SAFETY DATA SHEET

PRODUCT NAME: GASOLINE, UNLEADED
February 8, 2003

Page 4 of 6

SECTION 11 - TOXICOLOGICAL INFORMATION

Hazardous Ingredients	%	CAS #	LD50 of Ingredient (Species and Route)	LC50 of Ingredient (Species)
Gasoline	100	8006-61-9	18.8 ml / kg Oral - rat	20.7 ml / l Inhalation - rat
Contains or may contain:				
Toluene (a,b,c,e,f,g)	0 - 35	108-88-3	5000 mg / kg Oral - rat	7525 ppm / 4H
Xylene (mixed) (a,b,c)	0 - 25	1330-20-7	4300 mg / kg Oral - rat	5000 ppm / 4H Inhalation - rat
Pentane	0 - 20	109-66-0	Not established	364 gm / m3 / 4H Inhalation-rat
Trimethylbenzenes, mixed isomers (a)	0 - 4	25551-13-7	Not established	Not established
Benzene (a,b,c,d,e,f)	0 - 5	71-43-2	930 mg / kg Oral - rat	10000 ppm / 7H Inhalation - rat
Butane	0 - 12	106-97-8	Not established	658 mg / L / 4H Inhalation - rat
Ethylbenzene (a,c)	0 - 5	100-41-4	3500 mg / kg Oral - rat	4000 ppm/4H(LCLo) Inhalation - rat
Heptane	0 - 2	142-82-5	Not established	75 gm / m3 / 2H Inhalation - mouse
Cyclohexane (a,b,c)	0 - 5	110-82-7	813 mg / kg Oral - mouse	Not established
n-Hexane	0 - 6	110-54-3	28710 mg / kg Oral - rat	48000 ppm / 4H Inhalation-rat
n-Octane	0 - 1	111-65-9	Not established	118 gm / m3 / 4H Inhalation - rat
Ethanol	0 - 20	64-17-5	3450 mg / kg Oral - mouse	20,000 ppm / 10H Inhalation - rat
Naphthalene (a,b,c,g)	0 - 1.1	91-20-3	1780 mg / kg Oral - rat	Not established
Trimethylbenzene 1,2,4 (a)	0 - 7	95-63-6	5 gm / kg Oral - rat	18 gm / m3 / 4H Inhalation - rat
Isopentane	0 - 20	78-78-4	1600 - 3200 mg / kg Oral - rat	Not established
Styrene (a,c,d,e,g)	0 - 4	100-42-5	5000 mg / kg Oral - rat	24000 mg/m3/2H Inhalation - rat
Methyl tert - butyl ether (a)	0 - 18	1634-04-4	4 gm / kg Oral - rat	23576 ppm / 4H Inhalation - rat
Ethyl tert - butyl ether	0 - 21	637-92-3	Not established	123 gm / m3 / 15M Inhalation - mouse
Tertiary - Amyl methyl ether	0 - 20	994-05-8	Not established	Not established

SECTION 12 - ECOLOGICAL INFORMATION

No data are available on the adverse effects of this material on the environment. Neither COD nor BOD data are available. Based on the chemical composition of this product it is assumed that the mixture can be treated in an acclimatized biological waste treatment plant system in limited quantities. However, such treatment should be evaluated and approved for each specific biological system. None of the ingredients in this mixture are classified as a Marine Pollutant. In general, non-oxygenated gasoline exhibits some short-term toxicity to freshwater and marine organisms, especially under closed vessel or flow-through exposure conditions in the laboratory. The components which are the most prominent in the water soluble fraction and cause aquatic toxicity, are also highly volatile and can be readily biodegraded by microorganisms.

SECTION 13 - DISPOSAL CONSIDERATIONS

WASTE DISPOSAL METHOD: Dispose of in accordance with Local, State, and Federal Regulations. This product may produce concentrated hazardous vapors or fumes in a disposal container creating a dangerous environment. Refer to "40 CFR Protection of Environment Parts 260 - 299" for complete waste disposal regulations for ignitable materials. Consult your local, state, or Federal Environmental Protection Agency before disposing of any chemicals. Do not flush to sanitary sewer or waterway.

Figure K-1. Sample MSDS (continued)

MATERIAL SAFETY DATA SHEET

PRODUCT NAME: GASOLINE, UNLEADED February 8, 2003	Page 5 of 6

SECTION 14 - TRANSPORT INFORMATION

PROPER SHIPPING NAME: Gasoline

HAZARD CLASS / Pack Group: 3 / II
    REFERENCE: 49 CFR 173.150, .202, .242
IDENTIFICATION NUMBER: UN 1203
    LABEL: FLAMMABLE LIQUID
HAZARD SYMBOLS: F

IATA HAZARD CLASS / Pack Group: 3 / II
    IMDG HAZARD CLASS: 3.1 / II
RID/ADR Dangerous Goods Code: 3
Canadian TDG Class / Division: 3.2

Note: Transportation information provided is for reference only. Client is urged to consult CFR 49 parts 100 - 177, IMDG, IATA, EC, Canadian TDG, and United Nations TDG information manuals for detailed regulations and exceptions covering specific container sizes, packaging materials and methods of shipping.

SECTION 15 - REGULATORY INFORMATION

TSCA (Toxic Substance Control Act)
Motor gasoline is considered a mixture by EPA under the Toxic Substances Control Act (TSCA). The refinery streams used to blend motor gasoline are all on the TSCA Chemical Substances Inventory. This product may contain methyl tertiary-butyl ether (CAS #1634-04-4) or tert-amyl methyl ether (CAS #994-05-8), both of which are currently undergoing review and testing under TSCA Section 4. Notification to the U.S. EPA Office of Toxic Substances is required prior to export of this material from the United States.

SARA TITLE III (Superfund Amendments and Reauthorization Act)
311/312 Hazard Categories
Immediate (Acute) Health Effects
Delayed (Chronic) Health Effects
Fire Hazard

313 Reportable Ingredients:
(a) Indicates a toxic chemical subject to annual reporting requirements of Section 313 of the Emergency Planning and Community Right-To-Know Act of 1986 and of 40 CFR 372.

CERCLA (Comprehensive Response Compensation and Liability Act)
(c) The Comprehensive Environmental Response, Compensation, and Liability Act (CERCLA) has notification requirements for releases or spills to the environment of the Reportable Quantity or greater amounts, according to 40 CFR 302.

CPR (Canadian Controlled Products Regulations)
This product has been classified in accordance with the hazard criteria of the Controlled Products Regulations and the MSDS contains all the information required by the Controlled Products Regulations

IDL (Canadian Ingredient Disclosure List)
Components of this product identified by CAS number and listed on the Canadian Ingredient Disclosure List are shown in Section 2.

DSL / NDSL (Canadian Domestic Substances List / Non-Domestic Substances List)
Components of this product identified by CAS number are listed on the DSL or NDSL and may or may not be listed in Section 2 of this document. Only ingredients classified as "hazardous" are listed in Section 2 unless otherwise indicated.

EINECS (European Inventory of Existing Commercial Chemical Substances)
Components of this product identified by CAS numbers are on the European Inventory of Existing Commercial Chemical Substances.

California Prop 65, Safe Drinking Water and Toxic Enforcement Act of 1986
Warning: This product contains a chemical known to the State of California to cause cancer.

EC Risk Phrases
R11 Highly flammable
R20 Harmful by inhalation
R36 Irritating to eyes
R38 Irritating to skin.

EC Safety Phrases
S16 Keep away from sources of ignition
S23 Do not breathe vapor
S26 Avoid contact with eyes
S28 After contact with skin, wash immediately with plenty of soap and water.
S29 Do not empty into drains

Figure K-1. Sample MSDS (continued)

MATERIAL SAFETY DATA SHEET

PRODUCT NAME: GASOLINE, UNLEADED
February 8, 2003

Page 6 of 6

SECTION 16 - OTHER INFORMATION

Values stated in "%" column in Section 2 and Section 11 do not reflect absolute minimums and maximums; these values are typical which may vary from time to time.

NFPA HAZARD RATINGS			0 = INSIGNIFICANT	3 = HIGH
	HEALTH	1	1 = SLIGHT	4 = EXTREME
	FLAMMABILITY	3	2 = MODERATE	
	REACTIVITY	0		
	PERSONAL PROTECTIVE EQUIPMENT	B	Safety Glasses, Gloves	

REVISION SUMMARY:
This MSDS has been revised in the following
sections:

Section 2 - Changes in quantities
Changes in product numbers

MSDS Prepared by: Chem-Tel, Inc.
1305 N. Florida Ave.
Tampa, Florida USA 33602
(800) 255-3924   Outside USA (813) 248-0573

DISCLAIMER: The information supplied in this data sheet is obtained from currently available sources, which are believed to be reliable. HOWEVER, THE INFORMATION IS PROVIDED WITHOUT ANY WARRANTY, EXPRESSED OR IMPLIED, REGARDING THE ACCURACY OF THE INFORMATION OR THE RESULTS TO BE OBTAINED FROM ITS USE.
Handling, storage, use or disposal of the above-referenced product is beyond our control and may occur under conditions with which we are unfamiliar. FOR THESE AND OTHER REASONS, WE DO NOT ASSUME RESPONSIBILITY AND EXPRESSLY DISCLAIM ANY LIABILITY FOR DAMAGE, INJURY AND COST ARISING FROM OR RELATED TO THE USE OF THE PRODUCT.

Product Number(s) :

05	20	74	133	269	354	1106
06	21	76	166	270	516	1286
08	25	77	167	281	517	1088
09	26	82	181	305	1037	1289
10	51	84	185	326	1038	1290
11	61	85	188	327	1039	1326
12	62	91	190	329	1040	
13	63	95	199	334	1041	
14	64	107	257	335	1042	
15	67	110	265	336	1043	
16	68	112	266	338	1044	
17	69	131	267	339	1045	
19	73	132	268	340	1098	

Figure K-1. Sample MSDS (continued)

This page intentionally left blank.

Appendix L

Environmental Program Resources

This appendix provides a listing of resources available for implementing and sustaining your unit environmental program. Information on training assets, significant references and Web sites, lessons learned, and points of contact are included.

TRAINING

L-1.   Training is key to ensuring that personnel integrate environmental considerations properly to protect both themselves and the environment. The implementation of general and specialized training programs, along with the integration of environmental considerations into training exercises, will ensure that units are prepared to meet environmental requirements.

ENVIRONMENTAL AWARENESS

L-2.   Environmental awareness training is required for all personnel. Such training provides basic information on installation and unit environmental practices. It leads to safer performance and establishes an environmental ethic among Soldiers and Marines. Awareness training should occur as early as possible following an assignment to a unit, and environmental officers reinforce environmental awareness training annually.

ENVIRONMENTAL-SPECIFIC TRAINING REQUIREMENTS

L-3.   In addition to general environmental awareness training, individuals with certain duties and responsibilities require specialized training. As part of their ongoing technical skills training, units provide some specialized environmental training through integrated instruction or supplemental material.

TRAINING RESOURCES

L-4.   A variety of resources are available to assist units in the development and implementation of environmental training programs. Check with the unit training officer or NCO for the resources available, which may include training aids, devices, simulators, and simulations.

United States Army Engineer School Products

L-5.   USAES has developed a catalog that consolidates most of the currently available products and is updated on a routine basis. It is intended for use as a quick reference and educational resource for Soldiers, Marines, and leaders and may be accessed on the USAES DEI Training Division Web site at <http://www.wood.army.mil/dei>.

Environmental Officer Training

Installation Environmental Trainer's Course

L-6.   The installation environmental trainer trains unit/activity-level Soldiers, Marines, and civilians in a unit environmental officer course. This course provides environmental officers with the tools required to advise unit commanders/supervisors on environmental considerations at their respective units. Working with the Installation Environmental Trainer's Course and the installation environmental office, the environmental officer acts as a liaison between the unit and the installation staff.

State Environmental Trainer Course

L-7. In April 1997, USAES completed an ARNG version of the Installation Environmental Trainer's Course. It was designed to support the unique requirements of the state area coordinators.

Web-Based Environmental Officer Course

L-8. This Web-based course trains designated regular Army, ARNG, and USAR environmental officers. It consists of the modules provided below. For further information, contact DEI at <http://www.wood.army.mil/dei>.

- Understanding the Role of the Environmental Officer.
- Identifying Environmental Hazards in the Unit.
- Protecting the Environment From POL Products.
- Managing Environmental Risk Assessments.
- Integrating Environmental Risk Assessment Into Predeployment Planning.

Installation Environmental Management Office

L-9. The installation environmental management office provides installation-specific environmental officer train-the-trainer training to allow environmental officers to inform unit personnel of compliance. The environmental management office staff may also provide unit personnel with specific training in proper response to environmental emergencies. Personnel must comply with environmental regulations while accomplishing their tasks in a manner that meets Army environmental standards. The environmental management office provides briefings and training to supervisors and small unit commanders to ensure that they understand what is required of them. For further information, contact the local installation environmental management office.

Resident

L-10. Resident training pertains to instruction presented in a formal setting by trained instructors. It may be presented by conventional methods, such as conference, advanced technology, computers, distributed learning methods, or a combination of these methods. USAES has developed training support packages (TSPs) for inclusion in various initial entry, precommissioning, and professional development courses. For more information, see the environmental awareness and doctrine, organization, training, materiel, leadership and education, personnel, and facilities product catalog at the USAES DEI Products Web site at <http://www.wood.army.mil/dei/products.htm>.

Nonresident

L-11. All nonresident training products may be found on AKO at <https://www.us.army.mil>. To support a nonresident version of the environmental TSPs, USAES has developed Army correspondence courses related to preparing junior enlisted, company grade officers, and NCOs to execute their environmental responsibilities outlined in this FM and AR 200-1. Soldiers and Marines may request the following correspondence courses through the Army Correspondence Course Program (ACCP). The ACCP Web site at <http://www.atsc.army.mil/accp/aipdnew.asp> lists the courses and subcourses administered by the Army Institute for professional development and outlines procedures and administrative functions affecting student enrollment. Individuals may obtain more information/register for these courses at <http://www.train.army.mil/>. Courses available include—

- ACCP EN5700. This correspondence course provides junior enlisted personnel with a basic understanding of environmental considerations and responsibilities associated with their duties.
- ACCP EN5702. This correspondence course provides company grade officers and NCOs with a basic understanding of environmental considerations and responsibilities associated with their duties.
- ACCP EN5704. This correspondence course provides senior officers and NCOs with a basic understanding of environmental considerations and responsibilities associated with their duties.

Graphic Training Aids

L-12. All GTAs are available through AKO at the Reimer Library Web site at <https://www.us.army.mil>. The following GTAs are quick references for environmentally related actions:

- GTA 05-08-002.
- GTA 05-08-003.
- GTA 05-08-004.
- GTA 05-08-005.
- GTA 05-08-012.
- GTA 05-08-014.
- GTA 05-08-016.
- GTA 05-08-017.
- GTA 05-08-019.

LESSONS LEARNED CENTERS

L-13. The collection and study of lessons learned is a valuable means of improving the techniques and procedures for integrating environmental considerations. The recent increase in operations, both at home and overseas, has resulted in a wealth of experience and knowledge. See the following:

- Center for Army Lessons Learned (CALL) Newsletter 99-9.
- CALL Newsletter 04-19.

CENTER FOR ARMY LESSONS LEARNED DATABASE

L-14. The CALL database contains additional data to support the needs of the commander in the area of military environmental protection. *Military environmental protection* **is the application and integration of all aspects of natural environmental considerations as they apply to the conduct of military operations.** A host of lessons learned and examples of other unit actions/experiences are available for use. See the CALL Web site at <http://call.army.mil>.

SOURCES OF ASSISTANCE

L-15. Many sources of assistance are available to help units develop command environmental programs. These sources include installation staffs, SMEs at other agencies (such as USACE), and various online tools.

INSTALLATION/OPERATIONS STAFFS

L-16. Most installations maintain environmental staffs available to assist military units with environmental requirements. Some of this expertise may be found in specific environmental offices, while other areas of expertise are embedded in installation agencies (such as DPW/facilities or range management offices).

Environmental Management Office

L-17. The environmental management office is staffed with scientists and engineers responsible for developing and implementing installation environmental programs. This office is usually a division within the installation DPW or the facilities management office of the state area coordinator for the ARNG. Many environmental management offices are organized according to the installation environmental program which encompasses five general components. The components include—

- Compliance elements that monitor current operations and ensure that units follow environmental guidelines.
- P2 elements that manage installation initiatives, such as source reduction, HW minimization, recycling, and materials substitution.

- Natural and cultural resources management elements that manage installation conservation initiatives for forests, wildlife, wetlands, and historical resources.
- Restoration elements that manage the cleanup of contamination sites on the installation.
- Planning and documenting elements that address the possible environmental impacts of future operations and activities.

Directorate of Logistics

L-18. The responsibilities of DOLs and G-4s include the management of POL and HM. The directorate/staff section also exercises environmental control and oversight of HM (including ammunition) maintenance, transportation, and storage activities.

Directorate of Plans, Training, and Mobilization

L-19. The responsibilities of the Directorate of Plans, Training, and Mobilization or the Assistant Chief of Staff, Operations and Plans (G-3) include installation/unit operations and training. These offices coordinate all training activities, to include budgeting, development, and maintenance of training areas, the ITAM program, and mission priorities. The directorate also coordinates the range division and maintains overall responsibility for range operations, maintenance, and construction.

Staff Judge Advocate

L-20. The SJA provides legal advice and assistance in the interpretation and application of environmental laws and rules to installation activities. This process/service is particularly important when assessing the environmental impact of a new initiative (such as construction).

Public Affairs Officer

L-21. The PAO is the official spokesperson for the installation/unit and manages public involvement activities and responses—particularly during public controversy—in close coordination with other key installation/unit members. This is particularly important when assessing the environmental impact of a new initiative (such as construction).

Safety Officer

L-22. The safety officer works closely with the environmental staff on programs to help prevent accidents that could threaten or damage human health and the environment. HAZCOM, MSDSs (see Appendix K), and OSHA-mandated training are the purview of the safety office.

Preventive Medicine Office/Surgeon

L-23. The preventive medicine office is the point of contact for the medical monitoring program and for work-related health problems. This office, often colocated with medical units or hospitals, can provide critical information concerning public health issues (such as the use of pesticides).

Fire Department

L-24. The fire department provides firefighting and spill response support to the installation. In many instances, the fire department is also staffed with highly trained spill response personnel who provide expert advice on spill reaction measures.

Defense Reutilization and Marketing Office

L-25. The DRMO works closely with DPW and DOL to store and provide for disposal of solid waste, including HW generated at the installation. This DOD organization becomes critical to units attempting to turn in potentially hazardous substances or HM. Unit personnel with questions on turn-in procedures for potentially hazardous substances or HM should check with the receiving DRMO facility to determine documentation and packaging requirements.

SOURCES OF ASSISTANCE DURING TACTICAL OPERATIONS

L-26. While units may be able to benefit from the assistance of standard installation or base operations support during tactical operations, the likelihood is that they will only be minor, perhaps supporting players to provide assistance. Tactical operations will shift more support requirements to operational staffs rather than to installation staff support. Some likely/potential sources of assistance are identified in the following paragraphs.

Operational/Deployment Staff Assistance

L-27. The unit staff takes on a much larger role in environmental assistance when a unit is deployed or in an operational status. The load will tend to rest on these staffs in the case of deployment to relatively remote OCONUS locations. As time goes on and the duration of stay increases, it is highly possible that the command will establish organizations like the base camp coordination agency and its subordinate base camp assistance/assessment team. These organizations will provide tactical/operational commanders with the military environmental protection support they need.

Base Camp Coordination Agency and Base Camp Assistance/Assessment Team

L-28. The base camp coordination agency and base camp assistance/assessment team concepts were developed and successfully tested by the United States Army Europe. These organizations perform an important and vital role, which in a tactical/operational arena essentially replaces the roles performed by installation staffs. They may draw on resources from either home base or theater installation sources since they are located at tactical/operational locations (such as base camps), which they typically support. See CALL Newsletter 99-9 for insights into how these organizations provide assistance in a tactical/operational setting.

Joint Environmental Management Board

L-29. Operational or tactical units may operate in-theater or as part of a joint task force. As participants in a joint force, units may be required to interface with the actions of a temporary board, the JEMB (which the joint commander or his designated commander, joint task force may activate). The JEMB establishes policies, procedures, priorities, and the overall direction for environmental management requirements in-theater according to the OEBGD/FGS in effect for the countries within the AOR. If appropriate, the board may assume responsibility for the preparation of the environmental management support plan. The JEMB is further explained in JP 3-34.

Foreign Nation

L-30. Depending on the capabilities of the foreign nation and agreements that have been made, foreign nation support to the commander is possible. Senior-level staffs will typically be responsible for initiating and securing this type of support.

Contractor Support

L-31. Environmental support assistance for the tactical/operational commander may be provided by a contractor. This type of contracting has already occurred in places like Bosnia. Coordination for this support will likely come through the base camp coordination agency, USACE, or a similar agency with contracting capability.

Other

L-32. Regardless of the location, a myriad of sources are available with access to a telephone, e-mail, or other electronic means of communication. The Defense Environmental Network and Information Exchange Web site contains additional information. This Web site, operated by DOD, is sponsored by the Department of Environmental Security Corporate Information Management. It provides timely access to environmental legislative compliance, restoration, cleanup, and DOD guidance. See <http://www.denix.osd.mil> for more information.

L-33. The Army Environmental Center implements the environmental program for the Army by providing a broad range of innovative and cost-effective products and services in support of Army training, operations, and sound stewardship. For further assistance, see the Web site at <http://aec.army.mil/usaec>.

L-34. USACHPPM has developed the Hazardous and Medical Waste Program Lending Library. See the Web site at <http://chppm-www.apgea.army.mil>.

L-35. The Defense Automated Visual Information System/Defense Instructional Technology Information System Web site contains a database for and descriptions of thousands of audiovisual productions and interactive multimedia instruction products used by DOD. See this Web site at <http://dodimagery.afis.osd.mil>.

L-36. AKO provides access to the Reimer Digital Library, which contains ACCPs, FMs, GTAs, and other current policies and procedures. See the Web site at <https://www.us.army.mil>. A password is required for access to the digital library.

Glossary

AAR	After-action review
ACCP	Army Correspondence Course Program
AKO	Army Knowledge Online
AO	area of operations
AOR	area of responsibility
AR	Army regulation
ARNG	Army National Guard
BN	battalion
CA	civil affairs
CALL	Center for Army Lessons Learned
CBRN	chemical, biological, radiological, and nuclear
CBRNE	chemical, biological, radiological, nuclear, and high-yield explosives
CCIR	commander's critical information requirements
CERCLA	Comprehensive Environmental Response, Compensation, and Liability Act
CFC	chlorofluorocarbons
CFR	Code of Federal Regulations
CJCS	Chairman of the Joint Chiefs of Staff
COA	course of action
CONEX	container express
CONUS	continental United States
COP	common operational picture
CP	commander's policy
CRM	composite risk management
CSB	Combat Support Battalion
DA	Department of the Army
DEI	Directorate of Environmental Integration
DOD	Department of Defense
DODD	Department of Defense directive
DODI	Department of Defense instruction
DOL	Directorate of Logistics
DOT	Department of Transportation
DPW	Directorate of Public Works
DRMO	Defense Reutilization and Marketing Office
DS2	decontaminant solution 2
DSN	defense switched network
DTG	date-time group

ea	each
EBS	environmental baseline survey
ECR	environmental conditions report
EHSA	environmental health site assessment
ENCOORD	engineer coordinator
EO	executive order
EOD	explosive ordinance disposal
EPA	Environmental Protection Agency
EPAS	Environmental Performance Assessment System
EPCRA	Emergency Planning and Community Right-to-Know Act
ESA	Endangered Species Act
ESOH	environmental, safety, and occupational health
FGS	final governing standards
FHP	force health protection
FM	field manual
FSE	fire support element
FTX	field training exercise
G-3	Assistant Chief of Staff, Operations and Plans
G-4	Assistant Chief of Staff, Logistics
G-9	Assistant Chief of Staff, Civil Affairs Operations
GSA	General Services Administration
GTA	graphic training aid
HAZCOM	hazard communication
HEMTT	heavy expanded-mobility tactical truck
HM	hazardous material
HQ	headquarters
http	hypertext transfer protocol
HW	hazardous waste
IED	improvised explosive device
IO	information operations
IPB	intelligence preparation of the battlefield
ISO	International Organization for Standardization
ITAM	integrated training area management
J-2	intelligence staff section
J-3	operations staff section
J-4	logistics staff section
J-9	civil-military operations staff section
JEMB	Joint Environmental Management Board
JOA	joint operations area
JOPES	Joint Operation Planning and Execution System
JP	joint publication

JRTC	Joint Readiness Training Center
JSI	joint staff instruction
LOW	law of war
MAJ	major
MANSCEN	Maneuver Support Center
MCO	Marine Corps order
MCRP	Marine Corps reference publication
MCWP	Marine Corps warfighting publication
MDMP	military decisionmaking process
MED	medical
METT-T	mission, enemy, terrain and weather, troops and support available, time available, and civil considerations (Marine Corps)
METT-TC	mission, enemy, terrain and weather, troops and support available, time available, civil considerations
MGRS	military grid reference system
MOS	military occupational specialty
MSDS	material safety data sheet
NAVSUPINST	naval supply instruction
NCO	noncommissioned officer
NCOIC	noncommissioned officer in charge
NEPA	National Environmental Policy Act
NIOSH	National Institute for Occupational Safety and Health
NOV	notice of violation
NSN	national stock number
NWP	naval warfare publication
OCONUS	outside the continental United States
OEBGD	overseas environmental baseline guidance document
OPLAN	operation plan
OPNAVINST	Chief of Naval Operations instruction
OPORD	operation order
OSHA	Occupational Safety and Health Administration
P2	pollution prevention
Pam	pamphlet
PAO	public affairs officer
PCB	polychlorinated biphenyl
PIR	priority intelligence requirements
POC	point of contact
POL	petroleum, oils, and lubricants
PPE	personal protective equipment
QM	quartermaster
RCRA	Resource Conservation and Recovery Act

S-1	personnel staff officer
S-2	intelligence staff officer
S-3	operations staff officer
S-4	logistics staff officer
S-9	civil affairs staff officer
SARA	Superfund Amendments and Reauthorization Act
SITREP	situation report
SJA	staff judge advocate
SME	subject matter expert
SOFA	status-of-forces agreement
SOP	standing operating procedure
SPILLREP	spill report
STB	super tropical bleach
TB	technical bulletin
TG	technical guide
TIC	toxic industrial chemical
TIM	toxic industrial material
TM	technical manual
TSP	training support package
U.S.	United States
USACE	United States Army Corps of Engineers
USACHPPM	United States Army Center for Health Promotion and Preventive Medicine
USAEC	United States Army Environmental Command
USAES	United States Army Engineer School
USAR	United States Army Reserve
USMC	United States Marine Corps
UTM	universal traverse mercator
UXO	unexploded explosive ordnance
WMD	weapons of mass destruction
www	World Wide Web

SECTION II–TERMS

*critical habitat

A designated area declared essential for the survival of a protected species under authority of the Endangered Species Act.

*discharge

The accidental or intentional spilling, leaking, pumping, pouring, emitting, emptying, or dumping of a substance into or on any land or water.

*disposal (waste)

The discharge, deposit, injection, dumping, spilling, leaking, or placing of any solid waste or hazardous waste into or on any land or water. The act is such that the solid waste or hazardous waste, or any constituent thereof, may enter the environment or be emitted into the air or discharged into any waters, including groundwater.

*endangered species

Those species designated by the Secretary of the Interior that are in danger of extinction throughout all or a significant portion of their range.

*environmental area of interest

An environmentally sensitive area that may be deemed worthy of special consideration because of its unique and important qualities relative to adjacent areas (for example, the only forest within a large region) or the importance of its natural environment function (for example, a wetland, flood plains, permafrost area, or an endangered species critical habitat). The environmental area of interest includes man-made structures, such as wastewater treatment plants and dams.

*environmental assessment

A study to determine if significant environmental impacts are expected from a proposed action.

*environmental baseline survey

(Army) An assessment or study done on an area of interest (a property) in order to define the environmental state or condition of that property prior to use by military forces. Used to determine the environmental impact of property use by military forces and the level of environmental restoration needed prior to returning the property upon their departure.

*environmental compliance

The unconditional obeying of international, foreign nation, federal, state, and local environmental rules, regulations, and guidelines that affect current operations.

*environmental conditions report

A concise summary of environmental conditions at a base camp site, based on the environmental baseline survey, supported by maps and backup documents, prepared by base camp commanders for each base camp. The environmental conditions report documents conditions at the site if claims or other legal challenges arise against the government. Also called **ECR**.

*environmental ethic

Taking care of the environment because it is the right thing to do. This ethic is the operating principle and value that governs individual Soldiers, units, and the Army.

*environmental hazard

All activities that may pollute, create negative noise-related effects, degrade archaeological/cultural resources, or negatively affect threatened or endangered species habitats. They also include environmental health-related hazards.

*environmental impact statement

Detailed description of the effects, impacts, or consequences associated with designing, manufacturing, testing, operating, maintaining, and disposing of weapon systems or automated information systems. Under the National Environmental Policy Act, an environmental impact statement is required when cultural resources may be damaged or significantly adversely affected.

*environmental noise

The outdoor noise environment consisting of all noise (including ambient noise) from all sources that extend beyond, but do not include, the workplace.

*environmental performance assessment system

The examination of an installation's environmental program review to identify possible compliance deficiencies. It also includes designing corrective action plans and implementing fixes for identified deficiencies. Also called **EPAS**.

*environmental planning

Efforts that consider the impact of operation, training, exercises, or weapon system introduction on the environment and, where necessary, allow decisionmakers to take early action to eliminate or mitigate those impacts.

*environmental pollution

The condition resulting from the presence of chemical, mineral, radioactive, or biological substances that alter the natural environment or that adversely affect human health or the quality of life, biosystems, the environment, structures and equipment, recreational opportunities, aesthetics, or natural beauty.

*environmental protection

The application of human ingenuity and resources, through the disciplines of science and engineering, as required by environmental protection laws, regulations, and policies, to protect the natural environment.

*environmental protection level

The varying level of environmental protection that can reasonably be afforded at any particular time during military operations, given the absolute requirement that such a diversion of resources away from the mission at hand does not adversely affect that mission, any friendly personnel, or indigenous or refugee populations.

*environmental reconnaissance

The systematic observation and recording of site or area data collected by visual or physical means, dealing specifically with environmental conditions as they exist, and identifying areas that are environmentally sensitive or of relative environmental concern, for information and decisionmaking purposes.

*environmental services

The various combinations of scientific, technical, and advisory activities (including modification processes such as the influence of man-made and natural factors) required to acquire, produce, and supply information on the past, present, and future states of space, atmospheric, oceanographic, and terrestrial surroundings for use in military planning and decisionmaking processes or to modify those surroundings to enhance military operations.

*groundwater

A body of water, generally within the boundaries of a watershed, that exists in the internal passageways of porous geological formations (aquifers) and flows in response to gravitational forces.

*hazard communication

The responsibility of leaders and supervisors concerning possible hazards in the workplace and notification of hazards and necessary precaution to their personnel. Also called **HAZCOM**.

*hazardous material

Any substance which has a human health hazard associated with it. Special storage, use, handling, and shipment safety procedures and protocols must be followed to help protect against accidental exposure. Hazardous materials are specifically identified under federal law.

*hazardous substance

Elements, compounds, mixtures, solutions, and substances that, when released into the environment, may present a substantial danger to public health and welfare or the environment.

*hazardous waste

A solid waste that is either listed as such in federal law or exhibits any of the four hazardous characteristics— ignitability, corrosivity, reactivity, or toxicity.

*hazardous waste accumulation site

A specially designated site for the temporary collection of hazardous wastes where no container may remain on-site for more than 90 days. The site, and containers within it, must be properly marked and certain safety and management procedures apply. There is no limitation on the quantity of wastes which may be kept on site.

*medical waste

Any waste that is generated in the diagnosis, treatment, or immunization of human beings or animals.

*military environmental protection

The application and integration of all aspects of natural environmental considerations as they apply to the conduct of military operations.

*monitoring

(joint, NATO) 1. The act of listening, carrying out surveillance on, and/or recording the emissions of one's own or multinational forces for the purpose of maintaining and improving procedural standards and security, or for reference, as applicable. See FM 34-1. 2. The act of listening, carrying out surveillance on, and/or recording of enemy emissions for intelligence purposes. See FM 34-1. 3. The act of detecting the presence of radiation and the measurement thereof with radiation measuring instruments. Also called **radiological monitoring**. See FM 3-3-1. (Army) 1. An element of assessment: continuous observation of the common operational picture to identify indicators of opportunities for success, threats to the force, and gaps in information. (FM 6-0) 2. The assessment of emissions and ambient air quality conditions.

*natural environment

The human ecosystem, including both the physical and biological systems that provide resources (clean air, clean water, healthy surroundings, and sufficient food), necessary to sustain productive human life. Included in the natural environment are man-made structures, such as water and wastewater treatment facilities and natural/cultural resources.

*notice of violation

Formal written document provided to an installation by a regulatory agency as a result of environmental noncompliance. Also called **NOV**.

*restoration

The systematic removal of pollution or contaminants from the environment, especially from the soil or groundwater, by physical, chemical, or biological means. Also known as **remediation or environmental cleanup**.

*solid waste

Any material or substance (solid or liquid) that is inherently waste-like by being no longer suitable for its originally intended purpose.

*source reduction

The decrease of hazardous waste generation at its sources. This reduction is to be achieved through product substitution, recycling, and inventory control, and by developing new industrial processes that use less hazardous materials, such as bead blasting rather than solvents to remove paint.

*spill

A generic term that encompasses the accidental and the deliberate but unpermitted discharge or release of a pollutant.

*surface water

All water naturally open to the atmosphere (rivers, lakes, reservoirs, ponds, streams, impoundments, seas, or estuaries) and all springs, wells, or other collectors directly influenced by surface water.

*threatened species

Those species that are likely to become endangered within the foreseeable future throughout all or a significant portion of their range.

*toxic

Capable of producing illness, injury, or damage to humans, domestic livestock, wildlife, or other organisms through ingestion, inhalation, or absorption through any body surface.

*waste

Any discarded material.

References

SOURCES USED

These are the sources quoted or paraphrased in this publication.

ARMY PUBLICATIONS

ACCP EN5700. *Junior Enlisted Environmental Awareness Training, Edition D.* 1 September 2008.

ACCP EN5702. *Small-Unit Leaders' Environmental Awareness Training, Edition D.* 1 October 2008.

ACCP EN5704. *Senior Leaders' Environmental Awareness Training, Edition F.* 1 September 2008.

AR 40-5. *Preventive Medicine.* 25 May 2007.

AR 200-1. *Environmental Protection and Enhancement.* 13 December 2007.

AR 350-19. *The Army Sustainable Range Program.* 30 August 2005.

AR 385-10. *The Army Safety Program.* 23 August 2007.

AR 700-141. *Hazardous Materials Information Resource System.* 13 August 2007.

CALL Newsletter 99-9. *Integrating Military Environmental Protection.* 1 August 1999.

CALL Newsletter 04-19. *(O)Environmental Considerations During Military Operations.* November 2004.
https://call2.army.mil/default.aspx (Restricted Digital Library)

DA Pam 700-142. *Instructions for Materiel Release, Fielding, and Transfer.* 2 August 2004.

FM 3-0. *Operations.* 27 February 2008.

FM 3-34. *Engineer Operations.* 2 April 2009.

FM 3-34.400. *General Engineering.* 9 December 2008.

FM 4-25.12. *Unit Field Sanitation Team.* 25 January 2002.

FM 4-02. *Force Health Protection in a Global Environment.* 13 February 2003.

FM 5-0. *Army Planning and Orders Production.* 20 January 2005.

FM 5-19. *Composite Risk Management.* 21 August 2006.

FM 6-99.2. *U.S. Army Report and Message Formats.* 30 April 2007.

FM 7-15. *The Army Universal Task List.* 27 February 2009.

FM 10-67. *Petroleum Supply in Theaters of Operations.* 18 February 1983.

FM 10-67-1. *Concepts and Equipment of Petroleum Operations.* 2 April 1998.

FM 21-10. *Field Hygiene and Sanitation.* 21 June 2000.

GTA 05-08-002. *Environmental-Related Risk Assessment.* 1 March 2008.

GTA 05-08-003. *Hazardous Material Spill Response Procedures.* 1 September 2009.

GTA 05-08-004. *The Soldier and the Environment: Soldier's Environmental Ethic and Responsibility Card.* 1 September 2007.

GTA 05-08-005. *Leadership and the Environment: A Unit Leader's Field Guide, Assessment, and Quality Assurance Checklist.* 1 March 2008.

GTA 05-08-012. *Individual Safety Card.* 1 December 2005.

GTA 05-08-014. *The Environment and Predeployment: Unit Predeployment and Load Plan Considerations.* 1 January 2003.

GTA 05-08-016. *The Environment and Redeployment: How to Clear a Base Camp.* 1 September 2008.

GTA 05-08-017. *The Environment and Deployment: Tactical Risk and Spill Reaction Procedures.* 1 January 2003.

GTA 05-08-018. *Dust Suppression Alternatives.* 1 August 2006.

GTA 05-08-019. *The Soldier's Field Card: Checklist for Environmental Considerations During Training and Deployment*. 1 April 2008.

TB 43-0134. *Battery Disposition and Disposal*. 19 May 2008.

TB MED 593. *Guidelines for Field Waste Management*. 15 September 2006.

The Army Strategy for the Environment. 1 October 2004.

TM 5-830-3. *Dust Control for Roads, Airfields, and Adjacent Areas*. 30 September 1987.

TM 38-410. *Storage and Handling of Hazardous Material*. 13 January 1999.

USACHPPM TG-217. *Hazardous Material/Hazardous Waste Management Guidance for Maneuver Units During Field and Deployment Operations*. October 2000.

CHAIRMAN OF THE JOINT CHIEFS OF STAFF PUBLICATIONS

C JCSI 5810.01C. *Implementation of the DOD Law of War Program*. 31 January 2007.

CJCSM 3122.03C. *Joint Operation Planning and Execution System Volume II, Planning Formats and Guidance*. 17 August 2007.

DEPARTMENT OF DEFENSE PUBLICATIONS

DOD 4160-21-M. *Defense Materiel Disposition Manual*. 18 August 1997.

DOD 4715.05-G. *Overseas Environmental Baseline Guidance Document*. 1 May 2007.

DODD 4715.1E. *Environment, Security, Occupational Health (ESOH)*. 19 March 2005.

DODD 5101.1. *DOD Executive Agent*. 3 September 2002.

DODD 6050.7. *Environmental Effects Abroad of Major Department of Defense Actions*. 31 March 1979.

DODD 6050.16. *DOD Policy for Establishing and Implementing Environmental Standards at Overseas Installations*. 20 September 1991.

DODD 6490.2E. *Comprehensive Health Surveillance*. 21 October 2004.

DODI 4715.5. *Management of Environmental Compliance at Overseas Installations*. 22 April 1996.

DODI 4715.8. *Environmental Remediation for Department of Defense Activities Overseas*. 2 February 1998.

DODI 6490.03. *Deployment Health*. 11 August 2006.

EXECUTIVE ORDERS

EO 11987. *Exotic Organisms*. 24 May 1977.

EO 11990. *Protection of Wetlands*. 24 May 1977.

EO 12088. *Federal Compliance with Pollution Control Standards*. 13 October 1978.

EO 12114. *Environmental Effects Abroad of Major Federal Actions*. 4 January 1979.

EO 12580. *Superfund Implementation*. 23 January 1987.

EO 12856. *Federal Compliance with Right-to-Know Laws and Pollution Prevention Requirements*. 3 August 1993.

EO 13007. *Indian Sacred Sites*. 24 May 1996.

EO 13101. *Greening the Government Through Waste Prevention, Recycling, and Federal Acquisition*. 14 September 1998.

EO 13423. *Strengthening Federal Environmental, Energy, and Transportation Management*. 24 January 2007.

FEDERAL ACTS

Archaeological Resources Protection Act of 1979. 31 October 1979.

Clean Air Act. 14 July 1955.

Clean Water Act. 18 October 1972.

Comprehensive Environmental Response, Compensation, and Liability Act. 11 December 1980.

Emergency Planning and Community Right-to-Know Act. 17 October 1986.

Endangered Species Act of 1973. 28 December 1973.

Federal Facility Compliance Act of 1992. 6 October 1992.

Federal Hazardous Materials Transportation Law. 26 August 1994.

Federal Insecticide, Fungicide, and Rodenticide Act. 25 June 1947.

Marine Mammal Protection Act of 1972. 21 October 1972.

Military Munitions Rule. 12 February1997.

National Defense Authorization Act. 24 November 2003.

National Environmental Policy Act of 1969. 1 January 1970.

National Historic Preservation Act. 15 October 1966.

Native American Graves Protection and Repatriation Act. 16 November 1990.

Noise Control Act of 1972. 27 October 1972.

Oil Pollution Act of 1990. 18 August 1990.

Pollution Prevention Act of 1990. 5 November 1990.

Quiet Communities Act of 2005. 14 June 2005.

Resource Conservation and Recovery Act. 21 October 1976.

Safe Drinking Water Act. 12 December 1974.

Sikes Act. 15 September 1960.

Superfund Amendments and Reauthorization Act. 17 October 1986.

Toxic Substances Control Act. 11 October 1976.

United Nations Convention on the Law of the Sea. 10 December 1982.

JOINT PUBLICATIONS

AR 700-68/DLAI 4145.25/NAVSUPINST 4440.128D/AFJMAN 23-227(I)/ MCO 10330.2D. *Storage and Handling of Liquefied and Gaseous Compressed Gasses and Their Full and Empty Cylinders.* 16 June 2000.

FM 1-02/MCRP 5-12A. *Operational Terms and Graphics.* 21 September 2004.

FM 3-34.170/MCWP 3-17.4. *Engineer Reconnaissance.* 25 March 2008.

JP 1-02. *Department of Defense Dictionary of Military and Associated Terms.* 12 April 2001.

JP 3-0. *Joint Operations.* 17 September 2006.

JP 3-33. *Joint Task Force Headquarters.* 16 February 2007.

JP 3-34. *Joint Engineer Operations.* 12 February 2007.

JP 4-02. *Health Service Support.* 31 October 2006.

JP 4-02.1. *Joint Tactics, Techniques and Procedures for Health Service Logistic Support in Joint Operations.* 6 October 1997.

JP 5-0. *Joint Operation Planning.* 26 December 2006.

JP 5-00.1. *Joint Doctrine for Campaign Planning.* 25 January 2002.

JP 5-00.2. *Joint Task Force Planning Guidance and Procedures.* 13 January 1999.

MARINE CORPS PUBLICATIONS

MCO P5090.2A. *Environmental Compliance and Protection Manual.* 10 July 1998.

NAVY PUBLICATIONS

NWP 4-11. *Environmental Protection.* 1 March 1999.

OPNAVINST 5090.1B. *Environmental and Natural Resources Program Manual.* 1 November 1994.

PUBLICATIONS

Basel Convention on the Control of Transboundary Movements of Hazardous Wastes and Their Disposal. March 1989.

CFR, Title 29. *Labor*. 1 July 2006.

CFR, Title 32. *National Defense.* 1 July 2006.

CFR, Title 40. *Protection of Environment.* 1 July 2006.

CFR, Title 49. *Transportation.* 1 October 2002.

Convention on the Prohibition of Military or Any Other Hostile Use of Environmental Modification. 18 May 1977.

Environmental Modification Convention. 18 May 1977.

Geneva Conventions. 12 August 1949.

ISO 14001. *Environmental Management Systems.* 2004.

JSI 3830.01B. *Environmental Engineering Effects of DOD Actions.* 1 May 1998.

JSN 3820.01E. *Environmental Engineering Effects of DOD Actions.* 30 September 2008.

Uniform Code of Military Justice. 8 February 1949.

The Yellow Book: Guide to Environmental Enforcement and Compliance at Federal Facilities. February 1999.

DOCUMENTS NEEDED

These documents must be available to the intended users of this publication.

DA Form 2028. *Recommended Changes to Publications and Blank Forms.*

DA Form 7566. *Composite Risk Management Worksheet.*

DA Forms are available on the APD web site (www.apd.army.mil).

READINGS RECOMMENDED

These sources contain relevant supplemental information.

Habicht II, F. Henry. *Memorandum: EPA Definition of Pollution Prevention.* United States Environmental Protection Agency. 28 May 1992.

Index

standing operating procedure,
  iv

status-of-forces agreement
  (SOFA), 1-4, 4-11, 6-5, A-
  13, C-5

storage segregation, F-7, F-8

sustainability, v, 1-2, 1-4, 1-6,
  4-1, 4-2, 4-4, 5-1, 5-2, 6-2,
  6-7, A-2, A-6, E-2

sustainment, 1-4, 1-9, 1-10, 2-
  3, 3-1, 3-15, 3-16, 3-17, 4-2,
  4-3, 6-1, 6-6, G-5

T

tactical risk
  definition, 2-1

threatened species, 3-4, D-9

toxic industrial chemical (TIC),
  1-7, 3-13, 3-14, G-1

toxic industrial material (TIM),
  1-3, 1-7, 3-13, 3-14, 3-19, G-
  1

Toxic Substances Control Act,
  A-13

W

waste, 1-9
  disposal, 1-10, 3-9, 4-10, 6-
    7, E-5, E-6, F-9, G-3, G-6
  management, 2-11, 4-6, 4-
    12, A-10, A-11, B-3, F-1,
    F-2, G-5, G-6, H-3
  medical, 1-3, 1-9, 3-2, 3-9,
    3-13, 4-11, 6-3, L-6
  solid, 1-7, 1-9, 3-2, 3-5, 3-9,
    4-8, 4-11, 4-12, 5-4, 6-3,
    A-7, A-11, F-9, G-3, G-6,
    H-2, L-5

www.ingramcontent.com/pod-product-compliance
Lightning Source LLC
Chambersburg PA
CBHW081149270326
41930CB00014B/3091

* 9 7 8 1 7 8 0 3 9 1 5 6 4 *